THE
WORLD
HISTORY
OF
HIGHLAND
GAMES

THE
WORLD
HISTORY
OF
HIGHLAND
GAMES

DAVID WEBSTER

with photographs by Lynn Boland Richardson and others

Luath Press Limited

EDINBURGH

www.luath.co.uk

First published 2011

ISBN: 978 1906307 48 6

Printed and bound by
Graficas 94, Barcelona

Typeset in 9.5 point Quadraat by
3btype.com

Front cover images:
(*left*) Games at Mar Castle, 1834. Painting by George Mar
(*middle*) Bruce Aitken throwing a 28lb weight. Photo by Lynn Boland Richardson
(*right*) The Lonach Highlanders and Atholl Highlanders. Photo by David Webster

Contents

Acknowledgements

A great many people have co-operated over the years in the collection of information related to Highland games and I am very grateful to organisers, officials and office bearers all over the world for their help. It is fortunate that in Scotland priceless records of great, long-established games such as those at Braemar, Blair Atholl and Lonach have been kept, which have enriched my knowledge and helped me to perpetuate the history of the gatherings and games.

Illustrations are a very important part of this publication and the main contributors have been two Canadians. Lynn Boland Richardson took the superb modern photographs and the eminent artist Douglas Fales executed excellent images of participants. These photos and drawings could not have been produced to such an excellent standard without a good knowledge and a deep love of Highland games. Lynn's son, Matthew, is an active Canadian heavy who enhanced some photos of international throwers by adding national flags.

For the images in the book, we have credited copyright holders wherever possible. As can be expected in a history based book, many illustrations are old and in the public domain but we still like to acknowledge the importance of relevant works of art and images from the *London Illustrated News*, *The Graphic* and other such early publications.

I am grateful to have been allowed to photograph at Balmoral Castle, Scottish home of successive monarchs, and I am delighted to have permission to include photographs of some unique artefacts at Blair Castle. The Professors Todd of the Todd McLean Collection, with their incredible new archival facilities at the Stark Center for Physical Culture and Sports at the University of Texas in Austin, are always most helpful and encouraging. Mention must also be made of the interesting museums at Maxville, Canada, and Waipu, New Zealand. The well-informed ladies of the latter were able to provide information and illustrations of their settlement's links with Nova Scotia.

Over the years, the *Arbroath Herald* and various editors of the *Book of the Braemar Gathering and Scottish Annual* have been encouraging and most efficient in providing fine illustrations for our text. Bryce Scott of New Zealand, who has a collection that covers around 100 years of his family's success as all-round athletes at the games has made a major contribution. Other individuals deserving special recognition for their help include Charlie Allan, the late Gordon Dinnie, Alex Thomson, Wullie Baxter, Francis Brebner, John Burnett of the National Museum of Scotland, Andrew Rettie and John Robertson and his wife, Jean Swanston-Robertson. Greg Gillespie in Canada provided useful material on R. McLennan and band officials in Canada provided previously unavailable information on drummers.

Jim Jardine spent many months researching the history of the Caledonian Club of San Francisco. Nancy Maud and her daughter, Ann Elliot Smith, most kindly provided a wealth of information about their father (and grandfather) Launceston Elliot, and also the best collection of his photographs.

Gavin MacDougall and staff at Luath Press gave welcome guidance and understanding while Catriona Vernal and Christine Wilson provided perceptive scrutiny as editors.

To all of these and many others who co-operated, my very sincere thanks are extended.

List of Illustrations

Chapter Twelve: Queen Victoria's Highlanders

Chapter Thirteen: Caledonian Club of San Francisco Highland Games

Chapter Fourteen: Olympic Inspiration in Paris

Chapter Fifteen: War Games

Chapter Sixteen: Pipers and Piping

Chapter Seventeen: Scotland's Superb Dances and Dancers

Chapter Eighteen: 'An Ancient, Manly and Friendly Game'

Chapter Nineteen: Great Scott! A Speedie Competitor and a Big Mac

Chapter Twenty: Wrestling at Highland Games

An artist's impression of Braemar Highland Gathering.

Introduction

From very ancient origins, Highland games have grown to become one of Scotland's largest sports, in terms of attendance. They are this nation's most widespread tourist attraction. At home, they economically benefit many small communities, and further afield they can attract crowds of up to 50,000 people in the United States and Canada.

Various countries bid years in advance to hold the World Highland Games Championships, which attract numerous national and international athletic champions, Olympic Games competitors and some of the world's strongest men. There are huge attendances at pipe band competitions, often with over 1,000 bandsmen, while the major Highland dancing competitions can attract nearly 1,000 entrants.

Although over the centuries there have been laws and acts to ban such gatherings, the deep roots of tradition have held firm and, internationally, Highland games have never been stronger.

Where, why and how did Highland games begin? How did they become so popular internationally? This publication seeks to answer these questions, but first some more mundane matters require clarification.

The term 'Highland Games' is common in Scotland. Grammatically speaking, however, unless it refers to a specific name of an event it is more correct to write 'games', without the capital initial. The plural form, 'games', is also used rather than the singular 'game', as there are several disciplines within which are several competitions. 'Games' and 'gatherings' are now largely interchangeable, but I (perhaps in isolation) see a significant difference. In my view, a 'gathering' is not necessarily a games. Many ancient and modern clan gatherings may not have a 'games' element. An ancient gathering might have been for a hunt and a modern clan gathering simply a social occasion. In both cases, there would invariably be piping and often dancing and, if outdoors, perhaps even some informal traditional sporting contests – these would be Highland games.

Dancing and piping are both physically demanding, but in my view it is overstretching the language to define them as 'games'. Nor is it necessary to do so. These worthwhile practices are entertaining, traditional and autonomous activities in their own right, and should be an integral part of almost every gathering or games. I prefer to think of piping and Highland dancing as Scottish *cultural* events.

In recording the history of Highland games, I have often referred to the 'formalising' of named gatherings on certain dates. As the term implies, this indicates a clear distinction from informal, sometimes spontaneous, participation in sporting activities. For example, King Malcolm III's famous hill race in the 11th century was to find a suitable *gillie-ruith* (a running footman, or courier). It could have been held as a single specific event for this purpose, or as the main attraction amongst others at that early gathering on the Braes of Mar. This is traditionally regarded as the first games, informal though it may have been.

The 'modern' Braemar Gatherings originated in the Wright Society, founded in 1800, whose members participated in an annual march round the district. During breaks in the march, be they for resting, recreation or simply 'comfort stops', there would inevitably be a stone to be put, a stick to substitute for pulling the swingle tree, a sprint to be run and even a wrestle in the back-hold standing style that 'widnae blad their claes'[1], as was said in the Doric. These Wrights had a 'gathering' but these were informal activities. However, documentation does make it clear that traditional throwing activities were practised and winners named at Braemar before the 'formalising' and codifying of events, prize lists and recording of names and distances that first took place in 1832.

This is a good example of a single important event in the 11th century developing over the years and gradually formalising to become an annual event still attended by the monarchy. There are numerous other gatherings and games starting informally and developing, some lapsing and some restarting, according to demand and the availability of enthusiastic organising officials.

Now, having addressed the formalities – LET THE GAMES BEGIN.

---

[1]   A literal translation would be 'would not dirty their clothes'. In back-hold wrestling, no part of the body other than the feet must touch the ground. Of course, in a fall in poor weather, the loser is very likely to 'hae his cleaes bladded'.

CHAPTER ONE

In the Distant Past

Scotland's ancient bards and *seanachies* (storytellers) could recite and record the names of all of Scotland's monarchs over the centuries. They told stories of clan histories and battles that are still well known today. Although there is mention of warriors of great strength and tales of mighty deeds, information dealing specifically with Scottish sport, games, piping and dancing is quite sparse. Accounts of Scottish activities and achievements were certainly committed to paper but certain monarchs made great efforts to destroy all things Scottish,

Queen Victoria takes the oath, 1837. From the book Queen Victoria, Her Grand Life and Glorious Reign. Published in Guelph, Ontario, 1901.

inlcuding books. This is particularly evident around 1715 and 1745, when castles and stately homes were taken over to house soldiers. In spite of this, those who are prepared to search diligently will find numerous references mentioning different activities and competitions that together comprise the Highland games we now know and love.

A little controversy and a lot of confusion surrounds the earliest days of Highland games. Clearly, the 'experts' who credit Queen Victoria with the introduction of Highland games to Scotland are well off course. Victoria's interest undoubtedly gave the games the greatest boost they had ever had, but the games had been well established long before then.

There have been many theories, legends, speculative reconstructions and a great traditional heritage, but solid facts and written reports of early formal Highland games are few and far between. We are sure that many, perhaps most, of these accounts have been based on fact but some accounts have undoubtedly been exaggerated over the years. There is very substantial evidence of the various elements of Highland games being in existence for centuries, so we wonder why it is so difficult for some people to accept the existence of gatherings to promote and enjoy these activities.

If a mystery must exist, it should be around the existence of the Highland games of *today*. It is a great mystery that such Scottish customs survived in spite of numerous difficulties and persecution over the centuries.

There is an abundance of evidence in specialist books dealing with the history of piping, dancing and sports, to show the very early development of these various elements of Highland games as disciplines in their own right. However, some people go to great lengths to prove otherwise. One very negative scribe, writing some 30 years ago, tried to debunk the myth of the traditional role of the great hereditary pipers of the past. He should have been very embarrassed at the amount of excellent and authentic information that was generated as a result of his declarations. The existence of hereditary pipers to clan chiefs can no longer be denied, thanks to the good work done in this field by the McCrimmons,

From an old and rare French book, Merveilles de la Force et de l'Addresse, 1869, (Wonders of Bodily Strength and Skill) *by Guillaume Depping (1829–1901).*

the most famous of the hereditary pipers, and their supporters. McCrimmon family trees go back to the 1500s and show many generations of the clan's notable pipers up to the present day. It is a very impressive historical family record – another treasure of Highland games.

To fully appreciate the phenomenon known as Highland games, it is necessary to understand what has happened over the years. The development of Highland gatherings and games will be reviewed – the ups and downs, successes and setbacks, and indeed the challenges of the present day, which are as great as ever. These matters will be addressed in chronological order to show that, despite all the trials and tribulations, our valuable activities have survived and are thriving to this day.

The Earliest Games

Amongst the best-known Celtic celebrations of sporting and cultural endeavour are the Tailteann Games, promoted to honour Queen Tailt or Tailltu, goddess of nature. The ancient form ran from 1829 BC to 1180 AD, ceasing after the Norman conquest of the British Isles. These sports festivals preceded the Olympics in Greece and they came to Scotland by way of Ireland. They lasted for many centuries and the beginnings of Celtic throwing events can be seen in these. History shows how early Scots came from Ireland, bringing with them such age-old traditions.

A Tailteann medal from the author's collection.

Accounts of Inveraray Highland Games have said that the first Scots coming from Ireland settled in mid-Argyll and held their earliest games at Inveraray. There are also accounts of Mary, Queen of Scots (1542–1567) visiting the castle and witnessing the games.

There is a great wealth of ancient tales of strong, athletic men in north-east Scotland. These are mainly set in Mar, which was an important area and much more populated than it is today, and there are several old books with legends of the Braes of Mar, now better known as Braemar.

There were many great hunts, lasting up to two weeks at a time, in and around the little town. Led by the nobility, with a host of gillies and other retainers, deer, wolves and a variety of birds such as grouse and pheasants were pursued. John Taylor, the Water Poet (1578–1653), who participated in one of these hunts, quantified the incredible 'bag' by the hunters. Between the

St Fillans, c.1819.

hunting, eating and drinking, retainers would wrestle and put the stones (see illustration of St Fillan's Games in Chapter 2), which were readily available wherever they went.

Taylor was very impressed and in one poem he wrote:

> Why should I waste invention to indite
> Ovidian fictions on Olympian games?
> My misty Muse enlightened with more light
> To a more noble pitch her aim she frames
> I must relate to my great Master James,
> The Caledonian peaceful war;
> How noble minds do eternize their fames,
> By martial greeting in the Braes of Mar.

Taylor continues in this flowery vein, praising the hunt and the sport. The final lines (with my italics) rise to an extraordinary climax:

> Lowland, your sports are low as in your seat,
> The *Highland games* and minds are high and great.

It is possibly the earliest existing reference to Highland games, and the fact that Taylor was writing this about his experience at Braemar makes the quote even more interesting.

King Malcolm III

As a young man, Malcolm Canmore was more like an uncivilised warrior than the king who would lead Scotland to new heights. The change in person was largely due to the influence of his queen, Margaret, who transformed his court and his way of life. Eventually, Malcolm's influential queen was canonised as St Margaret of Scotland, and the royal dynasty that they established lasted for two centuries.

In 1040 AD an important gathering took place at the foot of Craig Choinnich, the hunting grounds of Kenneth I (832–860 AD), one of Scotland's first kings. It was here that Malcolm III built Kindrochit Castle for his wife, Margaret. The main event on the Braes o' Mar that day was a hill race sponsored by Malcolm Canmore, later King Malcolm III (1058–93). Canmore was an adaption of his less-than-complimentary Gaelic nickname, *Calum a Chin Mhor* (Malcolm of the Big Head).

King Malcolm Canmore.

Malcolm required a good *gille-ruith*, a running footman or courier, to take messages swiftly from one place to another, so he ordered a hill race with the winner to be given the post, in more ways than one, as well as a purse of gold and a fine sword and belt.

According to tradition, the favourites to win were the three McGregor brothers of Ballochbhuie ('the beautiful yellow glen').

The story, as we know it from various descriptions, is that only the two eldest of the three McGregors were amongst those who lined up for the start of the race. When the trumpet sounded, the king beat his sword on his shield to start the race, and the two brothers immediately took the lead. They were still in sight when there was a stir at the starting point and the youngest of the three brothers

A runner in bare feet, Alexander Campbell, by Sir Joseph Edgar Boehm of Vienna.

came running up. He implored the king to let him run and Malcolm told him he could go if he wished, but that he was too late. Nevertheless, the youth bounded away 'as fleet as a stag', according

to a *seanachie*. He moved faster than the others across the plain but it was on the hillside that he was most impressive. The king is said to have commented on his sure-footed progress in the ascent and voiced the opinion that the springal would beat them all.

Young McGregor passed all but his brothers, who were still in the lead as they came to the brow of the steep slope as they approached the final elevation. According to the story, as he closed behind them he cried out, 'Halves, brothers, and I will yield'. 'Keep what you gain, and we will do the same,' was the retort. They fell out of the spectators' sight and as they reappeared the youngest caught up with his brothers, who tried to block his way as they approached the finish. It could be seen that all three were now physically exhausted, but young McGregor darted past them, the cheers of the judges renewing their vigour.

Archibald Brown throws a short sledge hammer. These statues were commissioned by Queen Victoria from her Sculptor in Ordinary.

Just yards from the post, the oldest brother stumbled and grabbed his young brother's kilt. Whether it was to try to save him from falling or to stop his adversary is not known, but the youth cast off his kilt and with feeble steps grabbed the finishing post and victoriously threw it in the air before collapsing. All three brothers lay on the ground gasping for air, but they must have heard the cheers of the crowd below.

Hill racing is now a well-organised sport in its own right, and is currently popular at

The start of Glenarm Games hill race in the new millennium. Although kilts are optional, most runners here wear them.

numerous Highland games. The athletic gathering at Craig Choinnich seems to be the first Highland games attended by royalty and it is a credit to the monarchy that they continue to support the Braemar Gathering, as they have done since 14 September 1848.

Malcolm Canmore is linked with many other Highland games traditions, including the dance known as the Gille Calum. This sword dance is said to have originated at the battle of Dunsinane, when one of his henchmen was slain by Macbeth's chieftain. When the fighting was over, the victor took his sword, placed it over the sword of his vanquished opponent and danced in exultation over them. The words of the bagpipe tune played for the dance mock Malcolm's tax gatherers.

The Battle of Bannockburn

Ceres Annual Highland Games in Fife were first held in 1314 to celebrate King Robert the Bruce's victory at the Battle of Bannockburn. This town in Fife is named after Ceres, the Roman goddess of agriculture and fruits of the earth, and it is especially appropriate that local Fifers, who lived off the land, played a crucial role in this landmark battle.

The English King Edward II had 3,000 cavalry and 15,000 infantry. With banners flying and shields glinting in the sun, they rode out to meet the Scots, led by King Robert the Bruce, at the Bannock Burn, as it was then known. Bruce waited amongst nearby trees with only 8,000 men in total, but they were just as experienced as the English and they had prepared deep pits

Henry VIII throwing the sledge hammer by Stanley Berkeley (1855–1909).

and scattered the ground with iron spikes. When the English army marched into these traps, the Scots attacked, and the battle raged long and hard. As night began to fall, tight ranks of Scots approached their enemy from higher ground, forcing them downhill in retreat, where they camped overnight.

Next morning, Midsummer's Day, King Edward and his men were astonished to see several thousand spearsmen advancing on them. The Scots suddenly stopped and kneeled on the ground. King Edward and some of his leaders thought their opponents were begging for mercy and were heartened. Their joy was short lived. The Scots were receiving blessings from their priests, and those of their enemies who knew what was happening were already scrambling for their horses.

The Earl of Gloucester charged with the English cavalry but many were impaled on the unbroken lines of spears. The Earl was one of the casualties and the cavalry dropped back. Proud Edward's army, with little room to manoeuvre, were soon in disarray, but fought back bravely. 'On them! On them!' called Bruce and

William Thomson putting the stone. Sculpted by Sir Joseph Edgar Boehm.

the Scottish leaders, and on this the peasantry (or what was called the 'little people') rushed forward. These were ordinary lay people who came to support Bruce with nothing but pitchforks, axes and home-made pikes, bows and arrows. King Robert previously realised that the crofters and labourers armed mainly with home-made weapons would be no match for their well-equipped opponents. Not wishing to endanger them, they had been asked to stay back behind the hill and out of sight in reserve until required.

On the first shout of 'On them!', the patriotic peasants rushed over the hill en masse, shouting and roaring at the top of their voices. They must have been a fearsome sight for it seemed as if strong, fresh reinforcements were now entering the fray. The English, deciding that discretion was the better part of valour, hastily retired, giving victory to Bruce and his men.

When the victorious contingent of around 600 Fifers returned home, they were given the freedom of Ceres and games were organised at the Bow Butts in their honour. This became an annual tradition that has continued to this day. As the Scottish folk song says, the Flower of Scotland had stood against them, proud Edward's army, and sent him homeward to think again.

Incidentally, in Highland games parlance, a faulty caber throw, known as a Fifer, is a sneaky way of trying to achieve a victory.

Other early accounts
Amongst the early snippets of Highland games information we find that

in the early 16th century the Fraser clan held a large gathering at Beuly, near Inverness. Lord Lovat, head of the clan at that time, was an easy winner in putting the stone and throwing the hammer. Some have questioned whether he really was the best or if other competitors, for one reason or another, did not wish to exceed his throws.

In 1534, Henry VIII (1509–47) sent to Scotland his envoy Lord William Harwood, accompanied by 60 horsemen including specially selected sporting specialists in shooting, shot putting, wrestling and leaping. They were devastated when defeated by the Scots. In a return match, in which there was a wager of 100 crowns and a 'tun of wine pundit' on each side, the Scots won again.

Mary, Queen of Scots (1542–67 abdicated), the daughter of King James V (1513–42), contributed greatly to Highland culture during her reign. Several of the steps seen in Highland dancing competitions and in Scottish country dances are said to have been introduced at her court (the *pas de basque* is the best known). After a two-day visit to Linlithgow, she had to take to bed with a pain said to be caused by too much dancing at her 21st birthday party. She maintained that praying too long in a cold chapel was the cause of the problem. At Inveraray Castle she watched the

Inveraray Castle, 1780.

proceedings from under the gallows tree. This was long before she was tried and sentenced to death.

Inveraray Games

It has been claimed that the Inveraray events are the oldest games, or one of the oldest, having been brought to Argyllshire by the Gaels. History books say that the earliest settlements of the Gaels in this area were around 498 AD, and their

Michael Caine, Roger Moore and company in Bullseye! (1990), directed by M Winner. Grant Anderson, Scottish Champion, is second on the left.

culture and beliefs had a lasting effect on the Highland descendants.

Inveraray Games are still going strong and because of the beauty of the area the famed producer Michael Winner selected the castle grounds as the location for his film *Bullseye!*. The cast featured several international athletes, along with the famous actors Michael Caine and Roger Moore.

This £10 million movie production included a scene where one of the stars bumped into Grant Anderson and caused him to throw a 28lb weight onto the roof of a parked car where two tourists were sitting eating sandwiches. Actually, when Grant was faking the throws, he showed his accuracy by placing six throws exactly as required by Michael Winner – and you could have covered all six holes with one dinner plate. Jon Pall Sigmarsson was equally accurate with the caber, but he certainly put the fear of death into a cameraman who had to film him as he ran and threw the caber directly towards him. In another scene, Michael Caine stepped over a tug o' war rope as the men lifted the rope and began to pull. Michael's undercarriage suffered injury and he cut the rope, causing the pullers to fall in disarray into a sea of mud.

The Reformation

The Reformation was a time of change, with religious reformers doing everything in their power to discourage and ban sport, particularly on the Sabbath, while others tried to encourage it. Opponents within Scotland included the leading Protestant John Knox (born c.1505–14, died 1572). He and his ecclesiastical counterparts preached against recreational activities and were particularly specific regarding Scottish dancing. 'The music of the devil' was another recurring theme amongst those who seemed to promote the view that anything enjoyable in life was evil. In 1574, the kirk authorities appointed representatives to severely scrutinise all written material and, as a result of this censorship, a great deal of literature was confiscated and burned.

Putting the stone by the often wild actor and artist R.R. McIan (1803–56) in 1845.

Also in 1574, Lord Hugh Fraser was guarding Inverness, commanding 200 men. While waiting for a possible attack by Lord Huntly and the Gordons, the men had tough, but enjoyable, training. It was reported that:

> At intervals they used swimming, arching, football, throwing the barr [caber tossing], fencing, dancing, wrestling and such manly sprightly exercises and recreations very fit for polishing and refining yowth and to keep from effeminacy, baseness, loitering and idleness which fosters vice and inclines men to evill.

Following the Union of the Crowns in 1603, James VI King of Scots became King James I of Great Britain, reigning until 1625. Although not particularly popular in many quarters, he was a most enlightened monarch who was interested in several sports. He not only personally participated in sports but he also strongly encouraged his son to follow his example.

THE WORLD HISTORY OF HIGHLAND GAMES

On discovering that the Puritans were banning the practice of Sunday sport, even after church services, James VI had the Bishop of Chester put on paper his views in *The King's Book of Sports* (1618), which attacked those who sought to rob citizens of physical recreation. Realising that workers, exhausted after long hours of hard work and with little, if any, free time from Monday to Saturday, the monarch posed the question, 'For when shall the Common sort of people have leave to exercise if not on sondaies and holidaies, seeing they must plie theire labors and winn theire living in all workinge daies?'

I am fortunate enough to have a copy of this important and thought-provoking book, the rules of which applied to Scotland as well as England. In spite of royal support, the opponents of sport, including religious zealots, kept on the pressure. However, this rhyme from 1633, by William Lithgow (1582–1650) of Lanark, expressed a common view:

> For manly exercise, is shrewdly gone
> Foot-ball and Wrestling, throwing the Stone;
> Jumping and breathing, practices of strength
> Which taught them to endure, hard things at length.

Pipe bands and hereditary pipers have long played an important part in ceremonies and celebrations of all kinds, not just in Scotland but also overseas. Many lairds had their own pipers and some posts were passed down through several generations.

The best known and documented hereditary pipers are the MacCrimmons, who served the MacLeods and who have lived in Dunvegan Castle on the Isle of Skye since 1255. The lands at Boreraig were given to the McCrimmons at some time between 1500 and 1600, probably nearer the end of the 16th century. The great MacDonald of the Isles sent Charles MacArthur, a talented young piper, for a seven-year course at McCrimmon's

College of Piping at Boreraig, and MacArthur started another piping dynasty as hereditary pipers to the MacDonalds of the Isles.

It is well known that hereditary pipers will welcome a laird's bairn into the world and play appropriate music at funerals, but it is hard to imagine how Highland games could play any part in the grieving process.

Yet funeral games took place long before Christian times. The Roman poet Virgil (Virgilius Maro, 70–19 BC) graphically described the exercise of various games conducted in the intervening time between death and burial. There is a very interesting example of this in Scottish Highland games. According to our calculations, this would have occurred around the 1650s.

Jean Campbell, the mother of Robert of Glenlyon, returned to Chesthill after the death of her third husband. When she died there, her three sons, all lairds in their own right, assembled their men for the funeral.

In the foot races, sword exercises, fencing, wrestling, tossing the caber and throwing the hammer, the Glenlyon men acquitted themselves with honour. However, in putting the stone they and the Stewarts were, as reported, 'put to the blush' by one of the McGregors, who pitched the stone over a high branch of a tree making a better, more lengthy cast than all the others. Robert, anxious for the honour at stake, delayed the proceedings and sent for Robert McArthur, one of his shepherds, who was famous for his athletic feats. The shepherd immediately walked 15 miles to Chesthill and surreptitiously practised some putts. The original account says he was 'rehearsing' but in modern terms this is more likely to have been some last-minute training or warming up.

The stone putting event was resumed and McGregor, casting as before, challenged all present to top his feat. McArthur picked up the stone very casually and, without even removing his plaid, heaved the stone in the same direction as McGregor and sent it several feet beyond the latter's previous best mark.

Robert was so overjoyed that he gave all the gillies double allowances of whisky. The fun and games waxed fast and furious and mirth was so prevalent that the whole purpose of their meeting, *the funeral*, was nearly forgotten. Indeed, it was necessary to delay the interment for another day!

A Braemar Gathering in 1715

The period encompassing the Jacobite rebellions is one of the most important in Scotland's turbulent history. It began on 6 September 1715, in the clachan of Castleton, Braemar, when John Erskine, Earl of Mar, raised the Stuart standard and began a Jacobite rebellion:

> The Standard on the Braes o' Mar
> Is up and streaming rarely;
> The gathering pipe on Lochnagar
> Is sounding lang an' sairly,
> The Highland men
> Frae hill and glen,
> In martial hue,
> Wi' bonnets blue,
> Wi' belted plaids
> An' burnished blades,
> Are coming late and early.

So wrote Alexander Laing (1787–1857), and while the history of the Jacobite cause and its wars are outwith our remit, it is significant that this rebellion started at Braemar.

Games at Mar Castle 1834 by George Bryant Campion (1796–1870).

THE WORLD HISTORY OF HIGHLAND GAMES

With the intention of a hunt, a fine gathering was announced, with great sport, as previously described by John Taylor, the Water Poet. This Braemar Gathering of 1715, however, was merely a cover for the real purpose – a call to arms. Some of the famous McHardy family of Highland games athletes from Braemar were involved, and at least one sword used in battle is still in family hands. The struggle was short lived, but 30 years later the same cause was resuscitated with far more serious consequences, as will be seen.

Metal statue owned by Charlie Allan, former caber-tossing world champion.

The clergy feature in several true Highland games anecdotes and one of these referred to is the Reverend James Leslie, who was appointed as minister to the parishes of Moy and Dalarossie in 1716. There, in Strathdearn, between Inverness and Aviemore, Jacobitism was a topic on many people's minds. The Reverend Leslie was an unknown quantity. Not only was the preacher new to the area, he was also new to the ministry – so he was not made particularly welcome. When Leslie went to Dalarossie to preach for the first time, he found the men of the village putting the stone. It was a popular sport in the area and 100 years later the local *clach neart*, or stone of strength, was still to be found lying at the entrance of Moy Hall.

The local men were reluctant to interrupt

Braemar Gathering and Games at Invercauld in 1848.

their sport to listen to Reverend Leslie's sermon, so he challenged them to a contest. The deal arranged was that if he could beat them all they would come to the church and listen to his sermon. He won easily and became a legend in the area. The last of many stories of his exceptional strength was 30 years later, when he saved the life of Anne McIntosh, the laird's wife, from a band of soldiers who were plundering following the Battle of Culloden. He died in 1766.

Around 1743, before the Jacobite rebellion, another minister, this time in Moulin, Perthshire, had observed the Scottish interest in manly pursuits. In 1743 he wrote:

> It is observable that gymnastic exercises, which constituted the chief pastime of the Highlands 40 or 50 years ago, have almost entirely disappeared. At every fair or meeting of the country people there were contests of racing, wrestling, putting the stone etc.: and on holidays all the males of the district, young and old, met to play football, but oftener at shinty. These games are now practised only by schoolboys, having given place to the more elegant but less manly amusement of dancing.

Later, the Reverend Alexander Johnson (1746–1813) of Monquhitter, Aberdeenshire, writing of his farm servants, wrote that around the 1750s they 'frequently met to exert their strength in wrestling, casting the hammer, and in throwing the stones, and their agility at football, and their dexterity at coits (quoits) and penny-stane'.

This was a time of great change and Jacobitism had never completely dissipated. In June 1745, Charles Edward Stuart, better known as Bonnie Prince Charlie, sailed from Nantes in France and landed in Eriskay in Scotland, thus beginning the Jacobite rebellion of 1745.

The consequences of this war had very severe implications for Scottish traditions and culture, and Highland games might have ceased to exist.

Tales are told of the prince and his allies watching their troops compete in spontaneous challenges. One such clash took place on 15 August 1746, the eve of the battle of Culloden. The challenge is given some credibility as it includes the 'who, what, when and where' looked for by researchers.

In order to take his mind off the pending battle, a Lowlander issued a challenge in putting the stone. It was particularly aimed at the Highlanders, who often indulged in such sport. A Highlander, McGregor of Inverigny, had in his company a mighty man, Malcolm Durward of Mulloch, but Durward was indisposed. He had a large boil on his thigh and he was lying on his plaid among the heather, feeling angry and very sorry for himself. It was only with the greatest of difficulty that his companions persuaded him to uphold their honour and, to his surprise, a large number of officers had joined the troops to witness the event. A man named Lewis Gordon bid the spectators to stand back and give the champion from Mar plenty of room for their own safety and to let Durward be uninhibited in his efforts.

Malcolm Durward made only one throw but it soared three feet beyond the Lowlander's best mark. 'Mar forever!' roared Lewis Gordon, as applauding spectators showed their appreciation. The great effort caused the boil on Malcolm's leg to burst and by dawn of the next day he was fully ready for action.

That next day, the fateful 16 August 1746, not only put an end to the Stuart cause but also led to devastating, long-lasting implications affecting Highland games, dancing, and the wearing of kilts and any kind of tartan. All Scottish sporting activities were banned. The authorities in London even defined bagpipes as a weapon of war, and speaking in Gaelic was also forbidden.

This was a disastrous age for all Scottish activities and culture. There was more than suppression. A major strategy of that time was to destroy the image of Scotland as a nation and the identity of Scots so that they would become totally indistinguishable from other nations. This is very clearly indicated by the fact that there was no distinction made between Jacobite clans and supporters and the clans who had always been loyal to the government. Perhaps this was a major factor in the response to the reward offered for the capture of Prince Charles. In spite of the offer of £30,000, a vast sum in those days that would keep many families for life, not one Scot claimed the reward.

The Abolition and Proscription of the Highland Dress

The Disarming Act (1716) and the Act of Proscription (1746) went further than simply declaring that it would be a punishable offence to carry a gun or wear a kilt. No weapons of any kind were allowed and this put an end to hunting, which was an important part of life and domestic economy in the Highlands. Although plaids were a necessity for keeping warm in the cold mountains of the north, this article of clothing was also banned. The wearing of any tartan clothing or any item of Highland garb was punishable.

These were poor people with little in the way of clothes and these draconian laws affected the poor more than the rich.

It did not cost much for some yards of cloth that, uncut, could be wrapped round the body to make a kilt and a plaid that could be used as a warm cloak by day and a blanket by night. This one piece of cloth lasted a lifetime and, unlike a lowland suit, was affordable. Furthermore, the men of the mountains valued the freedom of the kilt in the rough terrain where they frequently had to walk and wade through streams and rivers. They did not relish the thought of having to remove their trousers many times a day, or alternatively wear wet 'breeks' for hours on end.

But the English had yet another humiliating measure to rub salt in the clansmen's wounds. All had to take this appalling oath:

> I ... do swear I have not, nor shall have in my possession, any gun, sword, pistol or arm whatsoever, and never use tartan, plaid, or any part of the Highland garb: and, if I do, may I be cursed in my undertakings, may I never see my wife or children or relatives: may I be killed in battle as a coward, and lie without Christian burial in a strange land far from the graves of my kindred.

'A Tour in Scotland, 1769'

Thomas Pennant was born in Flintshire, Wales, in 1726 and died there in 1798, at the age of 72. He wrote of two trips to Scotland – the first of which was one of the first major writings after the Jacobite Rebellion of 1745. He had a reputation of being scrupulously fair, although Scotland was obviously hostile to Hanoverians like Pennant.

Although Pennant has been a much-quoted writer,

An extract from The Act of Proscription.

ABOLITION AND PROSCRIPTION OF THE HIGHLAND DRESS
19 GEORGE II, CHAP. 39, SEC. 17, 1746

*

' That from and after the first day of August, One thousand, seven hundred and forty-seven, no man or boy within that part of Great Britain called Scotland, other than such as shall be employed as Officers and Soldiers in His Majesty's Forces, shall, on any pretext whatever, wear or put on the clothes commonly called Highland clothes (that is to say) the Plaid, Philabeg, or little Kilt, Trowse, Shoulder-belts, or any part whatever of what peculiarly belongs to the Highland Garb; and that no tartan or party-coloured plaid or stuff shall be used for Great Coats or upper coats, and if any such person shall presume after the said first day of August, to wear or put on the aforesaid garments or any part of them, every such person so offending ... shall be liable to be transported to any of His Majesty's plantations beyond the seas, there to remain for the space of seven years.'

REPEAL OF THE ACT PRESCRIBING THE WEARING OF HIGHLAND DRESS
22 GEORGE III, CAP. 63, 1782

*

' Whereas by an Act made in the Nineteenth year of the reign of his late Majesty King George the Second, entitled "An Act for the more effectual disarming the Highlands in Scotland and for more effectually securing the peace of the said Highlands and for restraining the use of the Highland dress" ... it was, among other things enacted that from and after the first day of August One thousand seven hundred and forty seven no man or boy, within that part of great britain called Scotland other than such as shall be employed as officers and soldiers in his majesty's forces, etc., etc. And whereas it is judged expedient that so much of the Acts above mentioned as restrains the use of the Highland dress should be repealed. Be it therefore enacted by the King's most Excellent Majesty, by and with the advice of the Lords Spiritual and Temporal and Commons in this present Parliament assembled and by the authority of the same. That so much of the Acts above mentioned or any Acts of Parliament as restrains the use of the Highland dress be, and are hereby repealed.'

There is much to see in this old print by Lance Calkin (1859–1936).
This is not an itinerant, begging piper; he is recruiting.
The recruiting sergeant will soon be talking to the young men.

I have not seen any previous reference to the following interesting observations. He pointed out that although many of the former pastimes of the Highlander had died out, amongst those retained was 'throwing the putting-stone, or stone of strength, as they call it, which occasions an emulation who can throw a weighty one the farthest'.

In Gaelic, a language spoken all over the Highlands at that time, this would be *clach neart*, *clach* being stone and *neart* being strength. However, in his footnote, Pennant quoted *cloch neart*. This quote is important because it shows that, in spite of the Jacobite Rising in 1745, Highlanders continued to practise heavy events.

In 2006, David Pennell kindly invited a small group of heavies and an official to Invercauld Castle, which he now occupies. Amongst the many interesting treasures the group saw in this historic building was an original 'Act of Proscription' bill poster, personally signed by General Wade. More than a century ago, the castle was the site of Highland games attended by royalty.

After the '45 rebellion, many Scots were tempted into the British army because soldiers could wear the kilt without being punished. Many regiments had their own Highland games and this tradition has continued to the present day. Soldiers took their Highland games all over the world, some of which will be described later (Chapter 6). There was usually a recruiting drive after significant problems in Scotland (e.g. after the Highland Clearances, although on that occasion there were some stern rebuffs). Many Highlanders were put off their land to make way for sheep and some Highlanders had the philosophy, quoted by John Prebble: 'If they prefer sheep to men, let the sheep defend them'.

After the Act of Proscription was repealed in 1782, the Gaelic bard Duncan Ban MacIntyre wrote:

> Indulgent laws at last restore
> The noble dress our fathers wore.
> Exulting then let us resume
> The bonnet blue and eagle plume,
> The tartan coat and jaunty vest
> And belted plaid becomes us best,
> With limbs unchained and footsteps free
> The pleated kilt just shows the knee.
> In hose or brogues we'll roam at will.
> O'er purple moor and heather hill.

The Highland Society in London had played an important role in campaigning for a relaxation of the laws outlawing Scottish cultural activities, but for many years after the repeal of the Act of Proscription the authorities in power were still highly suspicious of large numbers of Scots getting together for national activities. They were very conscious that the Jacobite Rebellion started at Braemar under the guise of a gathering for sport. The Highland Society Gathering at the Falkirk Tryst in 1781 was a landmark occasion. The location was chosen because Highland cattle were gathered here annually for the major sales of the year. Many of the animals were then transported

Cowal Champion's trophy.

to England. While sports and social gatherings were not permitted under the Act, there were some important events that affected the English economy such as pre-rebellion cattle sales. After the '45 rebellion, the Falkirk Trysts became the biggest cattle market as this town was more convenient than others for English buyers. In 1777, an estimated 30,000 cattle were sold in total at the August, September and October sales. By 1850, sales had increased to 150,000. The commercial aspects were accompanied by recreational pursuits and, not surprisingly, the social activities, dancing and sports were of an ethnic nature.

Although the Act of Proscription was not repealed until 1782, no action was taken to prevent these gatherings from proceeding. Furthermore, bagpipes were now being made and played illegally, and when the first Great Gathering took place at Falkirk in 1781 to coincide with the tryst, the main event was a bagpipe competition and the first prize was a fine set of bagpipes, won by Patrick MacGregor of Ardradour, Perthshire. This is significant on two counts. First, the unofficial relaxation of legislation and second, it is clear that this was bagpipe playing for competition purposes, not for entertainment or to accompany dancing. Competition is at the very heart of Highland games.

The effect of the Act of Proscription diminished, but national dress had largely died out and only gradually did area and family tartans become popular. Gatherings and games were very low key and usually ancillary to other events. It is a big step from piping, social dancing and traditional recreational sports being grouped to create formalised competitions that we now know as Highland games.

It was in this post-proscription era that a very young woman came to the Highlands and began writing about the things she saw and the people around her. Her correspondence was to become famous and even great writers like Sir Walter Scott would find much of interest in her observations.

Letters from the Mountains

In 1773, Anne McVicar, later known as Anne Grant of Laggan, arrived at Inveraray in a horse-drawn coach. This young lady, a mere 17 years of age, revealed her extra-ordinary flair for writing and gave a fine description of the castle and its contents as they were then:

Anne Grant (1755–1838).

> Wet and weary, late and dreary, we arrived at Inveraray and through watery moonbeams saw the semi-circular sweep of the bay, on the very edge of which stands Inveraray, a mean looking yet cheerful and populace place. 'Tis one street facing the water and beyond it a fine road surrounded by a beautiful lawn sprinkled with prodigious beech-trees, sweeps from one horn of the crescent to the other.

Picking up her quill pen the next morning at 5am, Anne continued the letter to her friend Harriet:

> I am greatly tempted to worship the sun. His first appearance from the sea was so overpowering after his long absence. Whence are thy beams, O Sun? I am not mad, most gentle Harriet... but consider it is the spring of day, of life and of the year and indulge me in rejoicing a little after I have mourned so much and so truly.

Later, she enthusiastically described her visit to the castle, and there is one particularly intriguing sentence: 'Suddenly we were ushered into a beautiful summer parlour, which had a sashed door that opened into a beautiful lawn. For a moment I thought I was in *the open fields surrounded by people engaged in rural sports*' [author's emphasis]. It transpired that this was a room hung with a huge Gobelins tapestry with very lifelike figures so realistic they seemed to live and move.

This well-written snippet by a self-educated lady of 17, who had never been to school, helps convince us that Highland rural sport was well known in Inveraray.

It will be seen that, at a much later date in her prolific correspondence, she made a very specific quote regarding putting the stone.

There have been three fine Scottish historians by the name of Grant.[1] Anne Grant was the earliest of these and is best known for her *Letters from the Mountains*, which give authentic and valuable information and were probably the earliest comprehensive descriptions of Highland life over a period of time. Unlike many others, Anne Grant's writing style is as acceptable and enjoyable to present readers as it was to the original recipients. It was never intended that the letters be pub-

Inchmurrin. Ben Lomond can be seen in the background.

lished but from an early age she showed a natural literary talent.

One day, she was travelling by Loch Lomond in a horse-drawn carriage when she passed Inchmurrin, the little island. Around 160 years later, Inchmurrin was owned by two of Scotland's

Loch Laggan.

greatest Highland games athletes, Tom and Jay Scott. Tom still lives there, well over two centuries after Anne wrote that the island 'serves as a park for deer and is also inhabited by harmless maniacs who roam at large, and lodge with the forester'.

Anne and her parents, Captain and Mrs McVicar, stopped opposite the island in the beautiful village of Luss. In the inn late that night, while studying Ossian's poems, young Anne heard a plaintive singing voice and a strange instrument coming from the room below:

> Stealing down on tip-toe I beheld a great dark-browed highlander, sitting double over the fire, and playing Macgrigor na Ruara[2] on two trumps [jews harps] at once, while a nymph, half hidden among her heavy locks, was pacing round and round and keeping time with voice and steps to his mournful tones.

This is but one of the earliest samples from her quill pen, but in the context of this book there is one particularly interesting passage in a letter dated 1773:

> I should love my father not merely as such, because he was the son of the wise and pious Donald, whose memory the whole parish venerates, and the grandson of the gallant Archibald who was the tallest man in the district, who could throw the putting stone further than any Campbell living, and never held a Christmas without a deer of his own killing, four Fingalian greyhounds at his fireside, and 16 kinsmen sharing his feast. Shall I not be proud of a father, the son of such fathers, of whose fame he is the living record? What is my case is in every other Highlander's.[3]

It is important to note that she specifically refers to the 'putting stone', not often mentioned in existing early literature, and she does it in a familiar manner, a matter-of-fact way, indicating that even in this remote area this was a well-known pastime. She is obviously very proud of her ancestor, Archibald, who could have been putting the stone in the late 1600s.

From the title of her fine book, *Letters from the Mountains*, and the accompanying portrait by a contemporary artist, some may imagine Anne Grant to be an old lady in a small croft or

The old manse at Laggan as it was in 2006.

blackhouse. This was not the case. She married the Reverend James Grant in 1779, and they lived happily, but frugally, in a thatched cottage manse, apparently with maids. James Grant was a military chaplain and a scholar of high repute. The manse at Laggan still remains in very good condition after being modernised.

The Laggan connection is also interesting as it is in this remote area that Queen Victoria and her consort watched Highland games in August 1847, a year before her first attendance at Braemar.

The Northern Meeting

It was not easy to redevelop the traditional social fabric of the country after the '45 Rebellion.

The famous Northern Meeting in Inverness, however, was inaugurated in Inverness on 11 June 1788. It was mainly a social event 'for the Purpose of promoting a Social Intercourse'.

These were difficult times, as draconian measures to prevent Scottish gatherings of any kind had only recently been repealed. Before commencing activities, officials of the Northern Meeting were careful to obtain from Edinburgh

Northern Meeting, 1888.

details of regulations that were then in force. As a result, it was declared that *no games were intended* and so this high-society event focused largely on dining and dancing at formal balls. The original functions were held over one week at first. To fill the mornings, the Duke of Gordon and Sir Robert Munro of Foulis were invited to participate and, following this, their hounds and huntsmen were added to the programme. Horse racing was introduced next, and in 1816 competitions of the Inverness Harriers were greatly appreciated.

George IV's visit to Scotland, attended by Glengarry.

Glengarry's Games

In 1822, a momentous year for Scotland with the visit of King George IV, McDonnell of Glengarry personally organised and supervised the first properly documented modern-style Highland games in Inverness. This was held at Duneancroy, meaning the level stretch by the Hill of Birds, and it is sometimes overlooked that this took place *after* the Northern Meeting.

Alasdair Ranaldson McDonnell, the 15th Chief and recognised as the last of the great Highland chiefs, even did his share of judging the events. This laird was a law unto himself, enjoying the limelight but always finding it difficult to keep his temper and financial expenditure under control. Glengarry evicted his clansmen to make way for sheep, which were more profitable. He squandered a fortune and did not pay taxes, and when he died in 1828 his estate had passed from his family for financial reasons. He was a larger-than-life figure, accompanied on public occasions

THE WORLD HISTORY OF HIGHLAND GAMES

by his 'tail' – consisting of his bard, Allan Dall, and the whole party in national dress. His games could hardly be considered a family-orientated event, with half the runners in an 8-mile foot race passing the tape stark-naked. A particularly horrible part of the programme was when three cows were felled and stunned by a sledge hammer and then torn limb for limb. Sir Iain Colquhoun wrote, 'Even the most expert of the competitors took four or five hours in running and riving, tooth and nail before bringing off the limbs of one cow'.

The lifting of an 18-stone boulder over a five-foot-high horizontal bar is the earliest recorded example of a stone *lifting* contest at Highland games. Such stone lifting is now included in many international games and an identical competition with a heavier stone took place at Arnold Schwarzenegger's classic competition for the world's strongest men, held in Columbus in the United States, in 2007.

I have found two reports of the Glengarry Chief's dueling. One indicates that at a Northern Meeting, he had been caned by Flora McDonald's grandson, Norman MacLeod, and as a result Glengarry had killed him in duel. The other says he fought a duel with an army officer from nearby

Brian Bell lifting a Manhood Stone of Strength.

Fort George. The officer died from the wounds he received. McDonnell, who liked to be known by his Gaelic name *Alasdair Faidaich*, 'the Untamed', was arrested and taken to Edinburgh where he was tried but acquitted. Perhaps the two reports are of the same incident.

Suffice to say that in 1815 he was one of the initiators of The Club of True Highlanders (which I have mentioned in a past publication, *Scottish Highland Games*, Reprographia, 1973) and McDonnnell's aim was to take over completely from the Celtic Society, which he had left in anger.

In 1837, the Inverness Highland Games took place in Academy Park for the first time. Our careful reading of old reports indicates that the origin of these particular Highland sports sprang from private sources separate from the Northern Meeting but were patronised by members of this latter organisation and the two bodies amalgamated. Later games were held in the Longman until they moved to the field by the Ness. The Longman area had previously been the site of the gallows and its name is derived from the ghostly, long, white spectres said to be frequently seen here.

The importance of these Inverness events should not be overlooked. McDonnell of Glengarry's efforts at Duneancroy date second only to St Fillans, which were formalised in 1819.

The efforts of organisers of Highland games and gatherings like the Northern Meeting undoubtedly saved the demise of these festivals, but there were many other problems. The Highland Clearances, virtually depopulating the Highlands, was another calamity for the games, and as a direct result of this and the drift to the cities there are only ruins left where there were once thriving communities. The north-east glens, where Highland games were once exceedingly popular, are now truly the Land of the Lost.

Off to the games in style. Most people walked, rode a horse or cycled.

A fine book of this title, by Robert Smith, vividly tells of the deserted ruined settlements and vanished peoples and communities.

In Victorian Scotland, nearly every town and village had its own annual games. Queen Victoria attended the Laggan Games in 1847, Braemar Games the following year and in 1852 Highland games were held in her honour at Holland Park in London. Some of her favourite athletes, such as McHardy, Menzies and Kennedy, who she had seen at previous games, were invited. The Queen's influence certainly popularised these gatherings, and without such a boost things would have been very different. This can be seen clearly by comparing the Scottish and American situations. In America there had been great development with the visits of Donald Dinnie, James Fleming, Duncan Ross and other Scottish professionals and also George Goldie's initiatives with American universities such as Princeton. However, as has been shown, the impact and inspiration of these pioneers had resulted in the founding of amateur track-and-field athletics on a club basis and as American clubs increased in number, athletics and athletes literally took a new track and developed in another direction. There was now a wider range of amateur track-and-field events and, instead of having an annual celebration, athletes had their own numerous and regular competitions that specialised in sports or games – without the cultural aspects of piping, bands and dancing. English teachers probably played a part, for Oxford and Cambridge athletic rivalry, starting in the mid-1860s, supported Goldie's initiatives at Princeton.

Donald Dinnie at 69.

Scottish heavies have always had a number of events in which they competed

THE WORLD HISTORY OF HIGHLAND GAMES

After the war a two minute silence was observed at the games in respect for those killed. The apparently grieving athlete is the Norman Murray Braemar caber trophy, presented in his honour by this fine athlete's family.

but the new breed of American athletes were shot putters, or threw javelin, discus or hammer; they did not do a battery of tests like the Scots did. This type of specialisation led to the Americans becoming the best athletes in the world.

Highland games organisers met this challenge and E.A. Donaldson, a meticulous researcher and fine author, recorded a peak of 125 Highland games in the United States after the Civil War (1861–65). Before the end of the century, there was an excellent and successful project that proved that traditional sports could still be a big attraction. In Chicago, the World Fair of 1893 promoted a nationally advertised three-day Highland Games, hosted by the Chicago Caledonian Club. It was an outstanding success. In neighbouring Canada, which, as part of the then British Empire was quite clearly affected by Victorian interests and examples, there were hundreds of Highland games.

Back in Scotland, the drift to the cities brought one blessing for Highland games. The tall, lean Highlanders, noted by earlier writers, became a recruiting target of Edinburgh and Glasgow police forces. Police pipe bands and many athletes became famous, some at an international level. Although Queen Victoria's high profile at the games was no longer there, things were still looking good for traditional activities, but the history of Highland games is full of ups and downs and once again there was a major setback.

The First World War (1914–18) brought Highland games to an abrupt stop. There were enormous casualty lists in numerous battles. Some 10 million men died; as many as tens of thousands in a single day. A whole generation of young men lost their lives. The majority of young Scots volunteered for action without delay and the losses were very much out of proportion to the country's population. Hardly a family escaped and very often there were deaths on both maternal and paternal sides of the family. The war not only affected Scotland and the Commonwealth (or the Empire as it was then known) but had a worldwide effect. It was turning point in the lives of all Europeans of that age. The feelings of grief and revulsion of the horrors of life in the trenches was passed on to the next generation. The abrupt stoppage of everyday life was felt in all aspects of community life, Highland games included.

The season of 1913 was the last full games season, although a few bravely continued in the summer of 1914. The great Strathallan Games were held just a few days before the outbreak of war. There were but a few isolated instances of these summer gatherings during war years. Many deaths of pipers, dancers and athletes were reported. Rumours abounded of the loss of 'Big Mac' McKenzie, the famous all-rounder. This shocked and saddened many, but the rumour was untrue and eventually, when there was authentic news of him, he had actually been promoted to the rank of captain.

In 1917, there were efforts to raise morale with various sports but the response was mediocre. At one event there was to be a cycle parade in fancy dress from the centre of town to the field and in spite of incentives and handsome

Above

This image and the one below may be the two oldest existing photographs showing round-headed throwing hammers. Ordinary sledge hammers were still being used 25 years later! The men of the 93rd Regiment, above, are seen in 1853 with a hammer almost identical to those in use today.

Below

This picture, including throwing hammer, is claimed by John Millar, former secretary of the Braemar Gathering, to have been taken in 1866, the year 'Royal' was added to the organisation's title. To the right of the house in the picture there was a throwing area where young Castleton athletes trained.

THE WORLD HISTORY OF HIGHLAND GAMES

prizes on offer, only one young girl turned up. The games circuit did not get back in full swing until 1919, and even then an important part of the proceedings at the various gatherings was a lone piper playing a lament for those who had fallen in battle. Thousands, with heads uncovered as a mark of respect, listened in absolute silence. Many games added a happier measure adopted to restore the balance. After the lament, a cannon would be fired and then the joy-bells would ring in local churches in a celebration of peace.

It took a decade to bring competition back to the previous level. The Great Depression affected a number of competitors and spectators in the late 1920s and the Second World War halted progress once again. It is truly amazing that traditional activities have survived and flourished once more with little help from any national governments, regardless of political persuasion. The help of local governments in Scotland and generous sponsors has been appreciated but the greatest praise and thanks are due to dedicated individuals and committees whose collective contribution has been quite incredible.

This brief overview takes us to the point in the history of our gatherings and games where more detailed descriptions of events and participants will reveal the fascinating happenings and history of Highland games, Scotland's major contribution to world sport.

1   Elizabeth Grant of Rothiemurchas (1797–1885), *Memoirs of a Highland Lady*; Isabel F. Grant MBE, LLD, *Highland Folk Ways, Along a Highland Road* and *Early History of the Highlands*; and Anne Grant, *Letters from the Mountains*.

2   March played on the bagpipes, entitled *MacGregor of Ruara*.

3   Mrs Grant of Laggan, *Letters from the Mountains* (1773, Vol. 1, p.56).

St Fillans Games from an original etching c.1820.

CHAPTER TWO

Saintly Games: St Fillans and St Ronan's

At the east end of Loch Earn, on the north bank of the River Earn just before its efflux from the loch, there can be found a lovely little village formerly known as Meikleport (little port), or Port of Lochearn. There is an Iron Age fort on top of nearby St Fillans Hill, named after the Irish missionary who is said to have lived there. The hill is also known as Dunfillan and Dundurn.[1]

Meikleport lay within the Drummond Estate and in 1817 Lord Gwydyr married the heiress to the estate, Clementina Drummond, and decided to rename the village 'St Fillans'. Two years later, in this remote backwater, Gwydyr initiated a phenomenon that was far reaching: he formalised and structured the country's ancient folk pastimes into what would become world famous as Scottish Highland games.

The aim was to provide a diversion mainly for the folks of the estate at Drummond Castle, and the programme contained all the main elements of today's Highland games including Highland dancing, piping competitions and 'the usual many feats of strength'. There can also be seen quite clear connections with warlike pursuits of earlier gatherings, with the proceedings of early St Fillans Games opening with rifle shooting.

I am fortunate to have in my private collection the earliest examples of bills advertising Highland games and since a wealth of information on activities and prizes is to be gleaned from these, they are included in full in this chapter. Although the organisers and helpers were volunteers, as has almost always been the case, the main officials had to report for duty at precisely 8am and all the other members, in full Highland regalia, at 10am. Following long-established informal traditions, shooting competitions were primary functions, for the earliest games were closely linked with warlike preparations.

The prize for the winning marksman was a silver-mounted powder horn, the kind often seen in ancient portraits of chieftains and lairds. A handsome mounted dirk (large dagger) and a set of patent leather sword belts provide further emphasis of the games' warlike origins. Another shooting prize was a *queych*, usually spelled 'quaich', which is a shallow Scottish drinking vessel with a small, usually flat, horizontal handle at each side. These are still awarded at some games and in my collection I have a lovely quaich won by former American champion Fred Vaughan. This vessel is over six inches wide and about 1.5 inches deep, and inside the base is engraved with the symbolic 'crest' of the famous Grandfather Mountain Games.

Listed amongst the prizes is a *spleuchan*, a word that has greatly puzzled many people, who have looked in vain in Gaelic dictionaries and thought it was perhaps mis-spelled.

Prize quaich from Grandfather Mountain Games.

One person guessed that it was a telescope, but he was wrong. The word comes from the Doric, a very localised dialect of the north-east of Scotland, the area in which Highland games have flourished over the centuries. It is still spoken in daily life by athletes and officials such as the Aitkens, Andersons, Francis Brebner, Gordon Martin and myself. A spleuchan is a tobacco pouch, which would be considered an everyday object when pipe-smoking was popular.

The Scottish Society of Cambridge and the Highland Society of London presented several of the prizes. The latter had, for many years previously, encouraged activities popular at Highland games. Both organisations were eager to promote all forms of Scottish culture so Ossian's poems figured prominently in the donated awards. Today's winners would not be over-enthusiastic if they won three volumes of Ossian in Gaelic with a literal translation into Latin, but in those days it is almost certain that all the pipers, and many others, would have Gaelic as their first language and those with formal education would likely have a working knowledge of Latin. Donald Dinnie, the champion athlete, for example, was almost definitely fluent in Gaelic, Latin and English.

Further cultural elements in the programme are the competitions for the best essay or song in Gaelic and for the best singer of ancient Gaelic songs. Plaid brooches, snuff mulls and patterned kilt stockings are all indicative of the age.

There were, of course, some differences from modern Highland games and it would indeed be strange if there had not been some development since then. We must not change for change's sake or change the basic character of events, but I strongly believe that while we should maintain traditions of the past, there

Duncan Macpherson announcing at Lonach, Strathdon, 1929.

should also be improvements. To quote but one example, megaphones, microphones and radio mikes have been big improvements in communicating with spectators and are essential for the vast crowds of modern gatherings. In the past, many more people would have heard the Gaelic songs and recitals of poems, and the knowledge of the seanachies would be dispersed more widely had modern public address systems been available.

Even without such niceties, however, St Fillans Games were a great success and repeated annually. It is worth pointing out that these activities were conducted consecutively in 'blocks' rather than simultaneously, as is the case in most Scottish games nowadays.

Professor John Wilson, an eminent writer who became a keen competitor in traditional heavy events, wrote an excellent eyewitness account of St Fillans Games. He was the ideal

St Fillan's in 2004.

person to appreciate the format and performances, and he was to play an important role in developing the concept. 'In physical make, Professor Wilson was of immense and stalwart frame, and of most imposing and prepossessing appearance,' wrote a fellow scribe who knew him well. He continued, 'And these physical features seemed to be but a true reflex of his remarkable mental constitution. In disposition likewise, he was one of the most noble, honest, and straightforward of men, and generous to a fault'.

He was very disappointed with his own physical make-up for he was desperately eager to become a member of the Six-Feet Club but was half an inch too short to join this select group of Scottish sportsmen. Wilson was good at hammer throwing, 'His feat would not have

Professor John Wilson (1785–1854), who originated the once-fashionable phrase 'The sun never sets on the British Empire'.

disgraced Donald Dinnie,' reported *Health and Strength* magazine. The professor also excelled at combat sports such as wrestling and boxing, although the latter has never been included in games programmes.

Professor Wilson visited St Fillans Games and wrote:

The village of St Fillans is of recent origin. It is situated at the east end of Loch Earn, on the north side of the road leading from Perth into the West Highlands, through Strathearn, by Crieff, Comrie and Lochearnhead; and is distant from Comrie five-and-a-half miles, and from Lochearnhead seven miles. It consists of a single row of houses, extending in the form of an irregular semicircle, from the inn at the lower extremity of the lake, partly along the lake side on one hand, and partly along the river which, issuing from it, gives name to the strath, on the other. There is an air about it that is quite pleasing. Most of the houses are slated, and a few of them – at 'the west end' – are two stories in height. Each cottage has on either side of the door narrow strip of ground with a rustic timber-railing, and planted with flowers and shrubs; while ivy, honeysuckle and other creepers, have been neatly trained over the fronts and roofs.

The St Fillans Highland Society, instituted in 1819, was an association of gentlemen of the west of Perthshire who held an annual meeting in August at St Fillans for the encouragement and exhibitions of Highland games and costume. On these occasions, a large square stage was erected on a level piece on a haugh on the south side of the river, opposite the village, to which there is access by a timber bridge. Part of the ground surrounding the platform was railed in, and furnished with seats and awnings for the accommodation of judges and visitors of rank. Behind these, a clear space was allowed as a promenade for members of the society, and beyond the outer barriers the mixed multitude of spectators found a convenient station on a semi-circular sloping bank, from which they could easily see and hear the performances. On the opposite side of the ground, or that next to the river, the carriages and other vehicles of the members were drawn up; the whole being arranged in amphitheatrical order, and with a somewhat classical effect. The games were usually opened with a competition among the pibroch performers, the prize being a handsomely mounted Highland bagpipe. After this and some other prizes had been awarded, the competitors in reel and hornpipe dancing and the ancient sword dance claimed

attention; followed by putting the stone, flinging the hammer, leaping, running, wrestling, target shooting, boat rowing and a variety of other manly and athletic exercises. Prizes were also awarded for the best displays of full Highland costume. At the end of the day, the members of the association dined together in their hall, a commodious building capable of accommodating 140 guests (now the village hostelry). I am not aware that the St Fillans society has had any gatherings in recent years.

Immediately above the games arena towers an isolated rocky eminence, known as Dunfillan or St Fillans Hill. On the south and east it is inaccessible, but it can be easily ascended on the north and west faces. St Fillan – whose name has been given to so many chapels, wells and other monastic relics in Scotland – is said to have flourished in the 7th century. He is said to have filled the office of abbot at Pittenweem, where he died in the odour of sanctity, and amidst his affectionate converts, in 649 AD.

The saint had erected three chapels in the district, one at Strathfillan, another at Killin and a third at Dundurn, in the immediate vicinity of the present village of St Fillans. He died at Dundurn, but the people of both Strathfillan and Killin each thought themselves to possess a better claim to the saint's relics. Accordingly, they proceeded to transport the body through Glenogle, with all decent and devout ceremony. On arriving, however, at a point about two miles from Killin, where the road branches off to Strathfillan, the funeral train – as might have

A semi-silhouette of John Wilson's statue in Princes Street Gardens, Edinburgh. Thousands pass it every day without knowing who he is or what he did.

    THE WORLD HISTORY OF HIGHLAND GAMES

been expected – became divided in their sentiments as to which road they should pursue, and words speedily became blows. As the strife waxed warmer, and swords had been drawn and blood was shed, it was discovered that two coffins exactly the same in appearance were before them. Each party seized one, and it remains a question to this day whether Strathfillan or Killin possesses the true relics of the patron saint of Breadalbane.

Today, nothing remains of the old chapel or oratory of the saint at Dundurn except a circular stone font, which can be seen in the window of the present chapel. A rude stone on the top of Dunfillan has been designated as St Fillan's chair; and a spring of water at the foot, known as St Fillan's well, was long resorted to for its healing virtues.[2]

St Fillans Games lasted for 12 years, with only occasional less-formal activities in the 1830s, but they started a new style of presenting Scotland's indigenous sports to a wider public and from there this tradition gradually spread to every continent in the world.

Professor Wilson's important contribution to Highland games goes well beyond leaving us a splendid description of St Fillans Games: we believe that he, along with James Hogg, was the catalyst for literary greats who added prestige and credibility to Scotland's ethnic sports. These men and their links with these activities should not be forgotten.

Sir Walter Scott (right). John Wilson is at the back of the group.

Professor Wilson was the main writer for Blackwood's Magazine, first published in April 1817 as The Edinburgh Monthly Magazine, the name being changed to Blackwood's Edinburgh Magazine in October of that year. Most of Wilson's contributions were published anonymously, as was the policy of this periodical, or else under his well-known *nom de plume*, Christopher North. The reason for this anonymity was because this new publication was probably Scotland's first experience of investigative journalism. The new writers had rightly judged that many people, however virtuous, took a malicious pleasure in seeing the mighty fall and hardly an issue passed without Blackwood's hatchet men taking someone to task. The authors were

This poster shows the variety of games in which Wilson competed.

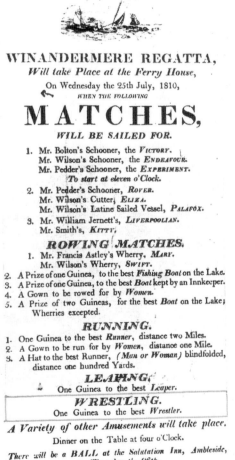

adept in the art. However, besides this selling point, there were wide-ranging articles on art, literature, politics, personalities and humour. The publisher relied largely on work by Professor Wilson and John Gibson Lockhart.

Wilson was born into a wealthy family near Paisley on 18 May 1785 and after private tuition went to Glasgow University at the early age of 14. Five years later, he entered Magdalene College, Oxford, where he became a

Bust of Sir Walter Scott (in author's collection).

distinguished poet and expert on Latin and Greek classical writers. It is interesting that he was no less distinguished in all sorts of outdoor sports and athletics 'and almost any amusement which permitted of an expenditure of animal spirits and energy, of which the young gentleman appeared to have rather much, if anything'. These qualities were amply displayed when he later competed in traditional games in Scotland. He was further enriched when he married a lovely English lady with a dowry of £10,000, a fortune in those days.

John Gibson Lockhart, who wrote 'Peter's Letters' for *Blackwood's*, described Wilson's appearance:

> In complexion he is the best specimen I have ever seen of the genuine ideal Goth. His hair is of true Sicambrian yellow; his eyes are of the brightest, and at the same time clearest blue, and his blood glows in his cheeks.

Although Wilson studied law, he did not practise but instead became editor of *Blackwood's Magazine* and professor of moral philosophy at Edinburgh University. His acknowledged extraordinary strength and energy was channelled into a variety of projects and amongst his close friends were Sir Walter Scott and James Hogg, the Ettrick Shepherd (1770–1835). All of this is relevant to Highland games.

Sir Walter Scott and Professor Wilson were very interested in St Fillans Games and others similar, and when Scott organised the proceedings for King George IV's visit to Scotland in 1822, the Strathfillan Society, which promoted St Fillans Games, was invited to take part in an elaborate welcoming parade. Led by Grahame of Airth and Stewart of Ardvoilich, the parade participants were resplendent in full Highland dress with lavish accoutrements and arms, including swords, targes and long-barrelled guns. The crowds of spectators were attracted especially to the gillies from St Fillans, described as tall, raw-boned, swarthy characters who looked as though they lived by hunting and slept in the woods. This great celebration was largely responsible for reviving enthusiasm for Celtic culture.

We can still see clansmen marching with ancient pikes and Lochaber axes at Lonach Games. At the modern Atholl Gatherings, Europe's last private army, the Duke of Atholl's Highlanders, parade with their now old-fashioned Lee Enfield rifles and ancient cannon.

Five years after King George IV's visit to Scotland, four literary giants – Sir Walter Scott, Professor John Wilson, James Hogg and William Blackwood of magazine fame – became deeply

Annual march of the Lonach men, 1954.

THE WORLD HISTORY OF HIGHLAND GAMES

involved in Caledonian sports in their own areas. This led the way to making Scottish traditional gatherings and games as we know them today, for these did not happen only in the Highlands but also in the Lowlands, right down to the border with England.

St Ronan's Border Games

Although born in Edinburgh, Sir Walter Scott was brought up in the Borders and in 1823 his novel *St Ronan's Well* transformed this quiet Scottish–English border area into a popular tourist destination. Four years later, the St Ronan's Border Club was established. The organisation's stated aim was to revive the old martial spirit of the Borders, to encourage the practice of outdoor sports and pastimes and to yield amusement to visitors of this sequestered watering place. The first annual gathering was held on 26 September 1827 and after nearly 180 years, these games are still held in Innerleithen, near Peebles.

John Gibson Lockhart left a good account of the proceedings for posterity. His sayings and writing were often incorporated into Professor Wilson's 'Ambrosian Nights' features in *Blackwood's Magazine*, Lockhart's aliases being William Wassel, Dr Ulrick Strernstare and Dr Peter Morris. In referring to Scott's *St Ronan's*

John Gibson Lockhart (1794–1854).

St Fillan's is in the parish of Comrie, in an area now known as Perth and Kinross. It is right off the beaten track and there is a hydro-electric station in a large underground cavern hewn out of the solid rock. The basin of Loch Earn, which goes down some 50m, was created by icy erosion during the glacial periods.

Well and its effect on the district, here is what Lockhart had to say:

> The notables of the little town voted by acclamation that the old name of Innerleithen should be, as far as possible, dropped thenceforth, and that of St Ronan's adopted. Nor were they mistaken in their auguries.
>
> Amongst other consequences of the revival of the place, a yearly festival was instituted for the celebration of the St Ronan's Border Games. A club of Bowmen of the Border arrayed in doublets of Lincoln green, with broad blue bonnets, and having the Ettrick Shepherd for Captain, assumed the principal management of this exhibition; and Sir Walter Scott was

well pleased to be enrolled among them. During several years he was a regular attendant, both on the Meadow, where (besides archery) leaping, racing, wrestling, stone-heaving and hammer throwing, went on opposite to the noble old Castle of Traquair, and at the subsequent banquet, where Hogg, in full costume, always presided as master of ceremonies. In fact, a gayer spectacle than that of St Ronan's Games in those days could not well have been desired. The Shepherd, even when on the verge of threescore, exerted himself lustily in the field, and seldom failed to carry off some of the prizes, to the astonishment of his vanquished juniors; and the *bon-vivante* of Edinburgh mustered strong amongst the gentry and yeomanry of Tweedsdale to see him afterwards in his glory filling the president's chair with eminent success, and commonly supported on this – which was in fact the grandest evening of his year – by Sir Walter Scott, Professor Wilson, Sir Adam Ferguson, and Peter Robertson.

Although writing styles have changed greatly since then, this shows that archery was still an important part of the programme and confirms that heavy and light events were prominent.

Papingo archery trophy, Kilwinning. This Ancient Society of Archers originated in 1483. Medals were added by past winners.

After all these years, we are pleased to be reminded of the ability and leading role of the Borders man James Hogg, the Ettrick Shepherd, during these formative years of the games.

Hogg wanted to spread some sweetness and light into the lives of ordinary people during a period of national unrest. Lords, dukes, earls and local gentry supported the shepherd. It was nobility at this level that became the first 'tone-givers' and offered sponsorship to the games, not Queen Victoria as so many believe. The Duke of Buccleuch and Lord Napier were members of St Ronan's Border Club and the Earl of Traquair was patron. Others, such as the publisher William Blackwood and Adam Wilson, captain of the Six-Feet Club, were also notables present on these occasions.

James Hogg was undoubtedly a key figure and bragged about how he had saved the demise of traditional manly exercises in the Borders. This should not be disputed; Hogg personally contributed prizes and augmented his prize fund with donations from well-to-do local farmers and his rich colleagues in Edinburgh.

At a celebration dinner after the first games, John Wilson took the chair, and as part of the proceedings James Hogg sang to the assembled company. Later, Sir Walter Scott was elected for life and was made 'Umpire of the Games'.

The results of competitions showed that Hogg's archery prowess was not quite up his abilities with the grey-goose quill. The Ettrick Shepherd enthusiastically entered the rifle shooting contests and tried his hand at wrestling but was unfortunate to be drawn against the mighty George Scougal, who 'couped him bonny'. This was the Scottish way of saying 'threw him beautifully'. Hogg always wrestled in his top boots, although sometimes he was criticised for doing this.

The best bowmen of that era were Robert Bell and Jed Water. Jed was also the champion stone putter and was said to be better than any man in the three kingdoms. Leading newspapers published challenges for a 12-month period, offering £100 to anyone who could beat him in putting with the 16lb or 21lb ball – Jed on his knees and his opponent on his feet! Nobody rose to the challenge.

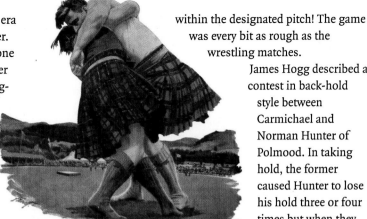

Backhold wrestling as practised in Scotland for centuries.

Several prizes in hammer throwing were won by the two Harper brothers, who farmed near Innerleithen. George Scougal, considered the champion wrestler of Scotland, also won three hammer throwing medals, and in the light events the champion leaper was Leyton of Denholme. He could spring 32 feet in three standing jumps and was also an expert in backward jumps. George Best, a tailor from Yarrow, was said to be more skilful than Scougal. Wilson's regular column had the Shepherd say about Best:

> The flying tailor o'Ettrick, sir – him that can do 15 yards [45 feet] at hap-step-and loup, back and forward on level grun' – stood second ae year in the ring at Carlisle – can put a stane within a foot o' Jedburgh Bell himsell, and fling the hammer neist best ower the border to Geordie Scougal in Innerleithen.

It has not been possible to find evidence of Best taking a second place at Carlisle.

Apart from the short sprints, shepherds generally won foot races at St Ronan's.

A popular part of the annual games was an Innerleithen versus Traquair football match, with anything up to 60 players on each side. As if that was not bizarre enough, the River Leithen was within the designated pitch! The game was every bit as rough as the wrestling matches.

James Hogg described a contest in back-hold style between Carmichael and Norman Hunter of Polmood. In taking hold, the former caused Hunter to lose his hold three or four times but when they finally closed, Hunter swept Carmichael off his feet as though he was a child and threw him down to win easily. It is also on record that the Ettrick Shepherd thought that Geordie Cochran's chip was invincible when properly applied. The ebullient shepherd poet was a vociferous supporter given to commentaries on the proceedings, laced with colourful encouragement to the competitors.

As a result of John Wilson's influence in the formation of the games and his particular interest in wrestling, this sport became one of the highlights of the annual programme and the Six-Feet Club awarded a fine medal for the winning back-hold-style wrestler at the inaugural games. In this style, the wrestlers put their arms round their opponent, one arm over his shoulder and the other under his arm, and thus clasp their own hands behind the other's back. The first winner was George Scougal (Innerleithen), who beat 31 competitors to win the award. He won again in 1828 and 1829 but was then barred from entering competitions at these games for the next three years. This was a common practice, not as a result of misdemeanour but done to prevent lesser competitors from being discouraged from entering. After Scougal, Robert Michie of Hawick won the main award – now a belt that became the customary champion's prize. Michie won this on two occasions.

Scougal was 5 feet 11 inches in height and he would usually compete at a weight of 15.5 stones (around 217lb or 100kg). He was a massive, powerfully built man who won his matches with the Herculean power of arms and shoulders rather than skill. The cross-buttock was the nearest approach to technique demonstrated by Scougal. Usually, he would pull his opponent into a rib-crushing bear hug and hold him there, squirming but helpless, until the champion saw an opportunity to put him on his back.

In addition to the six medals he won at St Ronan's, George had numerous awards at other sports meetings. From readings of Christopher North's (John Wilson's) writings, we find that Scougal was a butcher by trade. Many continental wrestlers and strong men followed the same profession and around a century ago it was said that if you wanted to find the strongest men in a village or town you had only to go to the blacksmith's smiddy or butcher's shop to find them. George Scougal's slaughter-house was right next door to a blacksmith's smiddy and this was where he demonstrated his favourite feat of lifting the heavy axle and wheels of a wagon with the heaviest men available sitting one at each end. He was described as a veritable Goliath of Gath in strength but as gentle as a woman in manner – unless he became excited, then it was a completely different situation, for he became very rough.

A powerful farmer, Abraham Clark of Calzie, came to the fore after the outlawing of Scougal and an even finer strength athlete was Robert Michie of Hawick, Scougal's successor at St Ronan's. Having served an 'apprenticeship' as an amateur, Michie began touring other Borders games, with great success in wrestling and with the hammer. At Hawick Border Games in 1831, he beat Carlisle's Thomas Emmerson, the north of England favourite. Emmerson was a powerfully built mason who wrestled with high-standard champions at Carlisle and other noted rings. He was moderately successful in these big tournaments.

Competitors in Scottish backhold wrestling clad in Cumberland and Westmorland dress code

Rob Michie, also known as 'Meikle Rab', was introduced to many by Wilson in his *Tales of the Borders*:

At a distance from the pavilion was a crowd of seven or eight hundred peasantry engaged in and witnessing the athletic games of the Borders. Among the competitors was one called Meikle Robin or Robin Meikle. He was strength personified. His stature exceeded six feet; his shoulders were broad, his chest round, his limbs well and strongly put together. He was a man of prodigious bone and sinews. At throwing the hammer, at putting the stone, no man could stand before him. He distanced all who came against him, and, while he did so, so seemed to put forth not half his strength, while his skill appeared equal to the power of his arm.

However, in 1831 the *Edinburgh Literary Journal* criticised the wrestlers at St Ronan's Games:

Wrestling is not a Scotch games, as will be conceded by every one who has been present at the Carlisle and St Ronan's games. There is strength enough amongst our peasantry, but this is the ore- it has never been moulded for a practical purpose. Men came forward on this occasion who never would have dreamed of thrusting their noses into an English ring; and they set to work in a slovenly unhandsome way- some of them armed *cap-a-pie* – hat, coat and shoes.

Still amid the motley crew you might recognise men who knew how to seize and to wield their antagonists. The art only needs encouragement; and we trust the next meeting will witness a better turn-out.

There is no doubt that wrestlers were much better dressed in later contests. The trend was set by English entrants, who took great pride in their outfits. At major back-hold wrestling tournaments, there were often prizes for the best athletic costumes, which raised the standard of dress.

The notable part in Scottish games history played by Sir Walter Scott, James Hogg and Professor John Wilson cannot be overlooked,

Statue of James Hogg, the Ettrick Shepherd, at St Mary's Loch.

The Scott Monument, Edinburgh.

but little can be served in comparing their respective roles and importance with the games – they all contributed in different ways. They salvaged what they could of Scottish culture and folklore after rebellions, wars and a rapidly changing way of life.

Fortunately, these three eminent figures have been appropriately acknowledged for their literary achievements. The Scott Monument dominates the view of Princes Street in Edinburgh and must surely be the greatest-ever memorial to a writer. There are also statues of him in various other towns. Professor Wilson died in 1854 and an impressive 10-foot-high bronze statue of him was made by John Steel and erected in the north-west corner of East Princes Street Gardens in Edinburgh in 1865. These are fine commemorations of great Scots and we should be proud to link their names with the early development of the modern concept of Scottish games.

The Border games at St Ronan's are still popular, with many competitors from the Highlands. Likewise, competitors from the Borders area compete in games in the Highlands. The rules of the activities are much the same and there is also integration in all aspects. These great men left a lasting legacy.

Dumfries Border Games

Several Borders games adopted the pattern established at St Fillans and St Ronan's. Amongst these the Dumfries Border Games were the most successful, attracting as many people as today's games in Scotland. Once again, wrestling played a prominent feature in the proceedings, which is not surprising considering the popularity of the sport in northern England and southern Scotland. The committee realised that the back-hold wrestlers were good 'box office' attractions and increased prize money for such events. As expected, those from south of the border took most of the awards. Jimmie Paterson was the best grappler in 1858, the year the Games were amalgamated with the Rood Fair on the dock by the River Nith.

Paterson of Weardale took home six and a half pounds, a splendid sum in those days. The organisers used a similar set-up to the Grasmere Games, with a large grandstand for local councillors, special guests and well-to-do

spectators. In other parts of the arena there was two-tiered seating and standing room around the ground. In total, crowds of up to 5,500 people could be accommodated comfortably, and more could be squeezed in if necessary. In addition, good prizes were also given in the piping competitions, Highland dancing and heavy events, all of which were popular with the public.

[1] In order to be consistent in this section we have used the spelling and punctuation St Fillans. This is how Professor John Wilson used it. Although St Fillan's is perhaps more correct, the committee in those days were not consistent and used various spellings.

[2] I am indebted to John Burnett, Curator of the History of Sport at the National Museum of Scotland, for providing a cutting of Professor Wilson's description of St Fillans.

These wrestling and caber tossing postcards are from Edwardian times, sent 1903–1905.

This original handbill is probably the oldest and most valuable Highland games document in existence. It contains detailed information on events and prizes etc. at the earliest formalised Highland games.

CHAPTER THREE

The Lady of the Lake

Sir Walter Scott's famous poem, *The Lady of the Lake*, contains one of the most important literary contributions to Highland games by one of the world's great writers who maintained the country's history in the old tradition. The games are not the main subject of his story, but Scott carefully researched his work and, in what would now be termed 'documentary drama', he included vital information for future readers. Most of the specific parts concerning the gathering and games are contained in the fifth canto, 'The Combat' (verses 20 to 27), while verses 13 to 19 give the lead-up to the event.

The scene of the poem is mainly the vicinity of Loch Katrine, in Scotland's beautiful Trossachs. As part of this story, Scott describes a journey well known to those of us who regularly attend Highland games at places such as Callander, Killin, Lochearnhead and Stirling. The time frame takes in six adventurous days and each canto describes one day.

As we have pointed out, in distant days our Scottish history was passed down by bards and seanachaidhs, and Scott's poem begins by lamenting that the harp has been hanging unused for too long. He asks:

> O minstrel Harp, still must thine accents sleep?
> 'Mid rustling leaves and fountains murmuring,
> Still must thy sweeter sounds their silence keep,
> Nor bid a warrior smile, nor teach a maid to weep?

Sir Walter, who became the most inspiring of all Scots tale-tellers, takes up the mantle of the ancient bards and goes on to give his rhyming account, beginning with a hunting party chasing a stag. After a long, exciting chase, one hunter sees a little skiff carrying the Lady of the Lake, who gave the poem its name:

> Eddying in almost viewless wave,
> The weeping willow twig to lave[1],
> And kiss, with whispering sound and slow,
> The beach of pebbles bright as snow.
> The boat had touched this silver strand,
> Just as the Hunter left his stand,
> And stood concealed amid the brake,
> To view the Lady of the Lake,
> The maiden paused, as if again
> She sought to catch the distant strain.
> With head up raised, and look intent,
> And eye and ear attentive bent,
> And locks flung back and lips apart,
> Like monument of Grecian art,
> In listening mood, she seemed to stand
> The guardian Naiad of the strand.

The continuing proceedings are related in this fashion. Verses 13 to 19 of the fifth canto lead up to the gathering before the games begin in what was variously described as Stirling's Royal Park or Castle Park, but is now described as the King's Park, which fits in well with the story. There, James V, King of Scotland, is attending traditional revels:

> To James, at Stirling, let us go,
> When if thou wilt be still his foe,
> Grant the grace and favours free,

A man hunting a Stag.

Loch Katrine's silver strand.

> I plight mine
> honour, oath and
> word.
>   That, to thy
>   native strength
>   restored.

Following this, there are several verses of an incredible fight to the death of the Highland chief Roderick Dhu. It is well worth reading for the vivid and exciting portrayal in poetry, but outside the scope of this resume. Stirling is eventually reached on the sixth day, at the end of verse 18, when the adventurous group career towards the castle on the rock that overlooks the games field:

> Right-hand they leave the cliffs, Craig Forth,
>   And soon the bulwark of the North,
>   Grey Stirling with her towers and town,
>   Upon their fleet career looked down.

As they go up the slope leading to the castle, the leader spies an impressive figure:

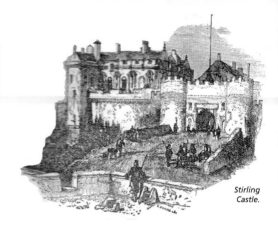
Stirling Castle.

> As up the flinty path they
>   strained,
>   Sudden his steed the leader
>   reined;
>   A signal to his squire he flung,
> Who instant to his stirrups
>   sprung:–
> 'Seest thou, De Vaux, yon woods-
>   man grey,
> Who town-ward holds the rocky
>   way,
> Of stature tall and poor array?
> Mark you the firm, but active stride
> With which he scales the mountain side?
> Know'st from whence he comes, or whom?
> 'No, by my word:– a burly groom
> He seems who in the field or chase
> A Baron's train would nobly grace.'
> 'Out, out, De Vaux! Can fear supply,
> And jealousy no sharper eye?

The Lady of the Lake.

> Afar, ere to the hill he drew,
> That stately form and step I knew;
> Like form in Scotland is not seen,
> Steps not such step on Scottish green.
> 'Tis James of Douglas by Saint Serle!
> The uncle of the banished Earl.
> Away, away, the court, to show
> The near approach of dreaded foe:
> The king must stand upon his guard,'–
> Douglas and he must meet prepared.
> Then right-hand wheeled their steeds, and straight
> They won the castle's postern gate.

Briefly, this explains that, as the mounted group get very close to Stirling Castle, a man of fine physique and athletic appearance catches their attention. Back in verse eight of the second canto, there are two lines indicating that the Douglases were driven to ruin and 'exiled from their native heaven'. In this account the particular representative of this illustrious clan had come from Cambuskenneth Abbey. This character plays a major role in our sphere of interest.[2] Douglas threads his way through the story, and as they see the castle towers:

> Ye towers within whose circuit dread
> A Douglas by his sovereign bled,
> And thou, O sad and fatal mound
> That oft has heard the death-axe sound,
> The dungeon, block, and nameless tomb
> Prepare– for Douglas seeks his doom!

THE WORLD HISTORY OF HIGHLAND GAMES

In the latter part of verse 20, the scene becomes animated, as it continues to do on games day:

> And see upon the crowded street,
> In motley groups what masquers meet!
> Banner and pageant, pipe and drum,
> And many morrice dancers come.
> I guess by all this quaint array,
> The burghers have their sports today.

Decapitation stone by Stirling.

These revels were an informal but clearly identifiable forerunner to what we now call Highland games. They included archery, caber tossing (hurling the bar) and other heavy events, as will be seen later. In his notes at the end of his book of poems, Sir Walter Scott explains:

> Every burgh in Scotland of the least note, but more especially the considerable towns, had their solemn play, or festival, when feats of archery were exhibited, and prizes distributed to those who excelled in wrestling, hurling the bar, and other gymnastic exercises of the period. The usual prize to the best shooter was a silver arrow. At Dumfries a silver gun was substituted, and the contention transferred to fire-arms. The usual prize for wrestling was a ram and a ring but the animal would embarrassed my story.

The poem, however, proceeds:

> As slowly down the steep descent
> Fair Scotland's King and nobles went
> Gravely he greets each city sire,
> Commends each pageant's quaint attire,
> Gives the dancers thanks aloud,
> And smiles and nods upon the crowd.

By now the poem has mentioned all the main participants in Highland games – pipers and drummers, dancers, heavies and wrestlers. As the poet continued to set the scene, he wrote:

> Now, in the Castle park drew out
> Their chequered bands the joyous rout,
> There morricers, with bell at heel
> And blade in hand, their maces wheel:

> But chief besides the butts there stands
> Bold Robin Hood and all his band –
> Friar Tuck with quarter staff and cowl.
> Old Scathelocke with his surly scowl.

In the past, I did not deal fully with Scott's story when researching Highland games. One part in particular made it lose credibility in my eyes, but I was wrong. The mention of the characters from Sherwood forest seemed out of context and totally inappropriate, but my discovery of Scott's very valid commentary encouraged me to take a completely new perspective – and then it sounded more than ever like a Scottish games.

Sir Walter Scott wrote:

> The exhibition of this renowned outlaw and his band was a favourite frolic at such festivals as described. This sport, at which kings did not distain to be actors, was prohibited in Scotland upon the Reformation, by a stature of the sixth parliament of Queen Mary, c.61 AD 1555.
> It would seem, however, from the complaints of the General Assembly of the Kirk, that these profane festivities were continued down to 1592.

Apart from the fact that archery and shooting were featured at the earliest formalised games, even in these modern times we often see similar,

Actors at Stranraer Games in 1960s. There was a cowled figure with a quarterstaff.

almost identical, groups and various re-enactments. As the archery drew to a finale, there was a challenge and the mighty James Douglas accepted it, won and reluctantly accepted the prize from King James:

> Their bugles challenge all that will,
> In archery to prove their skill.
> The Douglas bent a bow of might,
> His first shaft centred in the white,
> And when in turn he shot again,
> His second split the first in twain.
> From the King's hand must Douglas take
> A silver dart, the archers' stake;
> Fondly he watched with watery eye,
> Some answering glance of sympathy –
> No kind emotion made reply!
> Indifferent as to archer wight,
> The Monarch gave the arrow bright.

> XXIII
> Now, clear the Ring for hand to hand,
> The manly wrestlers take their stand.
> Two o'er the rest superior rose,
> And proud demanded mightier foes,
> Nor called in vain; for Douglas came

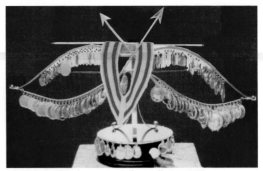

Kilwinning archers have competed annually since 1483. A medal is added each year.

> – For life is Hugh of Larbert lame,
> Scarce better John of Alloa's fares,
> Whom senseless home his comrades bear.
> Prize of the wrestling match, the King
> To Douglas gave a golden ring.
> While coldly glanced his eyes of blue,
> As frozen drop of wintry dew.
> Douglas would speak but in his breast
> His struggling soul his words suppressed;
> Indignant then he turned them where
> Their arms the brawny yeoman bare,
> To hurl the massive bar in air.

Wrestling is practiced world-wide in many different styles.

THE WORLD HISTORY OF HIGHLAND GAMES

When each his utmost strength had shown,
The Douglas rent an earth-fast stone
From its deep bed and heaved it high,
And sent the fragment through the sky,
A rood beyond the furthest mark; –
And still in Stirling's royal park,
The grey-haired sires, who knew the past,
To strangers point the Douglas-cast,
And moralise on the decay
Of Scottish strength in modern day.

XXIV
The vale with loud applauses rang,
The Ladies Rock sent back the clang;
The King with look unmoved bestowed
A purse well filled with pieces broad.
Indignant smiled the Douglas proud
And threw the gold into the crowd.

The poem continues in heroic vein, with proud
Douglas scorned by the king but winning the
hearts of the crowd who plainly showed their
admiration. The king was not amused and
created a diversion:

The Monarch saw the gambols flag,
And bade let loose a gallant stag,
Whose pride, the holiday to crown.
Two favourite grey-hounds would pull down,
That venison free, and Bordeaux wine,
Might serve the archery to dine.

Once again, Douglas outwitted the king, whose
plan now backfired and the games ended in
chaos:

'Break off the sports!'– he said, and
frowned,
And bid our horsemen clear the
ground.'–
Then uproar wild and misarray
Marred the fair form of festal day.
The horsemen pricked among the
crowd,
Repelled by threats and insults loud;
To earth are borne the old and weak,
The timorous fly, the women shriek;
With flint, with shaft, with staff,
with bar,
The hardier urge tumultuous war

At once round Douglas darkly sweep,
The royal spears in circle deep,
And slowly scale the path-way steep,
While on the rear in thunder pour,
The rabble with disordered roar.
With grief the noble Douglas saw
The commons rise against the law.

One of Walter Scott's explanatory notes gives us
an insight to the motivation leading to this
dramatic scene. He wrote of the downfall of the
Douglases of the House of Angus during the reign
of King James V:

The exiled state of this powerful race is not
exaggerated... The hatred of James was so
inveterate, that, numerous though there allies
were, and disregarded as the regal authority
had usually been in similar cases, their nearest
friends, even in the most remote parts of
Scotland, durst not entertain them, unless
under the strictest and closest disguise.

These are simply brief excerpts from an incredible
piece of poetry that exceeded all sales records.
Although statistics vary, it has been said that over
12,000 copies sold in a few weeks and 20,000 sold
in the first year. One report claimed that 50,000
copies were sold in 12 months. There is a telling
quote in Scott's main biography that shows that
all these claims may have been founded on fact.
It is explained that by July 1836 *legitimate* sales
were not less than 50,000 copies, since which
days, in spite of legal and illegal piracies,
the fair demand has been well kept up. Scott
was probably the first great writer to suffer
drastically from copyright piracy. The inclusion of the *Lady of the Lake* in hundreds of
books makes it not unlikely to be the
most published poem of all time.

The importance of this
poem to Highland games
enthusiasts lies in the fact that
Scott, a credible historian and
researcher, wrote most of this

*Archibald McIntosh
(b.1827). Detail from
MacLeay watercolour.*

poem in 1809, ten years before St Fillans Games, which is now widely accepted as the first codified, formalised games with specific documentation. It was written some 17 years prior to St Ronan's Games and describes a gathering and games during the reign of James V (between 1513 and 1542), more than 300 years before those at St Fillans. Also important are the mentions of King James's attendance and prize giving at the games. It is indeed very thought-provoking material from one of the most respected literary figures of all time.

1 *Lave*: to wash or bathe.

2 James V (1513–42)'s hatred of the Douglases is better understood with the knowledge that, soon after he was born at Linlithgow Palace on 10 April 1512, he became the object of a struggle between nobles who sought to use him to gain power. Douglas, the Earl of Angus, took him hostage and it was not until he was 16 years old that the young king escaped from the Douglases.

Throughout his life, the king harboured a grudge and took every opportunity to seek revenge. Perhaps the most chilling episode was when the beautiful sister of Douglas, Earl of Angus, Lady Glamis, was accused of plotting the assassination of the king. Although she may have been innocent, he had her burned at the stake in front of Edinburgh Castle.

King James had close relations with the French monarchy and generally, apart from the Douglases, he was well respected by Scottish nobility, most of whom admired the lavish buildings that became James's heritage to Scotland. He achieved a good deal in this respect in his short life, dying of cholera or dysentery at the age of 30.

Mary, Queen of Scots was his daughter.

James V.

Sir Walter Scott.

THE WORLD HISTORY OF HIGHLAND GAMES

CHAPTER FOUR

Laggan's Royal Games

In 1847, when Queen Victoria and her family visited Laggan, near Kingussie, she watched Scottish Highland games. At that time, illustrations of caber tossing, stone putting, high jumping and hill racing were published and names of some winners were recorded. Since then, these games at Laggan and their significance has largely been forgotten. This was the first time that Victoria and Albert had seen traditional Scottish games and it was the beginning of a lifelong interest that became extremely valuable to the development of such activities.

The visit to Laggan was marred by rain but the Queen took the opportunity to sketch Ardverikie[I], the house in which they lived, and also the surroundings and children. Her writings give many reminders of this totally different age.

In her personal diary of 21 August 1847, she wrote:

> Alas! A very wet morning. We were ready long before nine o'clock, but had to wait, as our carriages were not ready. At last we all landed at Fort William where there was a great gathering of Highlanders all in their different tartans, with

The Royal party watch the start of the hill race.

Lord Lovat and Mr Stuart Mackenzie at their head. We got into our carriage with Charles and the two children, there was a great crowd to see us off. We went by a very wild and lonely road, the latter part extremely fine, with mountains and streams that reminded us of Glen Tilt. We changed horses only once, and came at length in sight of Loch Laggan. It is a beautiful lake, (small in comparison to what we have seen) surrounded by very fine mountains.: the road by its side is extremely pretty. We saw Lord Abercorn's house of Ardverikie long before we came to it.

At Laggan there is only a small inn, and at the end of the lake, a ferry. Here in spite of the pouring rain, were assembled a number of Highlanders, with Macpherson of Cluny (always called Cluny Macpherson) and three dear little boys of his, Davidson of Tulloch, and others, with Lord Abercorn in full Highland dress. We stepped out of our carriage and stood upon

A. MacPherson of Cluny. By R. R. McIan (1803–1856).

the floating bridge and so crossed over in two or three minutes. We then drove on in our pony carriages, to Ardverikie, and arrived there in about 20 minutes. It is quite close to the lake, and the view from the windows, as I now write, though obscured by rain, is very beautiful, and extremely wild.

There is not a village, house or cottage within four or five miles: one can only get to it by the ferry, or by rowing across the lake. The house is a comfortable shooting lodge, built with stone and with many nice rooms in it. Stags horns are placed along the outside and in the passages; and the walls of the drawing room and ante-room are ornamented with beautiful drawings of stags, by Landseer.

On the 28th, about five o'clock, Albert drove me out across the ferry, along the Kingussie road, and from here the scenery was splendid: high bold hills, with a good deal of wood; glens with the Pattock, and a small water-fall; the meadows here and there with people making hay, and cottages sprinkled sparingly about, reminded me much of Thuringen. We drove to the small farm, where Colonel Macpherson now lives, called Strathmashie, and back again, 16 miles in all. We were delighted with the scenery, which is singularly beautiful, wild and romantic – with so much fine wood about it, which greatly enhances the beauty of a landscape.

Friday. 17 September. At two o'clock I left Ardverikie with the children, and reached Fort William at half past six, where I had the happiness of finding Albert on board the yacht.

In between these two entries in the Queen's diary, she celebrated her beloved husband's birthday with an event that was unique for them both.

The Laggan Games of 1847

On 27 August a very special treat was arranged to coincide with Prince Albert's birthday. That day, the estate became the venue for a traditional Highland gathering and games, and the public and athletes turned out to watch, participate and share in the Queen's delight in the proceedings.

One enthralled spectator was six-year-old Edward, Prince of Wales, later to become monarch. On a fashion note, he was resplendent in a Royal Stewart tartan kilt. The programme consisted of 'all sorts of ancient and warlike games'. These, of course, were the ethnic sports that were to become a regular part of Victoria and Albert's itinerary while in Scotland.

There are two important points that must be noted. First, although Queen Victoria's great interest in Highland games is almost inevitably linked with Braemar and 'Balmorality', she and the Royal family's first experience of a traditional Highland games was there in the grounds of Ardverikie by Laggan. Second, it started a boom, and a rapid development of such events not only in Scotland but also in other parts of the world where Scottish immigrants abounded.

The winner of the high jump was Gunn, a bank clerk in Inverness. He took two or three unhurried steps and sprang over the bar, landing 'as lightly as a cat'.

Such activities had been taking place in Scotland long before Queen Victoria was born. She was aware of this because one of her favourite books was Sir Walter Scott's *Lady of the Lake*, which strongly features royal games in the park below Stirling Castle. In her library at Balmoral she had 32 copies of this book so that her guests could share her passion. The Queen was very well acquainted with the content and would quote passages from this epic poem in her diary.

The national press were most interested and supportive of the Highland Games. Even staid London papers enthused and covered the events

THE WORLD HISTORY OF HIGHLAND GAMES

in text and illustration. They did, however, complain about the remoteness of the location, and Prince Albert seemed to relish their grumbling. 'The reporters call it an un-come-at-able place,' he wrote to the Duchess of Kent. 'They are quartered on the other side of Loch Laggan, which is only to be crossed on a flying bridge that belongs exclusively to ourselves.' In those days, the bridge floated on the loch but long afterwards was replaced by an iron bridge.

Putting the stone at Laggan. These athletic images were made in 1847 to illustrate Laggan Highland Games.

On a fact-finding trip to the area, it was found that Ardverikie is as unapproachable as it was in Victorian times, but the unsurpassed scenery and opportunity to follow the royal footsteps to Cluny MacPherson's Strathmashie and local beauty spots adequately compensate for minor disappointments.

Originally it had been hoped that by exploring the area, and hopefully Ardverikie estate, there could be found on-the-spot evidence, archives and graphics relating to the Queen's visit in general and Laggan Highland Games in particular. However, this was not possible. Set in the Cairngorms National Park, surrounded by the Monadliadh Mountains, Ardverikie is built close to the shore of beautiful Loch Laggan, which lies in Glen Spean between Kingussie and Fort William. It has, as a distant background, the impressive peaks of the Ben Nevis range.

Travelling from the south, one must leave the A9 at Dalwhinnie and continue north through some splendid scenery still unspoiled by man. Because of this, it has become the setting for a number of films, including *Mrs Brown* and the very popular BBC television series *Monarch of the Glen*.

Mrs Brown dealt with the relationship between Queen Victoria and her faithful personal servant John Brown, played by Scottish actor Billy Connolly. Dame Judi Dench, who has also attended Highland games, played Queen Victoria. Connolly, the country's greatest comedian and Highland games enthusiast, has his own beautiful estate in Scotland and has been responsible for a great upturn in development and attendances at the picturesque Lonach Highland Games on Donside. His daughter, Scarlett, is a multi-prize-winning junior Highland dancer. Incidentally, the Lonach Games go back long before Laggan Games; the Lonach Society was formed over 180 years ago.

A visit to the MacPherson Museum at Kingussie is very worthwhile from a historic point of view. Here, there is an original painting of Cluny MacPherson and a magnificent piece of silverware featuring a MacPherson speaking with Montrose on a horse. The army were

Laggan hammer thrower.

searching for MacPherson and had not recognised him. MacPherson claimed he had no knowledge of where the outlawed noble was hiding and if he had known he would not have told them. He was

Cluny MacPherson, as seen at the MacPherson Museum.

would formally present her children to the monarch. The youngsters looked splendid, with the girls in their prettiest frocks and the boys in kilts as they lined up in front of the Queen. It had been well rehearsed that on a signal they would bow, and the three eldest children followed instructions to the letter. Four-year-old Claud had other ideas though, and, still resentful of being displaced, stood on his head, displaying to one and all that he was truly traditionally dressed! He was determined to show how long he could stay upside down and he had to be physically encouraged back on to his feet. The well-known

The outlawed MacPherson meeting a soldier.

given a shilling for his 'honesty' and that shilling is also on show in the museum.

Lord Abercorn, the Second Marquis and the first Duke of Abercorn, had rented Ardverikie from Lord Henry Bentinck, presumably so he could have the full benefit of the deer forest that he had rented on a long lease from Cluny MacPherson.

The presence of the royal entourage stretched the facilities beyond their normal limit so the Marchioness had some of their own staff and four of their own children vacate their rooms and nursery at Ardverikie to allow more space for the royal guests. The youngsters, not grasping the importance of the visitors, were quite put out, especially young Claud. To compensate for this disturbance, it was arranged that the Marchioness

THE WORLD HISTORY OF HIGHLAND GAMES

phrase 'The Queen was not amused' was never more appropriate than on this occasion.

However, there is a sequel to the story. The boy was most certainly reprimanded; it is not known if he was chastised but he did eventually apologise to his elders. He was later given a second chance and taken to the Queen once more with an opportunity to make amends. Instead, he immediately stood on his head again.

At some stage the Queen must have forgiven him, for afterwards, as Lord Claud Hamilton, a Member of Parliament and a Lord of the Treasury, he became an aide to Her Majesty from 1887 to 1897. The original Ardverikie visited by the royals was destroyed by fire in October 1875. The rebuilt building also went up in flames. The loss is incalculable. The evidence of a Royal visit and its associated activities, Landseer's wall paintings, which were part of the very fabric of the building, and so much more were lost forever. The bad weather and midges experienced by Queen Victoria during her visit and the fires that destroyed an irreplaceable heritage have all been factors leading to Laggan Highland Games being forgotten, while Her Majesty's patron-

Queen Victoria and Prince Albert. Original carte de visite in author's collection.

age of Braemar Games helped this annual gathering to flourish and become famous throughout the world.

1   Ardverikie: in Gaelic, *Ard-mheirgidh*. 'Ard' means a height or a promontory. The last part could be related to rust, perhaps as a colour.

The caber was made from a 14 foot length of a young fir. It was about 20 inches in circumference at the top and had a little bit of a taper.

*The Lonach Highlanders and Atholl Highlanders, Europe's last
private army, opening parade. Note the length of the parade
around the field and Blair Castle in the background.*

CHAPTER FIVE

The Atholl Gathering and Games

The Atholl Gathering is one of the oldest annual gatherings still in existence and one that was very nearly lost. The Association of Atholmen was inaugurated on 28 November 1824 when a number of gentlemen of the Stewarts and Robertsons of Athole (we use the spelling as in the original minutes of a meeting) met at the New Inn in Bridge of Tilt.

It was agreed that these clans of the district would meet annually to promote and cement a generous, manly and brotherly friendship as existed between their ancestors. They would engender and cherish a proper Highland spirit and feeling among clan members and encourage every aspect of industry for which their part of the country was well adapted. There was to be special emphasis on the 'manufacture at home and the general adoption of Dress of those fabrics that have ever been peculiar to the Highlands'. The ancient and worn copy of the aims in my possession is stated exactly as it is here. The final sentence of the aims states, 'Likewise to revive our National Athletics, Games and manly exercise, amusements, as well as the encouragement and improvement of our National Music.'

There can be no doubt of the intention, and they went even further by stating [my italics]:

> It is expected that the *greater number* at least, of the two Clans will appear... *in the plaids or Tartans of their Clans* and that such as cannot provide themselves in time with the pattern of their clan, will appear dressed in Plaids or Tartans of other patterns.

It was agreed that the first meeting would take place on 4 July. In the following years the annual competitions would be widely reported.

The names of the events used in the 1820–40 era include: sledge hammer, cabbar (as used then), leaping, foot race, reel dancing, and the battle or ancient sword dance. The spectators included members and their families, numerous guests and 'the resident nobility and gentry of Athole and a number of distinguished strangers'.

There was another great force in the area in the form of the Atholl Highlanders, sometimes reported in their early years as the Royal Athole Highlanders. The Dukes of Atholl have long been the chiefs of Clan Murray, and the Sixth Duke of Atholl raised this private army. As it was his private property, it was not in the regular army infantry of the line.

In 1777, the Fourth Duke of Atholl went to London, offering to raise a regiment of 1,000 men from the Vale of Atholl to serve in the United States in the War of Independence. The offer was accepted but the regiment was diverted to Ireland. The Highlanders were disbanded in 1783 and returned to their homes, but the seeds had been sown and this was the forerunner of the Atholl Highlanders as we know them today.

In 1839, a jousting tournament on medieval lines took place at Eglinton Castle in Irvine, Ayrshire, and the young Lord Glenlyon, the 25-year-old nephew of the ageing Duke of Atholl, enthusiastically accepted the invitation to participate. This was a very important event that attracted many thousands to south-west Scotland and Glenlyon was determined to meet the high standards set by the organiser, the Earl of Eglinton, and he raised a Highland bodyguard of volunteers that shaped the Atholl Highlanders, which is now Europe's last private army.

Eglinton
Tournament

1839

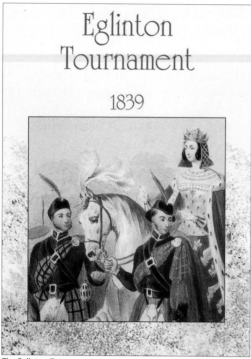

The Eglinton Tournament.

The wonderful Eglinton trophy.

Today, by car, it takes a little over two hours to travel from Blair Castle, headquarters of the Atholl Highlanders, to Irvine. In the days of the tournament, modern transport was unknown and the Highlanders marched 40 miles from Blair Castle to Perth, then took a riverboat to Dundee. A coastal vessel took them to the outskirts of Edinburgh and then they went via the Forth and Clyde Canal to Glasgow. They then took a steamer down the coast to Ardrossan from where they marched the last five or six miles to Eglinton Castle. What a journey! Lord Glenlyon was a brave leader and personally entered the lists as the 'Knight of the Gael' in this dangerous tournament. It all perfectly duplicated the knightly contest in days of yore and, not surprisingly, he was but one of the many wounded. His protective gauntlet was smashed in combat and his hand

was badly injured. A massive solid silver trophy, which, with its beautifully carved wooden base, stands over seven inches high, can still be seen in Cunninghame House, Irvine, commemorating this contest.

The Revival

The Atholl Gathering lasted for many years but gradually faded out and was not resumed again until 1982, when Douglas Edmunds and I brought an international line-up of heavies to star in the modern heavy events circuit. Of course, there was much more than just the heavies. The Atholl Highlanders always open the event in parade from the castle to the games field. Sometimes there have also been the pipes and drums of well-known bands such as the Vale of Atholl or Lonach Highlanders. The heavies follow the bands in

THE WORLD HISTORY OF HIGHLAND GAMES

Hercules at Blair Castle.

Jón Páll Sigmarsson.

parade and after the athletes are introduced, the Duke of Atholl starts the games in the traditional fashion, beating a sword on a shield. This is the signal for the Highlanders to fire their cannon and the mighty explosion can be heard for miles.

It would be difficult to find a better location. In the lovely Vale of Atholl, almost equidistant from the east and west coasts of Scotland, the games are held in a natural hollow adjacent to the historic castle. At the top of the little hill, just behind some shrubs, is a life-size statue of the Farnese Hercules. It is an area steeped in history and was one of Queen Victoria's favourite places, having stayed there on her first visit to Scotland, and was included in her future itineraries.

The modern series of games got off to a great start with some very popular strength superstars, such as Jon Pall Sigmarsson of Iceland and Ilka

Kinnunen of Finland, joining top Scottish heavies competing in the traditional heavy events.

The games have continued to change and develop and, although early in the season, often attract some overseas entries, such as Bill Crawford of New Hampshire and Anthony Lordi of Switzerland in 2006.

Blair Castle has been the venue for some very high-class piping competitions and the dancing competitions, so well organised by Jean Swanston-Robertson, are of a consistently high standard. Ever since the revival of the games, these fine piping and dancing contests have been an essential part of every Atholl Gathering. Another highlight is the hotly contested tug o' war events and the 'Kilted Sprint', in which the Highlanders always ensure that the finishing line is very close to the beer tent.

Excellent tug o' war competitions by competent teams are always very well supported by spectators, and a very demanding hill race was introduced to the programme in 2006 with the Star of Atholl Football Club providing a necessary core of competent runners who could safely meet the Beinn A'Ghlo Challenge for a very fine trophy. The race starts in the games arena and the course leads to the summit of Cairn Liath, 3,168 feet above sea level, then back to the games by the same route. The total distance of the course is estimated to be around 12 miles. It is definitely not for the faint hearted.

The 10th Duke of Atholl, Iain Murray, who graciously agreed to become the first patron of the International Federation of Heavy Event Athletes, never missed an Atholl Gathering until his untimely death in February 1996. His successor, John Murray, cousin of the 10th Duke, has been an equally gracious, and always supportive, chieftain. He is always present to start the games in colourful, traditional style. The Atholl Gathering is a very friendly gathering and a joyous beginning to Scotland's annual international circuit of Highland games.

The Atholl Highlanders in former times.

CHAPTER SIX

Spreading the Gospel

A detail from an old print of the New York Highland Games in 1867.

Between 1750 and 1850, Scottish emigrants played an important role in maintaining their national culture and traditions. When they left Scotland, they took with them their music, dance and healthy physical recreation in the form of traditional throwing events (see Chapter 1).

Most of the early development of Highland games in other countries was promoted by Scottish societies with various names: St Andrew's, Highland and Caledonian clubs or societies were common. The first Highland Society in Canada was formed in Glengarry in 1819. Many successful gatherings were held then lapsed and started again. Currently, excellent Glengarry Highland Games are still held annually in Maxville, featuring a huge number of pipe bands, fine dancing and heavy events.

In 1836, the Highland Society of New York had their first 'Sportive Meeting', a title later changed to 'Caledonian Games'. The aim was 'to renew the Sports of their native Land'. Two years later, the Caledonian Club of Prince Edward Island, Canada, held their first games.

Also in 1838, the Caledonian Society of Halifax, Nova Scotia, was formed. The following year, Toronto had a games full of pageantry that enthused all associated with the project. Next came Cape Breton, Nova Scotia, in 1848, with games held in Sydney, now called Antigonish and this fine event remains a jewel in our Highland crown.

A Caledonian Club was established in Boston in 1853, and its first formal games were held later that year. Its previous Highland games had been informal affairs, as they were in Montreal. By 1855, however, Montreal had a society in which a formal Highland games were of prime importance.

Another series of New York Caledonian Games commenced in 1857 at Jones Wood, New York City, and The Philadelphia Society in 1858. The development of games was accelerating.

The objectives of the various societies were to maintain the traditions, culture, customs and

America's first Amateur Athletic Club, inspired by Highland heavies. Be-whiskered Bill Curtis is seated in the centre at the back. Right: H.E Buermeyer, who often judged at Highland games.

literature of Scotland. The enormous popularity of the games allowed them to become the most important aspect of clubs and societies; the financial success of the gatherings subsidised the organisations' charitable and educational endeavours.

There were more such games in Canada.

Before the American Civil War in 1861, there were at least four Caledonian societies holding annual Highland Games in the United States. After the Civil War, in 1867 to be precise, the first international Highland Games competition was held, in the form of an America versus Canada competition.

Several newspapers observed an important aspect of Scottish games, mentioning, for example, the good humour and sportsmanship 'which evinced no bad or envious feeling amongst competitors'. The camaraderie amongst even the keenest contestants is still valued by all concerned.

The interest being created by Scottish competitions inspired some enthusiastic Americans in New York to form their own club in 1868. Since these Americans were mainly strong men, they were particularly influenced by the Highland heavy events, and they called their new organisation the New York Athletic Club. It was the forerunner to the Amateur Athletic Union, which became one of the most influential sports bodies the world has ever known.

The Highland Society of

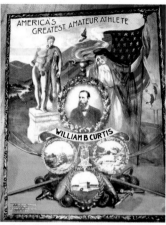

Father Bill Curtis was inspired by the Scottish games.

New York continued to set trends when, in 1870, it began inviting to its annual gatherings noted Scottish athletes such as Donald Dinnie and James Fleming. These box office attractions had an enormous effect, drawing tremendous crowds of around 30,000 spectators. This American vs. Scots competition was the first-ever such sporting clash.

A conspicuous athlete at many Caledonian Games in Canada and America was George Goldie (1841–1920) who, as a lad aged 13 years, had left Edinburgh with his family and emigrated to New York in 1854. Goldie lived in Canada for a while and in addition to competing at various Highland games was also a circus performer for a short while. He became North American Caledonian Games Champion, winning at the New York Caledonian Club annual games in 1869, 1870, 1871 and in 1874, when 20,000 spectators applauded his versatility in taking first-place awards in caber tossing and high jumping and other awards in pole vaulting and throwing the 56lb weight for distance.

Most important, however, was his appointment as the first physical director to Princeton University, a much respected seat of learning. Caledonian Games were instituted in his honour. When other New England universities followed suit, inter-collegiate athletics became the basis for America's success in world sport in later years.

Donald Dinnie and James Fleming.

In their book *Athletics at Princeton: A History*, Frank Presbrey and James Hugh Moffatt state:

> With the coming of spring, throwing the hammer, putting the shot, pole vaulting, sprinting, jumping, etc. were added to the list of exercises heretofore known in the college; and thus began the athletic awakening which as the years have grown has added so much to the prestige of Princeton.

The first of a great many Princeton Caledonian Games was held in 1873. Although the activity had been long practised in Scotland, George Goldie was known as the 'Father of the Pole Vault' as the event was new to America. When pole vaulting is added to putting the shot and throwing the hammer, it clearly indicates that Scotland's Highland games have significantly influenced the content of international athletics and even Olympic Games programmes.

For nearly two centuries, Highland games have been the principal manifestation of Gaelic ethnic identity in Eastern America.

George Goldie. Note the tartan ribbons on his medals.

It can be seen that there are great similarities in the development of Highland games in America and Canada, with an influx of Scottish immigrants establishing their own local games and gatherings. There has been a remarkable series of events, with a chain reaction that continues to develop, and there are superb games at Fergus, Ontario; Antigonish, Nova Scotia; Maxville, Glengarry, amongst others. These games grew from being local events to area-wide celebrations, then became of provincial importance. More recently, there have been several international Highland games in Canada that can boast over 1,200 competitors in piping, dancing and traditional athletics.

The games, the traditions, places and statistics are all very interesting but a vital element in the wonderful development of Highland games is the human factor – the people who made these games happen. Those earlier folks who travelled far from their native heath lived very different lives so their contribution is all the more notable. Travellers today often complain of delays, difficulties and hardships, be it confined spaces between aircraft seats or mediocre meals. Imagine, then, the hardships faced by followers of Reverend Norman McLeod (1780–1866) who, in 1817, led a group of people in emigration from the remote village of Assynt, Sutherland, in northwest Scotland, across the open Atlantic Ocean in a small sailing ship to Nova Scotia, a relatively uninhabited part of Canada. He became known as the 'Lion of Scotland'.

McLeod's pioneers were not the first to reach this location, but they became important because of their fiery leader, who later led another emigration of 800 people to Australia, and subsequently to New Zealand. There, McLeod reformed the community, settling at a place named Waipu. The followers of the controversial clergyman must, like their leader, have been exceptionally strong willed and very, very brave.

What, might be asked, has this to do with Highland

Piped ashore at Pictou. Settlers brought old traditions to their new life. Painted by John David Kelly (1862–1958), who depicted Canada's heritage.

games? Those keenly interested in our traditional activities may immediately have realised the connection, for Highland games at the highest level have been prominent in these places. Scotland (the birthplace of the games), Antigonish in Nova Scotia (where formalised athletic traditional games have been held continuously since 1862), Australia, and Waipu, in the North Island of New Zealand, have all hosted the World Highland Games Heavy Events Championships, thus forever ensuring their place in traditional sports history.

The good Scottish folks of Assynt were largely herring fishers or lived off the land, and before he became a minister, McLeod was a fisherman in the harsh environment of the Atlantic Ocean. Religion played little part in their lives at this time – they enjoyed ceilidhs (evenings of music and dance) more than sermons – but things began to change rapidly. An evangelistic parish minister, Reverend Kennedy, preached with great fervour and converted McLeod. The latter developed a lifelong burning force that motivated people to follow him to the ends of the earth. In July 1817, he sailed on the *Frances Ann* from Loch Broom to Pictou, Nova Scotia. There were many trials and tribulations on the long journey, sometimes tedious and sometimes fraught with danger, but eventually the emigrants arrived at their destination.

Norman McLeod was tall, powerfully built, very opinionated and articulate.

The settlers built a new community based on that at Loch Broom, but McLeod did not like this replica of the old ways. He wanted a new beginning that would meet his own high standards. He moved to the east coast of Cape Breton Island, where there were very few people, and there he built a formidable reputation but was not entirely accepted. It was reported: 'Though so wildly fanatical, he was a man of great power, and gained influence over a large portion of the Highlanders such as no other man in the country possessed.'

Norman McLeod's personality offended some people but despite this his congregation grew in size and strength over time. He moved several times, and taking up a block of land at South Gut, he built a church that held 1,200 worshippers. Often it was full and overflowing, with people standing in the corridors and on the stairs. People attended regularly, from as far as 20 miles away, considering McLeod as their chief as well as their minister. Surprisingly, he did not expect nor receive any payment for his services or financial contributions but the men of the congregation built his house and church, women did domestic chores and he was kept well supplied with fish from the sea and crops from the land.

These people recognised that their dynamic leader was completely unselfish and extremely concerned for their welfare. He criticised all kinds of 'frivolities', the pride of young women in the clothes they wore, and how they dressed their hair, dancing and various forms of entertainment. Many people disliked him because of this.

Canadian historians have acknowledged that immigrants from Scotland to Nova Scotia brought with them hammer throwing, caber tossing, stone putting, Highland dancing, piping and kilts, and that these activities were common long before the forming of a Highland Society in Cape Breton in 1848. Their motivation for this innovation was clear:

> They feared that the people might forget the songs, customs, and traditions that had brightened their existence during the strenuous

The Hector, one of the first ships to take Scots to Pictou.
There is a fine museum in Pictou depicting the immigration
of Scots. The images from Pictou are courtesy of the Ship Hector
Foundation, Pictou.

pioneer days... there was a danger that the old
ties, the feeling of kinship and affection for the
Scottish homeland would disappear.

A.A. MACKENZIE

There is a prime example of 'spreading the
gospel' in more ways than one. On the eve of the
Heavy Events World Championships of 2003 in
Nova Scotia there was, as so often happens,
a church service to mark this special occasion.

One of the many attending was the newly
installed Bishop of Antigonish, His Excellency
Raymond Lacey, and in a superb sermon the
University priest told me of one of Bishop Lacey's
predecessors. The following sticks very closely to
the original text of the sermon:

> About 200 years ago, the Strathglass Highland
> Games were taking place in Scotland. Strathglass
> and the surrounding district is home to many of
> the Chisholms in the Antigonish area and to
> many gathered here this week. Every year people
> from Strathglass and the surrounding
> community competed in tests of strength,
> agility, speed and endurance.

In 1804, just as the throwing commenced,
a heavily clad and hooded man approached
games officials and politely asked if he could join
in the final events. Permission was granted.
When the stranger finally took his turn, people
were amazed as he was so powerful that the stone
and hammer flew further then ever before in the
history of the games.

Just as the award ceremony began, the
stranger pulled back his hood. To their surprise,
spectators saw that this was their native son,
William Fraser, one of 12 siblings of a well-known
local family. William, now a Roman Catholic
priest at the age of 24, had just returned to the
Highlands after eight years of study at the Royal
Scots College near Madrid in Spain.

William Fraser, the strongest man in
Strathglass (about 20 miles from Inverness),
became Bishop of Antigonish in 1827. The priest
holding the position before William came on the
scene could not speak a syllable of Gaelic, so
when Father Fraser, a tall, strong, handsome,
well-educated, Gaelic-speaking native son, strode
into town, the local populace turned to him with
unqualified enthusiasm.

When Fraser preached, everyone showed up.
Even the Scottish Protestants attended those first
Eucharistic celebrations, declaring that 'if Fraser
were to remain in Antigonish we would convert to
Catholicism and immediately commence financial
support of his parish'.

The facts and story of the Strathglass
celebrations had previously been quoted in *Every
Popish Person: The Story of Roman Catholicism in Nova
Scotia and the Church of Halifax*. Apart from being an
entertaining account, the dates are of great
interest as 1804 was before the recognised
formalisation of Highland games.

Some of the Scots settlers in McLeod's
congregation decided to move on to New Zealand

to join friends and family there. Neil Robinson, McLeod's meticulous biographer, had this to say:

> They went to New Zealand because they felt that, in this community whose ways they know, there was a better chance of their families welfare; but they objected to the minister's rigid control of the private life. If they wanted to dance or sing the old songs they would do so. If they wanted to drink whisky, no edict from the minister would prevent it.

Norman McLeod and his flock remained in Nova Scotia for 34 years, and in time there developed a better balance between work, religion, leisure pursuits and sports, which naturally included traditional activities of their homeland. There were celebrations linked with the harvest and country dancing with old tunes on fiddle or bagpipes. Nowadays, Scottish music is distinctive and very attractive when played by Nova Scotian musicians. Being more remote and eager to remain true to their roots, their rendering of tunes are perhaps nearer to the original versions than can be heard anywhere in the world.

In passing, mention must be made of Angus McAskill, the Nova Scotian Giant, whose history has been well documented.

Born in the Outer Hebrides on the island of Berneray, when he was around two years of age his parents and their children moved to Harris. Four years later they all sailed for Canada. Angus grew to be 7 feet 9 inches and weighed 425lb (over 30 stone or 193kg) – he was immensely strong.

His exploits are well known amongst heavy event competitors and Scottish athletes visiting Antigonish Highland Games invariably visit Angus's grave and the small museum where his memorabilia is on show.

In 1848, there had been poor crops and near famine when Norman McLeod received a letter from his son Donald, writing from South

Australia. The letter praised the climate, the soil and the people. After much discussion, Norman McLeod, now 70 years old, and 800 of his followers, who had built two wooden ships by themselves, set sail to the other

Angus McAskill (1825–1863) with an average-sized man, Parson Taylor.

side of the world. It was one of the longest and most daring sea voyages ever undertaken by migrating people.

It proved difficult for them to locate a place where they could all stay together and found a new colony. There was a good deal of lawlessness and Norman McLeod had first-hand experience of this. In his search for suitable land, he got lost in the bush (forest) and encountered a party of bushrangers of the kind that killed travellers for their money and possessions. They decided that because of his calling they should spare the minister's life and gave him a place at their fire for the night. McLeod delivered one of his fiery sermons, urging them to change their evil ways. At dawn, they put him on a horse and directed him towards Melbourne – the bushrangers were probably more relieved than Norman McLeod.

Angus McAskill's grave, Cape Breton.

Meantime, a reconnaissance party went on to New Zealand, where earlier settlers had travelled from Nova Scotia, and before long the news returned that a good location had been found where they could resume their community lifestyle in the manner to which they had been accustomed. Without much ado, Norman McLeod and his flock moved on. They settled in Waipu, and from there spilled out slowly across the North Island. Even today the settlement that grew in Waipu seems truly Scottish in almost every way. These

Canadian Champion Doug McDonald of Antigonish in Waipu T shirt. The links remain in the 21st century.

descriptions have, by necessity, been kept as short as possible. It is, however, a tale of enormous courage and overcoming of handicaps by Scottish settlers to carve out a new life. In this young country they integrated completely, while still maintaining ancient traditions and ways of life.

Highland games are still very important in Antigonish, Nova Scotia. At every entrance to the town can be seen a large wooden sculpture of a piper, Highland dancer or caber tosser; there is a clan commemoration cairn here and a Highland games mural there. 'It's more Scottish than Scotland,' said Highland heavy Francis Brebner.

The World Heavy Events Championships have been held here and there is no doubt about the 'roots' of Don MacEachern, the athletic director and other Highland games officials. The link with religion is also clear, with a 'Kirkin' o' the Games' before the games commence. Over in Waipu, it is much the same story. There is another long tradition of Highland games. A fine large wooden notice board on the main road advertises the next games and a lovely eye-catching old poster is

Permanent Highland games mural on a house on Main Street, Antigonish.

displayed in what was previously called the House of Memories, a museum specialising in Scottish family history, with artefacts from the days of Norman McLeod and his compatriots.[1]

Religion still has an important place in the lives of the people. When the World Championships was held in Waipu in 1996 the great Scottish heavy, Francis Brebner, was invited to read the lesson at a church service broadcast throughout New Zealand. Although Frances was not a public speaker at that time, he accepted the invitation and his broad North East accent went down a treat.

Commemorating the early Scottish settlers in Antigonish.

There are still strong links between Nova Scotia and Waipu and through the co-operative staff at the Waipu Museum I was provided with information and photographs of John Kaiser of Baddock Bay, Cape Breton. Mr Kaiser, a descendant of Nova Scotia ship-

Francis Brebner (Scotland) loves Waipu and would like to live there.

wrights, has fashioned a splendid scale model of the *Margaret*, the ship that took Norman McLeod and his followers round the world to the southern hemisphere. The replica is made almost entirely of wood from his own property. He cut and carved every rib and knee-sawed all the planking. There are over 100 tiny belaying pins and literally thousands of parts and pieces – capstan, sails,

The Margaret, by John Kaiser, Nova Scotia. With thanks to Waipu Museum.

rigging and even barrels, bunks and supplies in the hold. He even forged his own anchors. The passion and dedication shown by their ancestors has been passed on to today's counterparts in Nova Scotia and New Zealand.

Let's have a closer look at Waipu and Antigonish Highland Games.

Waipu Highland Games

There is no doubt that early immigrants from Scotland practised traditional activities in New Zealand from an early date. Amongst the best known are the famous McHardys from Aberdeenshire, including the celebrated heavy Charles McHardy and Highland dancer Alexander McHardy. The great Donald Dinnie appeared at many Highland games in New Zealand, the first of these being at the Ashburton Caledonian Society Games of 1883 and the Annual Caledonian Society Games at Dunedin.

In the earlier pioneering days, little thought was given to maintaining records or having accepted rules and generally conducting proceedings on a formal basis. The Waipu Caledonian Society changed all that by establishing its first games on 1 January 1871 and becoming the largest and longest established gathering in New Zealand. Only once in its long history has the annual games been cancelled. This was in 1942, during the Second World War,

Games day in Waipu.

Waipu Highland Games.

but even then the society organised a similar games solely for children.

Held on 1 January each year, Waipu Highland Games is always the first on any comprehensive list of such annual Highland events. The motivation for the first Waipu games is interesting because it shows an aspect of community involvement that few people have considered. In the 1860s, there were not even simple sports fields, recreational or cultural facilities for settlers to practise the activities they enjoyed. The Caledonian Society addressed this problem and resolved to improve things by staging Highland games as a fundraising event.

Most sports nowadays look to local government to provide and maintain such facilities but the efforts of the Waipu Caledonian Society have long provided finance and maintenance for Caledonian Park, where the games are held. There is always a full programme of piping, dancing and heavy events and their own version of the *clach cuid fir*, the stone of strength. The 'rock scramble', as they call it, entails lifting and carrying a variety of boulders from one point to another while being timed.

The late Steve Barry was probably the first New Zealand modern heavy to compete overseas.

He first competed at Waipu at the age of 15 and was coached in caber tossing and other activities by Guy Ritchie in Waipu. In 1993 Steve won the New Zealand Championships and his main prize was a trip to Canada to participate in the Nova Scotia circuit. He took part in 10 competitions, competing at Antigonish, Pugwash, Halifax and Judique.

He did well with the hammers and weight for height, and managed to place in the top six overall. In a new solo drumming competition in 1993, 17-year-old Debbie Coutts also won a trip to Nova Scotia to attend the Gaelic College at St Ann's, Cape Breton, and New Brunswick Highland Games.

In recent years, Pat Hellier of Auckland has been the national champion. Putting the stone is his favourite event and he always does well in this. Although the days of awarding trips to overseas games are now gone, Pat has competed in several world championships and is popular with his contemporaries.

Waipu has a record that will not be beaten in this century, and the concept clearly showed the historic links with Scotland, Antigonish and Waipu. In the very last minute of the 20th century, Highland games athletes, including Francis Brebner of Scotland and Doug Macdonald of Antigonish, Nova Scotia, lined up with cabers as the last seconds of the century ticked away. A fraction before the century closed, they tossed the cabers in the 20th century and the big logs landed in the 21st century, pointing to 12 o'clock. New Zealand was the first country to see the dawn of the new millennium and, later that day, the World's Heavy Events Championships was the very first world title of any sport in the new century. That cannot be repeated until the next millennium.

Of course, many emigrants travelled directly from Scotland to the Antipodes and one such expedition was when the *Philip Laing* sailed from Greenock to New Zealand in 1847. It had 247 immigrants on board and they passed the time by dancing jigs and reels and listening to the fiddlers and pipers, while the most energetic men wrestled. A year later, having settled in Otago, the Scottish settlers celebrated the anniversary with a Highland games and in 1863 they founded the first Dunedin Caledonian Society. Within ten years they had produced a very firm foundation of traditional games with their own sporting heroes.

J.E. Lowe was the first man in Otago to teach callisthenics, deportment and Scottish country dancing. He was the son of the dancing teacher who had taught Queen Victoria's family when they were at Balmoral.

The full story of Otago Games, Bendigo Games and other fascinating early developments in far-flung places must surely be told at some future date.

Steve Barry.

1   I am very grateful for the willing co-operation of the current staff at Waipu Museum. They have been most helpful in providing information and illustrations.

Bendigo Games, Australia, 1860, nine years after the gold rush.

THE WORLD HISTORY OF HIGHLAND GAMES

CHAPTER SEVEN

Rory of the Hammer

Canada's first great heavy was Roderick McLennan (1842–1907), or 'Rory Mor' as he was known in Gaelic, the language spoken at that time in Glengarry, Canada. He had three very athletic brothers – Angus (1839–1912), Farquhar (1849–1917) and Alexander (1852–1911) – but Roderick, famous 'Rory of the Hammer', was the most athletic of all. He pioneered throwing the wire-handled hammer in the turning style, which, with the introduction of proper athletics arenas, became accepted by track-and-field amateurs worldwide. Roderick's throws with various sizes of hammers were records – probably world records – in those days.

Roderick's grandfather, Farquhar McLennan, emigrated from Kintail in 1802 and his father, Roderick (1803–93), fought in the 1837 rebellion. Both sides of the family were big and strong and Roderick grew to be 6 feet 4 inches and weighed approximately 238lb (17 stone or 218kg).

I have previously written at length in positive fashion on McLennan's very noteworthy abilities and achievements on the games field, in business and in politics. Because we did not make comparisons with Donald Dinnie (1837–1916), it is somewhat irksome that some have mis-interpreted this to assume that Dinnie came out worst in encounters with McLennan.

The truth is that:

- in spite of what many Canadians may think, *they never competed against each other*;
- Dinnie was a professional throughout his lengthy career of 1852 to 1912, while McLennan professed to be an amateur[1] in his relatively short athletic career of 1859 to 1873;
- Dinnie used the traditional wooden-shafted hammer, while McLennan used a wire and ring handle;
- Dinnie used the traditional standing style while Rory used what appears to be an unlimited approach with a turning technique called the run-and-swing style;
- Dinnie used the standard 16lb (light) hammer and the 22lb (heavy) hammer while McLennan, and his partner 'Jarmy', often used 12lb and 14lb (light) and a 16lb (heavy) hammer; and

Big Rory McLennan (1842–1907). Painting by Doug Fales, a famous Canadian artist.

- much of Rory's reputation centres on his competitions with a showman called Thomas Jarmey (also known as Jarmy), who was known in Scotland as Rice. Jarmy had a doubtful reputation and was certainly never Scottish hammer-throwing champion, as he claimed.[2] He persuaded the unwitting McLennan, who was undoubtedly superior, to do a series of events and, although billed as challenges and championships, they were actually more like shows or exhibitions. They agreed that McLennan would deliberately lose one of three competitions to build up interest. In many decades of experience in Highland games all over the world, we have never heard of any other such blatant arrangement.

This response to assumptions should not in any way be considered as an attack on Roderick McLennan; he was a great athlete whose speciality was throwing the hammer, unfortunately not in the traditional style. The Scottish style used at Highland games was a standing throw from behind the trig, using a wooden-shafted hammer. Roderick and his brothers seemed to be about the only competitors at the games to use the turning style. When American and Canadian Highland games rules were standardised and formalised in 1870, no doubt remained that the standing style of hammer throwing was the only style recognised in North America. It has been so ever since.

McLennan's appearances did a great deal for Highland games as he became one of the first, if not *the first*, Canadian cult sporting hero. Newspaper publicity about him heightened public interest in Highland games. Rory was a pillar of the community, successful in politics and in business – an ideal sporting ambassador. Even in those days the press loved controversy, and the story of the local lad versus the world champion sold many newspapers and had a positive effect in attracting more spectators to the games.

Even the tragic end to his sporting career did not, and should not, change public opinion.

Roderick McLennan's competition career ended in 1873, but at the Cornwall, Ontario, Highland games held annually to celebrate Queen Victoria's birthday, he was judging the heavy events. After the presentation of prizes he was persuaded to give an exhibition of hammer throwing. He made his massive effort and the hammer flew through the air to the applause of the crowd. The cheers stopped suddenly as the hammer sped towards 13-year-old Ellen Kavanaugh, who had moved forward inside the arena to get a better view.

The hammer fell and killed her and it was a stunned and silent crowd that filed from the games field that fateful day. McLennan was traumatised. A local newspaper reported the athlete's reaction:

> I shall never again, under any circumstances, allow myself to be dragged into athletic contests of any description. I am not, now, nor never was, a professional athlete, and for the future I shall cease to be even an amateur.

Donald Dinnie and R.R. McLennan.

Some time earlier, the poet Alexander McLachlan had penned an ode titled 'Roderick of the Hammer':

[Verse 6]
As if the whirlwind in its wrath
Its awful power had lent him,
He gathers on his whirling path
A terrible momentum;
While every heart is still as death
In fearful expectation,
He hurls it on its sounding path
'Mid shouts of admiration.

[Verse 5]
Words cannot ring his mighty swing.
It's the sublime of throwing!
Transformed into a living wheel,
The demon of the centre,
He gathers power, yet guides the steel
Where mortals dare not enter.

In this order, these selected lines seem almost prophetic, for poor wee Ellen did enter. Like many other tragedies, she was in the wrong place at the wrong time. It was not in any way Rory's fault, nor was it the style he used, but he paid a high price for this demonstration that went so tragically wrong.

He always kept the vow he made at the time – he would never participate in sport again. Instead, he became active in politics and defeated the local Liberal candidate to represent Glengarry in Ottawa. In 1896, McLennan moved up the political ladder, trouncing the opposition to become the Member of Parliament representing Winnipeg. A year later, he became Lieutenant Colonel Officer commanding the Glengarry militia, holding this position until 1900. He died seven years later.

McLennan in his later years, by Canadian artist Doug Fales.

Big Rory's titles and awards in Canada

Cornwall 1865	Champion of the world. Match with Thomas Jarmey. Prize: $1000 cash. 12lb, 14lb and 16lb hammers
Toronto, 8 August 1870	American Championship, 12lb hammer
11 August 1872	Montreal Hammer Championship medal
20 August 1872	Heavy hammer, standing style. Longest throw on record (distance not mentioned)
August 1872	World championship in throwing 56lb. Gold medal presented by Hon. George Brown

Alexander John MacDonald, or Big Alex McIsaac, as he was known, has been described as Rory's protégé, but there is not a great deal of information on him that is readily available. Indeed, the details we have gleaned give rise to more questions than answers. It is known that he was an excellent all-round heavy and that he was also a fine pole vaulter. In his time, poles were thick and heavy and it took a strong man to carry them at speed.

On 24 May 1900, he competed in every event in Canada's Glengarry Games and won the all-round championship. Nineteen years later, he won five gold medals.

Some of his medals are displayed in Maxville's excellent hall of fame, along with fine images of Big Alex by Doug Fales, an artist whose portrayal of Highland games heavies is unsurpassed anywhere in the world.

There are reports that McIsaac won a world caber-tossing championship at Devon, Canada, in 1919 and Queen Mary, wife of George V, is said to have presented him with a gold watch. I have searched archives thoroughly for any contemporary reports but there are none available, nor does there appear to be any mention of the leading Scottish caber tosser who would have been appropriate and available for such a world championship.

I do know that Rory taught Alex, who in turn taught Lloyd Kennedy, a local athlete, the same methods of tossing the caber. At his first opportunity at the Glengarry Games, Lloyd won the event, and won the caber championships a total of ten times.

Alexander John Macdonald – pioneer caber tosser, by Doug Fales.

In Canada, during the Victorian era, apart from throwing the weights, all the Scottish heavy events were practised in the traditional methods, with the notable exceptions of those inspired by Rory McLennan. A number of lads in Fergus, Ontario, copied the style, and James Perry was the one who best mastered McLennan's technique. While in the army, he won the 12lb hammer throw at the 13th Battalion of Hamilton Games by using the spinning or rotating style. His main opponent was a burly blacksmith who threw in the usual standing position.

Fergus's links with Scotland are very strong. In the early 1830s, two adventurous Scots were exploring Canada, seeking land on which they and their families and friends could settle. On the beautiful banks of the Grand River in south-west Ontario, they found an idyllic spot with good soil, luxurious vegetation and all the natural elements required to develop and sustain a community.

These pioneers were Adam Ferguson and James Webster. Adam had made a reconnaissance in 1831 and published a descriptive book telling would-be emigrants about this new land.

In addition to describing the country, he included information detailing the equipment that settlers would require and the costs involved. This handbook wasn't exactly a bestseller, as most of the target audience were illiterate. However, Ferguson's writings, including his excellent journals, have proven to be superb sources for historians over the years.

In an area originally known as Little Falls, the settlement founded by Adam Ferguson and his colleague and friend James Webster became known as Fergus. James Webster lived in the first log cabin built in the area in December 1833, and one hard winter he gave so much of his own money to needy neighbours that there was a petition to change the name of the settlement to Websterville.

These were hard times and both men injected substantial sums to offset the difficulties of settlers unaccustomed to the harsh winters and the problems of beginning, literally, from scratch. Life was also exciting; Native Americans camped nearby and bears would wander into the schoolyard. Although there was not what we would refer to as a population explosion today, many new townships sprung up in the area.

As land owners, their policy

Detail from a full-length image, Big Alex, by Doug Fales.

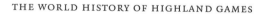

THE WORLD HISTORY OF HIGHLAND GAMES

was to allow only Scots to purchase sites, and all the streets were given Scottish names, a practice that is still in evidence today. In 1840, Webster further developed the Celtic connection by founding the nearby town of Arthur, which he designated for Irish settlers.

The Caledonian immigrants took with them their age-old love of rural Scottish games and James Webster himself, the first Fergus settler, left documented evidence of putting the stone and caber tossing. These sports may or may not have been formalised in those early days in Ontario, but we can say for sure that they were known and practised before 1840.

In Scotland during the 1800s, the MacIntoshes, including Lawsie, were renowned Highland games athletes, and it was no different in Fergus.

Dougal, James and John MacIntosh were the local champions, hotly challenged by Henry Michie and the Clarks of Bona Cord. ('The Reminiscences of James Perry' as recorded by Pat Mestern in one of her excellent books). This statement interests us greatly. The great traditions of Highland games have been at their strongest in north-east Scotland at places like Braemar, Ballater, Aboyne, Lonach and other parts of Aberdeenshire. The motto of Aberdeen is 'Bon Accord' ('happy to meet, sorry to part, happy to meet again') so Bona Cord, which Canadians have puzzled over, just means that they came from Aberdeen, the city of Bon Accord. These are expressions regularly used to this day in Scotland's Granite City and it is an excellent observation on the spirit of Highland games.

Permanent billboard on the old field in Victoria Park, Fergus, Ontario.

Duncan C. Ross, of Scottish stock, was one of Canada's best athletes. He became Police Chief of Coburg, Canada in Victorian times.

One wonders if one of the stalwarts of modern Fergus Highland Games, Steve Clark, is a descendant of the Clarks of Bona Cord.

Highland games were very well established in Fergus during the 1880s, with an annual event every July. The First World War had devastating effects on these indigenous activities and while there was a revival in Scotland, this was not in evidence in other parts of the world. Fergus Games were not revived until 1946.

Matt Richardson about to toss the caber.

1   In Victorian times, the distinction between amateurs and professionals was largely a social one, particularly in England. Gentlemen like Roderick could compete for wagers without infringing their amateur status. Artisans, on the other hand, who occupied a lower social position, were deemed to be professionals, even though their love of the sport was their main reason for participation. In north-east Scotland there was no such distinction. Young people automatically competed for prize money or prizes in kind without even contemplating their status.

2   Jarmey (also known as Jarmy, Jermy and Rice). Thomas Jarmey of Guelph, as he was known in Canada, did visit Scotland under the name of 'Rice', challenging all comers at throwing the hammer. Unfortunately, Jarmey's conditions allowed throwing with the turning style. This style had been banned at Scottish games after an accident in which two men were injured, and as a result committees and athletes were disinterested. However, John Tait had recently retired (which makes the date 1854 or 1855) and he accepted the challenge. The match took place at Stonefield Recreation Grounds in Glasgow. John had accepted 'Rice's' turning rule but was surprised when Rice (Jarmey) rejected the usual wooden-shafted hammer and produced one with a wire shaft some five inches in length and with a ball-like handle. This unexpected device left Tait beaten by 11 feet so he asked for a return match under standard rules but Rice was having none of this. The old timer, Tait, immediately practised with a similar hammer and beat Rice significantly. Rice/Jarmey then headed back across the Atlantic.

THE WORLD HISTORY OF HIGHLAND GAMES

CHAPTER EIGHT

Canada's Best All-Rounder

Once in a while there comes along an incredible character who does not easily fit into the standard categories. Highland games has had more than its fair share of these, in men such as Jay Scott, Bob Aitken, John McKenzie and our present subject, Canada's best ever all-round athlete, Walter Renwick Knox of Orillia, Ontario. The athletes named may not have been the 'best ever' throwers, runners or jumpers, but they could win first prizes in various categories and in their own times they could go home with better filled sporrans than the categorised champions.

Born in Listowell, Ontario, in 1878, Knox began his athletic career in 1898 and won many prizes during that season. In 1900, in Toronto, he annexed his first title as pole vault champion of Ontario and two months later won the Canadian pole vault championship in Montreal. He took 20 first places that season. From then on he competed year after year at national and international levels, with consistently good performances. Wishing to extend his sphere of influence, he began competing in wrestling in 1910 but then had a brilliant idea. Hearing of Highland games, he thought he should meet the Scots on their own ground, where there were opportunities for many different events.

Knox made his Scottish debut at Shotts Highland Games in June 1911, without any fanfare of trumpets. He just got off the boat after a transatlantic journey, turned up unannounced, ran, jumped, collected the prizes and left as quietly as he appeared. Naturally, he did not win all the first prizes but he did create a big stir, amongst the jumpers in particular. He loved the atmosphere of the Scottish games and in one season picked up the following prizes: 39 first places, 15 second places, 17 third places and one fourth place at 23 Scottish Highland games. One biography claimed he won 57 first places, 23 second places and 32 third places in Britain in 1911.

In 1912 he had other priorities as his considerable talents had been recognised at home

Walter Knox on a visit to Scotland. Photographed in 1912.

in Canada. With his great fund of technical athletics knowledge, he was appointed National Athletics Coach for Canada at the 1912 Stockholm Olympics. This did not stop him returning to Scotland.

I have before me a page of a cuttings book from 1913, when the feats of Jim Thorpe, Olympic gold medallist and 'the greatest athlete of the first half of the 20th century'[1] were fresh in people's minds. The headlines of these papers read 'Walter Knox worthy opponent of Thorpe in all-round athletics', 'Knox worthy rival of Thorpe' and 'Walter Knox some wrestler'. The *Toronto Star Weekly* headline is 'Knox, All-round champion, great little piece of stuff from Canada'.

The Scottish heavies, of course, teased the light events athletes about being beaten by this 'great little piece of stuff' but their turn was not too far away. Knox decided to enter heavy events as well as those in track and field and, to everybody's astonishment, in putting the stone he beat the famous A.A. Cameron and other leading athletes. There and then, Walter became very popular amongst the runners and jumpers, movers and shakers. There followed other such wins over John Mackenzie, Jock Nicolson and James Morrison.

Knox set many records in the light events and it is likely that he will still hold some local records, particularly in the pole vault, which has been largely dropped from games programmes. Knox very often exceeded throws of 11 feet, with hard landing areas, and picked up ankle and leg injuries along the way. This was a very common occurrence at Scottish games, where local committees acted irresponsibly by failing to produce proper landing areas for the vaulters. It is strange that organisers could not understand the dangers of falling from a height of 10 or 11 feet, in all kinds of positions, on to a hard surface. He was credited with personal bests of a vault of 12 feet 5 inches, 24 feet 2 inches in a long jump and 45 feet 6 inches in a triple jump, but he did not equal these in Scotland.

Up until, but not including, 1912, Walter Knox's prizes in Canada, the United States and Scotland totalled 337 first places, 90 second places, 53 third places and two fourth places. In 1912 he won a further 70 prizes.

Knox was so successful as Canada's national coach at the 1912 Olympics that he was appointed coach for Britain's Olympic training squad for 1916, which of course was cancelled because of the First World War. He was offered a three-year contract at £400 per annum – a very respectable sum in those far-off days.

The world's best all-rounders (pre-War)

The magnificent Jim Thorpe (1888–1953), mentioned in the newspaper headlines earlier in this chapter, never met Walter Knox in the arena, but comparisons of their best performances at that time can be made.

Thorpe has an Irish grandfather on his father's side and a French grandmother on his mother's side, but his mother and paternal grandmother were Native Americans. Throughout his life, Thorpe suffered from racism and he was never entitled to vote. It was not until 1954, a year after his death, that Native Americans were granted voting rights.

After the Olympics, he was stripped of his gold medals when it was 'discovered' that he had

Walter Knox (1878–1951).

played in minor league baseball before competing at the games. The Athletic Union, in stripping him of his medals, also rescinded his performances, on paper only because in reality he remained the best athlete in the world. Losing his Olympic medals had a devastating effect on Jim Thorpe and, although he became a star attraction as a professional baseball and basketball player, these were not lifelong careers. Depressed, he had to fight a battle against alcohol and sadly he died in abject poverty. In 1983, *30 years after his death*, Jim Thorpe's gold medals were restored. The comparison above shows their performances in

Knox featured in this magazine in 1915.

character, competing in Scotland in the summer months, hunting in Canada in the depths of winter and prospecting in an occasional gold and silver rush. Knox enjoyed moose hunting in the toughest of winter conditions and he was featured on the cover of *Health and Strength* magazine with his dogs pulling a sledge with a load of moose pelts. He had previously spent two nights out in the open without blankets. At one stage of his life, he lived amongst the Klondike gold miners, buying and selling claims but living rough as they did rather than with the lifestyle of a businessman.

	Thorpe	Knox	Winner
Height	6 feet 1¼ inches	5 feet 8 inches	
Weight	181lb	155lb	
100 yards	10.1/5 s	9.4/5 s	Knox
120 yard hurdles	15.4/5 s	15.4/5 s	Tied
Half-mile walk	3 min 27 s	Not attempted	Thorpe
One-mile run	5 min	Not attempted	Thorpe
High jump	6 feet 1 ¼ inches	5 feet 7 inches	Thorpe
Long jump	23 feet 3 inches	23 feet 7 inches	Knox
Pole vault	10 feet 7 inches	11 feet 9 inches	Knox
Discus	123 feet	133 feet	Knox
Shot put	42 feet	43 feet 6 inches	Knox
Wire hammer	125 feet	120 feet	Thorpe
56lb weight for distance	28 feet	25 feet	Thorpe

1913. We know of their better performances but this seems a good and fair result at that time – both equal winners.

The Canadian was a tough and colourful

The most successful part of Knox's career was from 1900 to 1915, but he continued to coach thereafter. In 1920 he was again appointed Canada's Olympic coach but his last competition

Dignatories present awards to W. Knox and B. Scott – great rivals and great friends. Crieff 1913.

was at the Ontario shot putt championship in 1933. Unfortunately, he did not return to the Highland games after the First World War. He was sorely missed.

This great all-rounder was inducted into the Orilla Hall of Fame, and always treasured happy memories of his days at Scottish Highland Games. Walter Knox died in 1933 at the age of 55.

[1] In 1950, Associated Press named Jim Thorpe the greatest athlete in the first half of the 20th Century.

Walter Knox, Canada's National Athletics Coach with some of the team at the 1912 Stockholm Olympics.

CHAPTER NINE

The Celtic Gathering

The first annual Celtic Gathering took place in Glasgow in 1857 and was organised by Glasgow's Celtic Society. The proceedings of this two-day event began each day with a procession to the College Park, where activities commenced at 10.30am.

Around 12,000 people attended each day, with the Duke and Duchess of Atholl and the Duke of Hamilton as the guests of honour. There was a full programme of piping, Highland dancing and traditional throwing and jumping events.

The results for the piping competitions included many clan and estate pipers from various parts of Scotland. Several of these pipers competed in the dancing events, and the names

of the estates employing them and the award winners' trades were recorded in the prize lists. The Highland fling was won by John McPherson, saddler; in second place was William Menzies, a farmer from Dunkeld; and in third place was a shoemaker from Edinburgh. The well-known heavy, James Paton, also featured in the dancing prize list, taking second in the reels. The contests, like others of the period, were for men only.

The champion heavy of the games was John Tait, the well-known gamekeeper to the Duke of Hamilton. He carried off half a dozen prizes, including both stones, both hammers and the caber. The light hammer was won with a distance of 101 feet 9 inches – but wait! 'Light' it most certainly was – only 12lb. The heavy hammer,

The Celtic Gathering on College Green, Glasgow.

16lb on this occasion, was won with a rather pathetic distance of 73 feet 4 inches by Tait, who was awarded a handsome medal and £4–4 – a sum equivalent to many weeks' wages in those days.

In keeping with the aim to encourage traditional dress, there were often competitions for the 'best-dressed Highlander at his own expense'. On this occasion, Duncan McDonald of Dunkeld won, and the best dressed at his master's expense was Alex Cameron, piper to Neil Malcolm Esq. Another unique competition in line with the aims of such societies was for the best Gaelic poem on the military service of Highlanders in the late war. However, the most obvious manifestation of the aims and objectives was at the first grand dinner of the Celtic Society, which took place after the games with around 100 guests in attendance, 'the greater portion of whom were dressed in the picturesque Highland costume'. The next year followed much the same pattern, with a procession of around 150 people clad in Highland garb marching through Glasgow from George Square via Buchanan Street, Argyle Street and High Street to the Upper College Park by the gate on Blackfriars Street.

The programme was much as before except for the addition of a very popular and exciting broadsword competition. This was won by James Paton of Murthly. The 16lb stone was thrown, a distance of 39 feet 9 inches, awarded to a wiry Highlander with longer arms than Rob Roy.

There were a number of well-known heavies in the prize list, including Paton and William Stewart, and there was a battle for the top places between William Tait and William McHardy, both from famous families of heavies.

Kenneth McLeay, the famous artist of Victoria's Highlanders, was one of those present and there was great excitement at the end of the day with the announcement of the successful laying of the *Atlantic Telegraph* and the playing of the national anthem by William Ross, the Queen's Piper, in honour of this momentous occasion.

William Ross, Queen Victoria's piper. Kenneth MacLeay, RSA.

James Paton (b. 1833) of Murthly, near Dunkeld, a versatile competitor who won many prizes in Highland dancing, heavy events and single sticks (fencing).

THE WORLD HISTORY OF HIGHLAND GAMES

CHAPTER TEN

The Best-Dressed Highlander

The Act of Proscription of 1746 could well have resulted in the disappearance of the kilt, plaid, tartans and other such Highland dress traditions. Indeed, this was largely the purpose of the act.

Fortunately, the danger of extinction was seen and measures were taken to counteract the effects of the prohibition. One of the main aims of many of the earliest Highland games was to encourage the preservation of traditional Highland dress as well as to maintain the traditions of the past. Apart from introducing an 'only kilties can play' rule to make the wearing of the kilt compulsory for competitors in piping, dancing and heavy events, many committees offered prizes in a 'Best-dressed Highlander' competition. Over 185 years later, this practice still continues at some games. Sometimes the prize is confined to a participant, often the competition may be open only to members of the organising society, and at other times it could be open to all and sundry.

The Best Dressed Highlander competition.

The popularity of the 'Best-dressed Highlander' competition was at its height in late Victorian times, when it was common to see advertisements such as 'A Prize of £5 to be awarded to the Best Dressed Highlander at his own expense'.

Satirical comedy is not as new as many people believe, and in 1936 the following ode amused Highland games enthusiasts. It truly captures the flavour of an unashamed teuchter:

The Best-dressed Highlander

My name is John Macleod – from Chiefs descended
Distinguished for their courage and their size.
A Highland Gathering lately I attended,
Because there I saw there was to be a prize
For the best-dressed Highlander,
The best-dressed Highlander,
The best-dressed Highlander at his own expense.
My kilt and stockings I was wearing,
My claymore and my dirk and my skean-dhu,
And when I sallied forth with manly bearing,
I heard admiring whispers not a few –
'He's the best-dressed Highlander,
The best-dressed Highlander,
The best-dressed Highlander at his own expense.'
The world has many shining paths of glory,
  And I have chosen out this path for me –
    That John Macleod, until he's old and hoary,
    Will always incomparably be
    Quite the best-dressed Highlander,
    The best-dressed Highlander,
      The best dressed Highlander, at his own expense.

On a more serious note, it can be seen that Highland games did not reach the stage of having such competitions without great care. The motive for this competition was not to provide fun or entertainment but to restore interest in the previously banned national dress so that it could be perpetuated for all time. This was exactly the opposite intention of the Act of Proscription and it was important that organisers did not antagonise the authorities.

The Northern Meetings in Inverness are amongst the best documented gatherings, and their procedures and progress are interesting. Captain Graham MC of Edinburgh provided Northern Meeting officials the regulations pertaining to organised societies and having studied these, the office bearers proceeded cautiously, for even in 1788 Highlanders had to 'ca' canny' (be very careful).

The utmost care was taken to remain within the law and to not jeopardise the future of the Northern Meeting, but a hidden agenda could perhaps be detected. At first, the rule was made that members should wear a specific uniform, which consisted of a grass-green-coloured coat with buff edging and white metal buttons. A black velvet cape was worn over the coat and a buff or fancy waistcoat under it. Silk breeches, either buff or black, were also required. Getting down to details, the coat had to have metal buttons and the capes had to have silver buttons, and all buttons had to be engraved with the initials 'N.M.', for Northern Meeting.

A little later, they showed their true colours on the retiral of their popular patron, the Duke of Gordon, when the gentlemen of the district invited him to a farewell dinner. 'Champagne flowed like water; *the Highlanders were in full costume of the mountains, and great excitement prevailed*' [my italics]. The dinner, though, was held at Kingussie, which could have been to distance them from an official society function.

However, in 1841, a year after these Highland games were officially started under the name of the Northern Meeting, piping and dancing were

Balmoral Highlanders at Braemar Gathering and Games in the early 1920s.

introduced into the programme and two extra prizes were allocated to the two best-dressed Highlanders, regardless of the person who paid for the outfits. The committee had perhaps been overcautious but members had much at stake. The main winner had been a member of the society for 50 years.

One of the many modern gatherings that continues to encourage high standards of national dress is the North Hampshire Highland Games at Loon Mountain, in the United States. As chieftain of these games in 2006, I had the honour of judging and awarding prizes for the best-dressed Highlanders, both male and female. Although many young people wore interesting variations of Scottish apparel, the two winners were mature individuals in clan societies. The female winner wore a long skirt and a traditional waistcoat in green velvet over a full-sleeved blouse. Clan Keith provided the winning male, Mr Hattenbrun, impeccably dressed and wearing personally made leather accoutrements of a very high standard. Judging took place informally over the weekend; there was no parade or inspection, so the result reflected their normal Highland dress on such a Scottish occasion.

CHAPTER ELEVEN

Ceremonial for Highland Gatherings

From time immemorial, clansmen have marched into battle or mustered to negotiate with other clans, while in times of peace they joined together in more sociable gatherings and games. This practice has been observed over the years, for example at Braemar, Lonach and Oban Highland games, and many other games begin with a 'March of the Clans' – an opening parade of participants.

Frank Adam states in his comprehensive work *The Clans, Septs and Regiments of the Scottish Highlands*, first published in 1908, that 'the principal is that clans or *Estaits* march junior first, but at the head is that of a Grand Officer, or (normally) the "tribe of the land" on which the gathering is held'. At Braemar, where the park is part of the old curtilage of the royal castle at Kindrochit, the Ardrigh's Balmoral Highlanders lead the march, and the Farquharsons and Duffs follow in the normal manner.

The quartered Royal Ensign and the tressured lion rampant of Scottish royalty are the best-known banners, but many chieftains and lairds use a personal banner near their tent or pavilion at games and gatherings. These flags carry the shield device of the owner and they are considered the rallying flags of the chief's following. There are also standards, developed since the 17th century and used by private followers such as the Lonach Highlanders, the colours of which have been inspected by Queens Victoria and Elizabeth.

Another form of banner is the pipe banner, attached, as the name implies, to the bagpipes. Unfortunately, these seem to be dying out, even more so as Scottish regiments diminish in numbers. There is a mistaken, relatively modern view that pipe banners, such as regimental banners, should not be used outside. Traditionally, such banners have always been used outdoors, although an especially expensive or valued one would not be used in inclement conditions.

Many games throughout the world continue to incorporate a parade as some part of the proceedings, and usually as part of an opening ceremony. There is a suitable set procedure for international circuit games, with heavy events championship contenders walking into the field behind the band. These athletes stop in front of the main platform and face the chieftain of the games, main guest of honour and other dignitaries assembled there. The professional athletes are each introduced briefly by name and championship titles where appropriate. Last to be introduced is the defending champion, who carries the chieftain's finely crafted sword and shield. He goes forward to the chieftain, who accepts the weapons and proceeds to beat the sword to north, south, east and west, inviting everyone from all four corners of the kingdom. If it is a two-day event, the chieftain will present the leader in the first day of competition with the sword and shield and he will carry them the next day. At the end of the games, the overall winner is the recipient, who takes them on to the next major event.

The pageantry of the opening ceremony at international circuit games was first introduced at a splendid Highland games in Shrewsbury, where over 30,000 spectators thoroughly enjoyed the proceedings.

This ceremony is based on the amalgamation

of two traditions. Firstly, that of around 1040 AD, when Malcolm Canmore initiated the first recorded gathering on the Braes o' Mar, beating his sword upon a shield to start the Craig Choinich hill race (see Chapter 1). Secondly, that the chieftain's champion would traditionally carry the sword and shield.

Over 300 years ago, fierce Alasdair Mor was one of the great champions. This was no fictitious character. Alasdair Grant, to give him his proper name in modern form, was a celebrated *ceann-tigh* of Clan Grant, well known for his strength and courage. A fine painting of him by Richard Waitt in 1714 shows Big Alasdair looking malevolent while wielding a dangerous-looking sabre. He is wearing a belted plaid in the fashion of the time, and the tartan is unlike that recognised as Clan Grant. It was described by John Sobieski Stuart as an 'owr Spey' tartan, worn predominantly on the south side of the Spey. Alasdair Grant's jacket and accoutrements worn in this painting are in keeping with a Highland gentleman of that era. Like other clan champions, the sword and targe comprise an integral part of his equipment.

Alasdair Grant, the champion in 1714. By Richard Waitt, 1714.

I have noted with interest that an issue of the *Inverness Journal* referred to the Clan Grant champion as Allister Moir Grant. His nickname 'Mor' (meaning 'big') had been converted to Moir. The article was written in 1812 when the former champion's son, John Grant, died at the age of 92. John had served under four Grant lairds and had a wealth of anecdotes on past times. He especially knew a great deal about cabers, as they are called in the old language. Known as the Admiral of the Spey, he was in charge of all the Glenmore Company's[1] transportation of timber. The cabers, or tree trunks, were floated down the Spey to the sea at Gartmouth and many believe the sport of caber tossing had its origins in the riversides of Strathspey, where, at one time, hundreds of woodsmen felled thousands of trees and floated them down the River Spey. It was a major industry for a remote area.

This traditional opening has become an annual task for the Dukes of Atholl at the Atholl Gathering. Numerous stars of stage, screen and television have performed the task, including Scottish favourites such as the late Mark McManus (most famously known as Taggart), Johnny Beattie, Bill McCue, Andy Cameron, Bill Simpson of *Dr Findlay's Casebook* and Diana Rigg of *The Avengers*. Terry Butcher, Hazel Irvine and various Scottish rugby captains have represented sporting interests in wielding this weapon in opening ceremonies.

THE WORLD HISTORY OF HIGHLAND GAMES

Sword and sash

World championships and Highland games on the international circuit are usually opened in full traditional style by the beating of the champion's sword against a shield, in accordance with the old ceremonial rite. It has become standard procedure for the chieftain of the winner of the most important events to be presented, albeit it temporarily, with the champion's sword, a finely crafted and authentic great Highland broadsword.

Over the years, royalty, heads of state, civic dignitaries and well-known personalities have enhanced the games in this ceremony – Prince Edward at the Commonwealth Games Highland Games, Prince William in Tokyo, Princess Alexandra in Sweden and San Francisco, Sir Billy Sneddon and Premier Dick Hamer in Australia,

Aaron Neighbour (Australia), World Highland Games Champion 2009, competed in the 1998 and 2006 Commonwealth Games.

the Sports Minister in Nigeria and the Icelandic Foreign Minister to name but a few.

Swords have a long connection with Highland Games, for in earliest times these weapons were one of the most coveted prizes, and some of the events were linked with swordmanship. Modern strength athletes groaned when they heard that the dreaded Inverarnon sword hold was in the programme as it had to be held horizontally until exhaustion! Fashioned after William Wallace's mighty weapon, the sword of strength provided one of the most demanding of all strength tests. This two-handed sword, or *claidheamh da laimh*, was most common in the 16th and 17th centuries, whereas the chieftain's sword is a basket-hilted broadsword, correctly termed by Gaels as the *claidheamh mor* (or claymore).

Swords and 20th-century Highland gatherings are linked to the warlike past by the *ghillie callum*, and on rare occasions by the Argyll broadswords – Highland sword dances of ancient origin. The champion's sword made its very first appearance in just such a dance to mark a Highland games heavy events championships.

The shield, which is beaten with the champion's sword by the chieftain, is referred to as a 'targe', or target.

The Jon Pall Champion's Sash is a perpetual trophy at international circuit Highland games, and commemorates one of the greatest and most successful competition strongmen the world has ever seen. Jon Pall Sigmarsson, four times the World's Strongest Man and five times the World's Muscle Power Champion, died tragically in January 1993. He was highly respected and popular among athletes and the public alike.

Winning strength athletes are proud to wear this trophy associated with his name. In 2007, a new sash was introduced at the World Championships in Inverness, presented by

Her Majesty Queen Elizabeth presents Bruce Aitken with the Heavy Events Trophy at Braemar.

The World Championship 2004. Winner, Bruce Aitken (Scotland); second place, Dave Barron (USA); third place, Dave Brown (USA).

Canadian Lynn Boland Richardson and Swiss American Anthony Lordi. It is embroidered with the names of all world champions.

A more formal victory ceremony was introduced at the New Hampshire Highland Games on the occasion of the 25th anniversary of the World Championships in 2004. This involved a proper three-tiered plinth that competitors mounted when bronze, silver and gold medal winners were announced. National flags were raised and after presentation of the medals, the national anthem of the winner's country was played. In Scotland's case this was *Scotland the Brave*, the anthem selected by Scottish team athletes and played over the years at the Commonwealth Games.

A sprig in a bonnet

Long before tartan and the widespread use of metal cap badges, clansmen wore a uniform and a distinguishing 'plant badge' in their bonnets. One of the snippets of folklore from the North East is that Montrose's troops wore sprigs of ripe

oats pinned to their bonnets in the sacking of Aberdeen on 13 September 1644. In spite of this early reference, the practice became much more common after 1745, and I speculate that this was perhaps one of the many secret ways in which Scots tried to maintain their identity when the Act of Proscription was in force.

The custom of wearing plant badges can still be seen at Highland games, particularly in the March of the Clansmen, for example at Lonach Games in Donside. Forbes men wear a sprig of broom, Farquharsons wear Scots fir or red whortleberry and Gordons wear ivy.

Today, it is considered most correct to affix the sprig behind the cap badge. Women should wear it on the shoulder of a tartan sash, often behind a plaid brooch.

[1] Glenmore still has remnants of the old Caledonian forest near Rothiemurchas, owned even today by descendants of the old Grant lairds. John Grant of Rothiemurchas hosted the first five world hammer-throwing championships.

Lonach Highlanders attach their sprigs.

GARNOCK INTERNATIONAL GAMES

WINDSOR CASTLE, ROYAL LIBRARY © 1992 HER MAJESTY THE QUEEN

LADESIDE PLAYING FIELDS
KILBIRNIE

ENTERPRISE AYRSHIRE

Archie McIntosh Strathnairn (b.1842) and Alex McIntosh Glenroy (b.1847).

THE WORLD HISTORY OF HIGHLAND GAMES

CHAPTER TWELVE

Queen Victoria's Highlanders

Queen Victoria genuinely believed, and put it on record, that 'the Highlanders are the finest race in the world'. This and other quotes are excerpts from her personal diaries through which she shows her attachment to her loyal Scottish staff and genuine interest in them and their families. Through Sir Arthur Phelps, clerk to the Privy Council, she made it known to members of her court and visitors to Balmoral that she ardently desired 'that there be no abrupt severance of class from class but rather a gradual blending together of all classes... and a kindly respect felt and expressed by each class to all its brethren in the great brotherhood that forms a nation'.

This was a very marked difference from the culture in English sport, where there was not only an emphasis on recognising socio-economic class differences, but *rules* were also made to maintain the differences between 'amateurs and gentlemen' and more lowly 'professionals and artisans'.

My good friend Professor John Fair pointed out that rich businessmen not only used sport to climb the social ladder but, having done so, pulled up the ladder to set themselves apart from clerks, shopkeepers and others who made up the rest of the middle classes. The Queen clearly disapproved of such practices.

Queen Victoria made numerous references to the Highlanders

Queen Victoria in Coronation robes.

looking very handsome in their kilts, and 'dancing Highland reels, which they do to perfection, to the sound of the pipes, by torchlight... It had a wild and very gay effect'. She wrote with feeling about a 16-mile row up Loch Tay to Auchmore, describing the voyage and the scenery: 'Two pipers sat in the bow and played very often. The boatmen sang two Gaelic boat-songs, very wild and singular the language so guttural and yet so soft.' It reminded her of the passage in Sir Walter Scott's *The Lady of the Lake*:

> See the proud pipers in the bow.
> And mark the gaudy streamers flow
> From their loud chanters down, and sweep
> The furrow'd bosum of the deep,
> As, rushing through the lake amain,
> They plied the ancient Highland strain.

The Royal Party passed Killin, which has long hosted a fine annual Highland gathering, and in her writing she mentioned the River Dochart, where every year clansmen and athletes begin their march to the games field.

Queen Victoria provided Highland dress for members of her staff and her Balmoral Highlanders paraded proudly at Braemar Highland Gathering and Games along with the Duff Highlanders from Invercauld. It made a splendid colourful sight. Often the Lonach Highlanders from Donside and the Atholl Highlanders from Blair Castle would join in the parade. Many of these men in the various contingents were participants in the Highland Games and some were highly ranked athletes or pipers. From her earliest days at Balmoral, Queen Victoria would visit her Highlanders' families in their own homes and get to know them all by name.

Her Majesty was very enthusiastic in promoting, developing and perpetuating various aspects of Scottish culture. So while she did not play a part in the origination of the games, as many people believe, her influence is still evident and she should be given the due credit. One of the best examples was when the Queen commissioned a very talented and prolific artist, Kenneth MacLeay (1802–78), to paint some portraits of her family. Having appreciated the excellence of MacLeay's work and his attention to detail, she extended his remit, giving him a major commission to paint some of the Highlanders working for her on the Balmoral estate. She also conceived the idea of extending this to include representation of important clans of the Highlands. The extension of this project allowed the inclusion of notable members of staff of various lairds and landed gentry who she had met on her Scottish travels.

MacLeay's watercolours for the Queen included a number of almost photographic likenesses of some of the greatest athletes of the period. The foresight of Queen Victoria, the skill of the artist and background information collected has provided a resource that will continue to be valued by current and future generations.

The results of this inspired idea have left a legacy that is only gradually being fully appreciated. It has given us an unrivalled pictorial record of many fascinating and important characters in certain spheres. The Queen wished authentic likenesses to specific individuals, so as

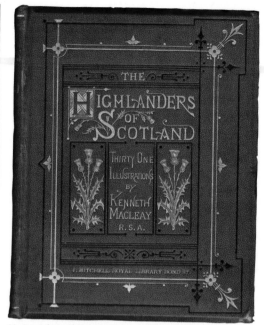

MacLeay's beautifully bound book, published 1873, in the author's collection. Rare original photos of his paintings are pasted in sepia into this fine publication. For a time they were very widely circulated as prints and cards.

well as real-life facial features of his subjects, McLeay's images show costume, weaponry, accoutrements and a plethora of useful detail for those seeking specific information in these areas. As this publication is focused on Highland games and gatherings, we will confine our attention to extracting such relevant information from *The Highlanders of Scotland*.

Kenneth MacLeay (1802–1878), born in Oban on 4 July 1802, was a founder member of the Royal Scottish Academy and his work was widely acclaimed over the years. His mother, Flora Macdonald (1729–1824) was a descendant of King Robert I and Alexander Macdonald.

Previously, it has been impossible to find images of the earliest heavy event champions, the stars of the Highland games arenas, but fortunately there were many athletes employed by the nobility and royalty and they were prominent in these commissioned paintings.

Most important are the portraits of two members of the McHardys, a north-east family of clan warriors who became pioneer athletes. The two retainers selected to represent the Earl of Fife were James Lamont and William McHardy, while Sir Charles Forbes of Newe's men were Charles McHardy and John Michie.

John Lamont and William McHardy

William McHardy (b. 1805) was the son of Allaster (or Alistair) McHardy of Auchallater, an isolated farm that still exists some four miles from Braemar. William and his brother John were amongst the first recorded prize-winners at Braemar Gathering and Games and their subsequent families were also great Highland games athletes. William had been forester and keeper on Mar Estate for 21 years for the Duke of Leeds, Mr Powell, and later for the Earl of Fife at Mar Lodge. William was the earliest authentically named lifter of the Inver Clach Cuid Fir, or Manhood Stone. This particular stone was the genuine forerunner to the McGlashen and Atlas Stones of Strength featured more than 100 years later in televised 'World's Strongest Man' competitions. On one occasion, carter John Lamont (b. 1830) was delivering goods to the Inver Inn. While the carter was inside, William, a practical joker, lifted the stone onto the back of the cart. On his return, Lamont could not understand how the cart could have been loaded.

James Lamont, (b.1830), and William McHardy (b.1805) by Kenneth MacLeay in 1865.

William McHardy's brother, John (b. 1806), was one of the first prize-winners of the formalised Braemar Gatherings and Games. He was one of the most notable heavy event champions and his descendants followed in his footsteps. John was the father of Charles McHardy (b. 1834), painted by Kenneth MacLeay to represent the Forbes men, a famous company of Lonach Highlanders whose annual marches continue to this day as a stirring reminder of ancient traditions. These two McHardys illustrate the integration of families and locations that creates great difficulties for historians and genealogists. According to tradition, there are two main branches of the McHardys. The Corriehoul McHardys of Corgarff were descendants of a French nobleman, Harde, who received a grant of land from King David II over 700 years ago. Within living memory, this family continued to occupy the same property. These athletically gifted men were from a dynasty of great warriors, and the name McHardy and its variations occur more often than any other clan or family name in the prize lists of the games of Lonach in Donside and Braemar in Deeside.

The other branch of the family is known as the Buie McHardys, *buie* meaning 'yellow' in Gaelic, a language that was still in daily use in and around Braemar until comparitively recently. The Deeside McHardys are linked in history with Norsemen and their fair hair and complexions contrast with the darker Corgarff McHardys of Donside. Charles McHardy, a Buie, was born at Auchallater and moved from Deeside to Donside. He was an athlete from a very early age and at 17 became a member of the Braemar Highland Society. Over the years, he won several champion's and gold medals. He cherished, above all, the awards won at the games held at Balmoral Castle in 1859, when Queen Victoria personally presented him with a fine sword for tossing the caber and a silver-mounted dirk featuring one large and two smaller cairngorms (local jewels) for throwing the hammer. These wonderful prizes, still in the family, are shown in MacLeay's superb painting.

Charles McHardy and John Forbes Michie
Portrayed alongside Charles McHardy is John Forbes Michie, another well-known athlete of the period. He was born at Burnside (part of the McHardy's land in Strathdon) on 6 April 1860. He joined the Lonach, Strathdon Friendly Society and won many prizes at their Highland games, being particularly good at putting the stone.

Queen Victoria's influence in the artistic project is very obvious in the inclusion of Willie Duff, an Athole Highlander who she mentioned

Charles McHardy, (b.1834), and John Michie, (b.1820), by Kenneth MacLeay in 1865.

several time in her writings. Willie was a heavy events competitor and two of his medals are on view at Blair Castle. He was a great character, a law unto himself. Fortunately, Duff was photographed as well as painted, and a comparison of images reveals a little-observed characteristic of MacLeay's technique and also perhaps the influence of his Royal patron. In *Highlanders of Scotland*, the subjects look well groomed and their dress and uniforms are invariably very smart. In reality, they were not so neat; Willie Duff's jackets, with bulging pockets, were more than a little rumpled and his hair and whiskers looked as if they were complete strangers to brush or comb. That did not stop the Queen from admiring him. Willie was born on 20 June 1810, on Stewart of Ballechan's property, and after serving his time as a cobbler he became a woodsman on the Atholl Estate. Joining the Atholl Highlanders, he was Lord Glenlyon's henchman at the Eglinton Tournament.

As he grew older and his big black beard became much longer and greyer, he was nick-named Beardie Wullie. It can be seen by these various examples that good Highland games athletes played quite prominent roles in the rural community, and especially with the landed gentry. The eminent artist Charles Landseer was also commissioned to paint a watercolour of Willie.

In 1873 the Royal train sped through Dunkeld without slowing down so nobody would catch a glimpse of Her Majesty. Nobody, that is, *except Willie Duff*. The Queen was emotionally touched when she saw that the shrewd old Willie, who she remembered well, had gone further up the line and had perched on a bank by a slope, which caused the train to slow down. There he was, in splendid isolation, waving fond farewell to his beloved monarch.

William's father, Alex (b.1785), was a crofter,

THE WORLD HISTORY OF HIGHLAND GAMES

Willie Duff, (b. 1810). A favourite of Queen Victoria, painted by Sir Edwin Landseer c.1865, but this image is a hand-tinted postcard of a photograph by A.F. Mackenzie (1846–1940).

woodsman and toll-keeper. Like his father and others before him, Alex, and then Willie, lived at Sock, near Balnamuir on the Athole estate. In passing, it should be pointed out that the spellings 'Athole' and 'Atholl' have both been in use over the years, largely depending on the preference of the duke of the period.

Willie was the oldest son of the family and after serving his apprenticeship as a cordiner (shoemaker) he entered the service of the Duke of Athole and became an Athole Highlander in 1839. This is now Europe's last private army and retains strong connections with Highland games. The Highlanders have an annual parade at the modern Atholl Gathering and Games, and often compete in an entertaining kilted race. The 10th Duke of Atholl was particularly interested in the

Atholl Games and was the first president of the International Federation of Heavy Event Athletes. His successor, the current Duke, is also very supportive and annually opens the proceedings in traditional style. This annual games marks the start of the new season for the international heavy events circuit.

Willie Duff was a very talented man, particularly in sports and outdoor activities. He was Lord Glenlyon's personal henchman at the famous Eglinton Tournament at Kilwinning in 1839. Fond of a dram and a free spirit, Duff wanted to go 'out on the town' but instead, much to his dismay, he was confined to camp. It was a very unusual, widely reported, disciplinary matter.

Duff was a very skilled angler and oarsman, and an expert in tying flies to attract fish. A most experienced otter hunter, he was always in demand to unearth these elusive animals. Apart from that, he had many social and domestic skills. The neat knitting and elaborate patterns on Willie Duff's kilt stockings were all his own work. He had a good singing voice for Port a Beul, the mouth music of the Gael, and Gaelic folk songs, which he sang with passion and pride. His musical accomplishments were further illustrated by his very competent playing of the violin and bass. When he heard a tune he liked, he could personally put the music on paper from ear. Duff added to his versatility by accumulating a great deal of interesting information and anecdotes from a wealth of reading over the years. Queen Victoria met Willie on her first visit to Scotland in 1842 and he always remained a firm favourite of hers.

Another athlete well known to the Queen was Charles Duncan, born in 1826. He had a long and successful career, competing and winning prizes at Braemar in hill races and heavy events such as tossing the caber. There are several mentions of

The Queen regularly visited her friendly neighbours.

Charles Duncan and other Highland games competitors in her diaries, some of which will be quoted. On Royal expeditions, Duncan kept notes of the names of the places, distances and times. The Queen also picked up some Doric words and expressions from such retainers, sometimes using them in her diary or in speeches.

Charles Duncan was still going strong at the turn of the century, by which time he had given up hill running to concentrate on shooting. He was still able to win the annual target-shooting contest held at Balmoral. In MacLeay's portrayal of Charles Duncan as one of Her Majesty's Keepers at Balmoral, the gillie is wearing two very large medals on his plaid. The possibility of these being shooting medals has been expressed but we personally feel that at the time the painting was created, it is much more likely that they would be won for his prowess on the hill and with the caber.

Donald Stewart and Charles Duncan by Kenneth MacLeay.

Duncan must have been a great favourite of the Queen as she also asked the great artist Sir Edwin Landseer to portray this athlete.

Farquharson's men in the MacLeay series were James Bowman and William Brown, two of the 266 members of the Braemar Society at that time. James Bowman was the better known of the pair because of his extraordinary leaping abilities. He and his father were the most spectacular jumpers in the north-east and were often called upon to entertain visitors with their celebrated athletic feats. Jumping clear over the back of horses was their most appreciated stunt. James Bowman, MacLeay's subject, was born at Invercauld on 12 March 1814, while his father, John, was born at Auchtaven, a property of his father, William (James's grandfather). As their name suggests, earlier members of the Bowman family were from the archers of Mar fraternity. The Bowmans intermarried with other noted warrior families, such as the McHardys and the Cattanachs, producing genetically superior physical specimens. James's mother was Margaret McHardy, daughter of Allaster McHardy of Auchallater. With such a pedigree, or gene pool, it is not at all surprising that he was such a fine athlete. Bowman was a valued stalker for the Prince Consort and a great mountain guide. In 1848, he was called upon to escort their Royal Highnesses on their first ascent of dark Lochnagar. It was a misty day and that night in September 1848 Queen Victoria wrote 'Bowman (Mr Farquharson's keeper) and MacDonald, who preceded us, looked like ghosts'.

Kenneth MacLeay painted many wonderful specimens of Highland men and two of his finest models were Lachlan and Ewan MacPherson. Not even the voluminous plaids and many accoutrements could conceal the magnificence of their physiques. From their massive calves to their broad shoulders and deep chests, they were shown to advantage by their proud but unassuming bearing. The two were not closely related. Lachlan was born in 1811 at Laggan. He lived for a

James Bowman and William Brown by Kenneth MacLeay in 1865.

Macdonald (1842–90) was said to be remarkably tall and handsome. By Kenneth MacLeay in 1887.

time at Blair Atholl, and then in nearby Dunkeld, before becoming a hotelier at Birnam. Lachlan Mor's two grandfathers, along with their fathers, joined Clan Chief Cluny MacPherson and the Jacobites in the 1745 Rebellion.

Amelia Murray MacGregor, in her contemporary notes supporting MacLeay's paintings, stated that for many years Lachlan was Champion of Scotland for all athletic games. It has not been possible to find acceptable evidence to substantiate this, but he certainly looked every inch a champion. His colleague, the swarthy Ewan MacPherson, had a large torso, and the accuracy of MacLeay's brush showed that this made Ewan's head look smaller by comparison. The target or shield carried by MacPherson is an interesting feature in the painting. Originally made in France for Prince Charles Edward Stewart, it was passed to Cluny MacPherson after the Battle of Culloden,

Lachlan McPherson and Ewan McPherson by Kenneth MacLeay.

who treasured it for many years. When the Queen attended Loch Laggan Highland Games on her second visit to Scotland, Ewan carried the targe as the MacPherson clan chief's henchman. In these modern times, such traditions are still maintained in international Highland games, when the champion's sword and shield are carried on to the field by the current champion. The historic targe in MacLeay's painting is now in the Museum of Scotland in Edinburgh. The banner borne by Lachlan MacPherson in the painting is the ancient green banner of the Clan MacPherson, carried throughout the 1745–6 Jacobite Rising.

Kenneth MacLeay declared that these were the two finest men of the series. Lachie Mor (Big Lachlan) was 6 feet 3 inches in height and Ewan was just one inch shorter. While much above the average height of town dwellers at that time, such heights were not unusual in Highland men, particularly in the north-east of Scotland. Completed and sent to Queen Victoria in November 1867, this is truly a historic painting.

The most interesting painting for many Highland games enthusiasts is that of Archibald and Alexander McIntosh with the *clach neart*, a stone of strength, or putting stone.

There is a great deal of artistic licence in composing this scene so, bearing in mind a mutual desire for authenticity, some observations seem necessary. In serious competition, an athlete would have removed his *sporan molach* (in this case made of fox skin), the heavy large buckled belt, neckerchief and his weskit (waistcoat). More often than not, his sleeves would be rolled up above his elbows. However, we do know that Highlanders on expeditions and marches would often indulge in informal competitions during breaks, and on such occasions they would toss cabers and put the stone, in whatever they were wearing. One old account reads 'without

THE WORLD HISTORY OF HIGHLAND GAMES

removing his plaid' and goes on to describe an athlete making a record throw while fully dressed. MacLeay's interpretation of the athletic stone-putting Scot is appealing even to Highland games purists.

In the painting we see Archibald McIntosh putting from behind a caber, which, interestingly, is being used as a trig or stopboard. Alexander, born on 16 August 1842, was 15 years younger than his companion in the painting. He was one of eight children and succeeded his father as ground officer of the McIntosh of McIntosh. Alexander was the grandson of Ewen McIntosh, a stalwart, powerful clan warrior who fought in most battles during the 1745 rebellion. He was badly wounded at Falkirk and from then on carried a musket ball in his shoulder throughout his life. Ewen was also noted for the defence of his captain, who was fatally wounded in battle. Donald Mor, Alex's great-uncle, was another famous fighter, serving as a lieutenant in America and fighting many battles, one of which was the taking of Quebec. Surviving these, he returned to Scotland and with his pension secured the tenancy of a farm. Such a heritage was common amongst Highland games athletes of that period and stone putter Archibald McIntosh was no exception. His great-grandfather, a gallant standard bearer in the government's army of the period in 1745, was killed in action during the '45, bravely carrying his flag until death. Archibald, the thrower, was born at Essich, near Inverness, on 19 July 1827. He was a farm manager who had a wife, Jessie (née Reid), two daughters and a son. This painting made a very favourable impact when it was exhibited at the Royal Scottish Academy in 1869.

Amongst MacLeay's subjects there are other Highland games personalities such as James Menzies (b. 1845), winner of the Best-dressed Highlander prize at the 1865 Athole Gathering.

His fine equipment has been well observed by the artist.

These Highland retainers are colourful and fascinating as personalities in their own right and Kenneth MacLeay made his models a joy to behold. The clan tartans and Highland accoutrements depicted by him with incredible attention to detail are full of ethnological treasures for observant investigators. Queen Victoria knew her Highland retainers very well and while she noted their fierce independent spirit and personal pride, she also observed their devotion to her. In a private letter after the death of her consort, Prince Albert, she wrote that she found their self-respect and gentlemanlike chivalrous feelings comforting and consoling (the plot for the film *Mrs Brown* was based on the Queen's bereavement at this time). The paintings and biographies of these men and Queen Victoria's

Alexander (b.1806) and James Menzies (b.1845) by Kenneth MacLeay in 1867.

personal perspective in her diaries greatly enrich our knowledge. They give us a fine legacy of information about Highland games participants and their backgrounds that would otherwise have been lost to posterity.

The Queen's enthusiasm for the games and competitors was matched by Prince Albert's. When the Consort wrote the brief for Braemar Castle, he included integrating with the building a collection of unique marble bas-reliefs designed according to his demands. One of the most attractive of these is seen high on the outer west front wall of the ballroom. This fine work shows a hefty Highlander putting the stone while other contestants wait their turn; one of these, on the far right, is seated and holding a heavy sledge throwing-hammer. It has been written that King Malcolm Canmore was one of the spectators in the bas-relief but this assumption is incorrect. There is no doubt that the main spectators are Queen Victoria, Prince Albert and their family. John Thomas (1813–62), was commissioned for this historic work by the Consort after the latter had seen Thomas's excellent works in the Houses of Parliament. This artistic depiction of Highland games pre-dates MacLeay's works. Further proof of Queen Victoria's very deep interest in Highland games was seen when she hosted the Braemar Games at Balmoral Castle, her own Scottish home, in 1859, 1887, 1890, 1898 and 1899.

Those who have read Queen Victoria's diaries will know that she had a genuine, unswerving admiration for the Highlanders of Scotland, and it must be said that this admiration was mutual and long lasting. Only her own words can adequately convey her sentiments.

October 3rd 1844

Lord Aberdeen was quite touched when I told him I was so attached to the dear, dear Highlands and missed the fine hills so much. There is a great peculiarity about the Highlands and Highlanders; and they are such a chivalrous, fine active, people. Our stay amongst them was so delightful.

Braemar Gathering

September 12, 1850

We lunched early, and then went at half-past two o'clock, with the children and all our party to the Gathering at the Castle of Braemar, as we did last year.

The Duffs, Farquharsons, the Leeds and those staying with them, and Captain Forbes and forty of his men who had come over from Strath Don, were there. There were the usual games of putting the stone, throwing the hammer and caber, and racing up the hill of Craig Cheunnich, which was accomplished in less than six minutes and a half: and we were all pleased to see our gillie Duncan, who is an active and good-looking, young man, win. He was far before the others the whole way. It is a fearful exertion. Mr Farquharson brought him up to me afterwards. Eighteen or nineteen started, and it looked very pretty to see them run off in their different coloured kilts, with their white shirts (the jackets and doublets they take off for all the games), and scramble up through the wood, emerging gradually at the edge of it and climbing up the hill.

After this we went into the castle, and saw some dancing; the prettiest was a reel by Mr Farquharson's children and some other children, and the

This fine bas-relief is still to be seen by visitors to Balmoral. Sculptor John Thomas (1813–1862).

THE WORLD HISTORY OF HIGHLAND GAMES

Ghillie Callum beautifully danced by John Athole Farquharson, the fourth son. The twelve children were all there, including the baby, who is two years old. Mama enjoys it very much, it is her first visit to Scotland.

Some time later, she made an interesting note about Charles Duncan:

> One of our keepers since 1851: an excellent, intelligent man, much liked by the Prince. He like many others spit blood after running the race up that steep hill in this short space of time, and he has never been so strong since. The running up hill has in consequence been discontinued. He lives in a cottage at the back of Craig Gowan (commanding a beautiful view) called Robrech which the Prince built for him.

The hill race was reintroduced in the Braemar programme many years later.

The day after the 1850 Braemar Games, Her Majesty gave an interesting account of salmon leistering (catching salmon with spears), a practice that was common in Scotland. There is an interesting comment:

> Duncan, in spite of all his exertions yesterday, and having walked to and from the gathering, was the whole time in the water.

This is most revealing. Charles Duncan had already walked the distance from Balmoral to Braemar (around seven miles) before competing in caber tossing and then a hill race, and walked back the same distance home after his exertions. The next day, he was back to energetic work on the river.

Charles Duncan later in life.

The Lonach Highlanders passed the Dee on their homeward march and seeing the fishing, hailed the Balmoral gillies. The Royals had departed but later the Queen, hearing of the incident, wrote:

Salmon leistering on the River Dee in 1880.

> We heard yesterday that our men had carried all Captain Forbes's men on their backs through the river. They saw the fishing going on, and being greeted by our people, said they would come over, on which ours went across in one moment and carried them over – Macdonald at their head carrying Captain Forbes on his back. This was very courteous, and worthy of chivalrous times.

These Highlanders, athletes and gillies alike, were certainly admirable characters.

As Queen Victoria wrote of Balmoral on 15 October 1856: 'Every year my heart becomes more fixed in this dear paradise.'

A Royal report

Prince Albert had presided over a conference of the British Association in Aberdeen on 22 September 1859, and as a result the members were invited to a Highland Games at Balmoral. Here is an extract of the Queen's perspective:

> At two o'clock we were all ready. Albert and the boys were in their kilts, and I and the girls in

The Philosophers' Highland Gathering at Balmoral, 1869, a little known Highland games.

royal Stewart skirts and shawls over black velvet bodices.

It was a beautiful sight in spite of the frequent slight showers which at first tormented us, and the very high cold wind. There were gleams of sunshine, which with the Highlanders in their brilliant and picturesque dresses, the wild notes of the bagpipes, the band, and the beautiful background of mountains, rendered the scene wild and exciting in the extreme. The Farquharsons men, headed by Colonel Farquharson, the Duff's headed by Lord Fife, and the Forbes's men headed by Sir Charles Forbes, had all marched to the ground before we came out, and were drawn up just opposite us, and the spectators (the people of the country) behind them. We stood on the terrace, the company near us, the 'savants', also, on either side of us, and along the slopes, on the grounds. The games began about three o'clock:

1. 'Throwing the Hammer'
2. 'Tossing the Caber'
3. 'Putting the Stone'

We gave prizes to the three best in each of the games. We walked along the terrace to the large marquee, talking to the people, to where the men were 'putting the stone'. After this returned to the upper terrace, to see the race, a pretty wild sight; but the men looked very cold, with nothing but their shirts and kilts on; they ran beautifully. They wrapped plaids round themselves, then came to receive their prizes from me. Last of all came the dancing- reels and the 'Ghillie Callum'. The latter the judges could not make up their minds about; it was danced over and over again; and at last they left out the best dancer of all! They said he danced 'too well'! The dancing over, we left amid loud cheers from the people. It was then about half past five. We watched from the window the Highlanders marching away, the different people walking off and four weighty omnibuses filling with the scientific men.

Lawsie

In Victorian times, Alexander (Lawsie) MacIntosh was one of Deeside's finest athletes. He had a superb physique, and as standard bearer to the Farquharsons he led them in the March of the Clansmen, in which he was most conspicuous. At 6 feet 1 inch, his massive build as a young man aroused much favourable comment. He never ventured far from home, but he became a legend in his own area and was immediately noticed by visitors to Braemar.

It has been said that he put the 16lb stone 40 feet 4 inches to take a first at Glengairn Games in 1863. In 1873, he achieved 32 feet 11 inches with the 22lb stone at Ballater Games.

Lawsie first competed at Braemar in 1871, and his best put with the 28lb stone, in Braemar (standing) style, was 26 feet 4 inches. His best event, however, was tossing the caber. He won prizes for over 50 years and, as a popular singer at ceilidhs in the old Mar Castle, he was often in the limelight.

Alexander rubbed shoulders with royalty and was a gillie for King Edward. His two sisters had been in service for King George V and Queen Mary

Lawsie at Braemar.

and Betty Gillin, who wrote for the old Braemar book, sought out the MacIntoshes looking for a photo of their noted brother. Later, she marvelled at their incredible collection of genuine royal memorabilia given to the MacIntosh ladies over the years, and one rather jealous, haughty local lady exclaimed, 'Oh them! They think they are Royalty!'

Alexander was often called 'Lawsie', the name of the croft he farmed at Crathie, near the church where generations of kings and queens worshipped. In later years, when he moved to Braemar, he was familiarly known as Sandy.

At the age of 71, he placed second in tossing the caber at Braemar and although best known for heavy events, he remained very supple and agile. When he was 74 years old, he could kick the lintel of a doorway, *keeping one foot always on the ground.*

His upper body diminished with age but his huge muscular legs were very noticeable when wearing the kilt. His calves measured a massive 18¼ inches and most of his adult life he weighed around 16 stones (224lb, nearly 102kg). His only weight-lifting feat on record is, at the age of 46, lifting three 56lb weights (total 168lb, over 75kg) with his teeth.

A London doctor seeing Lawsie toss the caber at Braemar when he was over 60 years of age decided to find out more about this remarkable man. The laird emphasised that he must not mention that

Right: Sandy (Lawsie) MacIntosh (1851–32).

he was a doctor or Sandy would be unwilling to discuss matters.

When they met, they walked briskly up the hill towards Sandy's cottage and the visitor began puffing with the exertion. 'Man,' said old Lawsie, 'Ye'r pechin an' gey sair made.[1] I think you should see a doctor!'

In 1923, the King's jeweller was commissioned to make Lawsie a special medal for having competed at Braemar for over 50 years. He was very proud of this medal and the fact that he had been in personal service to Queen Victoria, King Edward and King George v.

Lawsie passed away on 26 April 1932. He is now a Deeside legend.

While MacLeay was at work in Scotland with his paintings, in 1866 a new Caledonian Games was inaugurated in California; which would eventually prove to have long-lasting, worldwide benefits for games enthusiasts. The Caledonian Club of San Francisco's Scottish Gathering and Games, held annually on Labor Day weekend, is now one of the biggest and best in the world. The next chapter will tell us how it all began.

Lawsie competing at Braemar in 1905.

SANDY Mc INTOSH
age 74, the oldest competitor at the BRAEMAR GATHERING throwing the hammer

[1] Translating the Doric, 'You are breathing hard and physically struggling'. 'Sair made' is very close in sound and meaning to the German 'Sehr mude'.

The MacCrimmon family tree. For details from the document, see p.131.

THE WORLD HISTORY OF HIGHLAND GAMES

CHAPTER THIRTEEN

Caledonian Club of San Francisco Highland Games

A quiet Spanish mission town and Mexican port on the northern coast of California was caught up in the Gold Rush and rapidly expanded into a city by the influx of immigrants. The city became known for lawlessness, graft and corruption. This was San Francisco, El Dorado – a land of golden opportunity for those who could stand up to hardship and were willing to work long and hard. There was an abundance of Scots far from their native land who were willing to do just that. The impact they had has been well documented but the formation and early days of the Caledonian Club of San Francisco have largely been forgotten and this should be rectified to honour the founders and credit those who perpetuated the interesting history of this club.

One very stormy night in 1866, Clement Dixon braved the weather and, from his home in Fifth Street, went to his almost-new 'Ale Vault' in Summer Street, where he had arranged a meeting in a private room behind his bar.

Seventeen men, mainly Scots, had been invited and every one turned up eager to discuss a bold plan, little knowing that more than 140 years later, their brainchild would still survive and be famous internationally. The Caledonian Club of San Francisco was inaugurated that evening with the intention of initiating a Highland games in San Francisco. No time was wasted. The first games took place at Hayes Park on Thanksgiving Day, Thursday 29 November 1866, just five days after the meeting.

The park had a large pavilion with a sizeable hall, restaurant, various public rooms, shooting gallery, recreational facilities for billiards and a fine gym. A beer parlour was, of course, another important facility for the new Caledonian Club members. Sadly, a few short years later, a new venue had to be found as the great fire of November 1872 (see below) completely destroyed this location.

Although staged with almost indecent haste, the first games, with a modest attendance, were quite successful. This was, no doubt, largely because of the very fine prizes offered for the traditional competitions. The most interesting trophy was a silver quoit costing $50. This was a large sum in those days but at that time there was a great deal of wealth in San Francisco, with billions of dollars being raised in gold and silver. Other prizes went up to $300, a huge incentive to enter the seven athletic events and two novelty events. Dancing and piping did not feature in the first programme but that was quickly rectified. The events were quoits, putting the 26lb stone, throwing the light, 12lb hammer and heavy, 16lb hammer, high jump, long jump, triple jump, blindfolded wheelbarrow race and the three-legged race.

This programme may have been influenced by those in the initial group, including A.F. and A.S. McDonald, who were known as 'heavies'. The wealthy wool mill owner, Donald McLennan, came from Inverness; several came from Nova Scotia; Angus McLeod came from

The Caledonian Club of San Francisco produced this poster for their Highland Games.

Pictou, where many of the first Scottish pioneers landed; others were from Edinburgh, Lesmahagow, and so on.

A.F. and A.S. McDonald dominated in hammer throwing, A.F. McDonald doing 78 feet 6 inches with the 16lb hammer and, in second place, his brother doing 67 feet. With the 12lb hammer, the same winner did 92 feet. George Scott won the 26lb put with 22 feet 1 inch and the hop, step and jump with 35 feet 6 inches. Carmichael won the high jump with 4 feet and long jump with 15 feet 7 inches. It seems strange that there was no piping or dancing competitions but earlier historians pointed out that many games in Scotland developed in the same way.

In 1867, tossing the caber, hitch and kick and a piping event were added to the programme, and a 22lb stone was used in the putt. Christopher Chisholm was awarded a set of quartz sleeve buttons as his prize for winning the caber. In 1893, he became 10th Chief of the Club.

The Caledonian Club grew very rapidly, numbering 95 members by the following Thanksgiving Day in 1867, when the second games were held.

The second games were very well publicised in news-papers advertisements and articles. Advertising the games of 1867, it was stated that 'The object of the Club is for the practice and encourage-ment of the Athletic Games of Scotland'. Later this was amended to:

Ryan Vierra on the cover in 1999.

> The chief objects shall be the encouragement and practice of the games, and the preservation of the customs and manners of Scotland, the promotion of a taste of the language and literature, and the binding more closely in social links the sons and daughters, and descendants of our mother country.

In 1868, Highland dancing featured in the programme and in 1869 there were two stone putting competitions with 16lb and 22lb stones, just as in Scotland then and today.

The Highland games have remained the mainstay of the Club, moving to different venues over the years. The 1868 games were in Sausalito, held not on the sand but on a haugh, a level green very close to the shore, and to this day the street marking the edge of the field is called Caledonia Avenue. In 1869, the games moved back to San Francisco.

The winner of the handicap race for men over 45 in 1870 was given a cow and a calf. A ton of coal was often awarded and, because this was still frontier country, a pistol was not uncommon as a prize.

In 1871, a great fire was started when Mrs O'Leary's cow kicked over her lamp and destroyed three and a half square miles of Chicago. The Caledonian Club of San Francisco organised a second games that year, which raised $1,200 for victims of the Chicago Fire.

Athlete Andrew Foreman was the greatest athlete and 2nd Chieftain of 1871 and, like many Scottish champions, he sported immaculate Highland dress, with his medals that he won in Scotland and America prominently displayed.

The aims were amended in 1873 to include 'the promotion of a taste of literature, music, (etc)'. Club officials established cordial relationships with St

Andrew's societies and other Scottish organisations and this pattern remained over the years. Membership increased to 300 in 1870, 450 in 1874, and 1,225 names were listed in 1896.

The search for continuity of location for the games was almost fulfilled in 1873 when the Club booked Badgers Central Park across the bay in Oakland. This remained the games field until 1884, when the games moved to Shell Mound Park and remained there until well into the new century. The internationally acknowledged Highland games world champion, Donald Dinnie, the first sporting superstar, competed in the San Francisco Games in 1883. Although in his 47th year, he earned record sums in games competitions, record breaking and, outside the games, wrestling with William Muldoon, the father of American wrestling.

In 1893, the Columbian Exposition, a world fair, was held in Chicago to celebrate the 400th anniversary of Columbus' discovery of America. Part of the celebrations was a Scottish week, a Highland games being one of the main attractions. Scottish organisations worldwide were notified and teams solicited for open competitions. The Caledonian Club of San Francisco had made an incredible gold medal, in which was mounted a fine diamond. It was competed for at the Chicago Games and given to the Caledonian Club with the most points in the various contests. It was said that this medal was the finest award ever at any North American games and that it would become a permanent award. Participants competed on three consecutive days and, after some debate over ineligible competitors, the Caledonian Society of Dutton, Ontario, Canada, received the coveted award.

By the end of the century, the Caledonian Club of San Francisco was still expanding and had an incredible membership – one report

In 1868, when this painting by M. Donald was produced, the games were held in what is now called Sausalito.

quoted 1,500 members. In 1885, 12,000 people attended the games and there became a great need for club facilities to meet the demands of such a successful organisation. In 1885, joining with the St Andrews Society, they raised money and built a home of their own to be known as the Scottish Hall, a two-storied building with ample basement space. The first floor included a fine hall, measuring 48 by 72 feet. The fact that four out of five San Francisco newspapers reported the occasion reflects the impact of the Scots' initiative, for by this time the Caledonian Club was much respected in the community for its social and charitable work. Sadly, its value was short lived.

On the morning of 18 April 1906 an earthquake struck San Francisco, followed by many devastating fires. The Great Fire of 1906 destroyed much of the city and 'the Scottish Hall was but a heap of smoking ashes, gone forever'. Losses included club records, engravings and memorabilia, but fortunately, there were no human casualties. Since so much documentation was lost, we have been greatly indebted to Club historian Jim Jardine for his willing and meticulous research.

After the disaster, members showed amazing fortitude and determination. The annual games were not cancelled; they were merely delayed and moved to a new location. The annals of the club report the meeting of November 1906 and concluded 'The Caledonian Club was indeed the Caledonian Club again, fire or no fire!' This speaks volumes for the strength of character of its members.

Activities were resumed immediately and, although delayed, the annual Highland games were held, but on a reduced scale. Even an earthquake and a fire could not stop them.

The activities of the Caledonian Club deserve a book of their own. Here we can but mention a few highlights. One such highlight is the provision of a fine 11-foot-high granite statue of Robert Burns in a shady glade at Stanyan and Fell Street. Five thousand people, Scots and their friends, turned up for the unveiling on 23 February 1908. Two years later, a new hall was opened.

Club member James McEachran was the best known heavy of the post-war years, and the first of numerous Olympians that have competed in more recent times. McEachran threw the (wire-handled) hammer at the Antwerp, Belgium, Olympics of 1920 and again in the 1924 Olympics in Paris. This outstanding athlete was born in Prince Edward Island on 2 June 1881 and joined the Caledonian Club in 1910. He won many competitions and the club presented him with a diamond medal for his record-breaking feats in hammer throwing. McEachran was still competing and winning points at the age of 65 and in 1947, after the caber had been dropped from the programme for some time, his strong support of the event saw its inclusion in the programme once more.

Between 1914 and 1932, the Caledonian Club had its own pipe band, clad in Prince Charles Edward Stewart tartan kilts. It took less than $1,000 to outfit the bandsmen. After 1932, they simply gave generous donations to other pipe bands in the area.

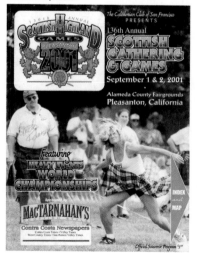

Cover girl Shannon Hartnett, former Olympic Games competitor.

THE WORLD HISTORY OF HIGHLAND GAMES

In similar fashion, the club fostered Highland dancing. The cost of dancers' costumes seemed to be a key factor in the lack of interest in dancing competitions but this was eased with the introduction of the Aboyne dress. There were not many dancing teachers in the area so in 1958 the club allocated funds to pay teachers and lessons were given for free. This was successful for a short time but a simple survey of entries in 1965 indicated that out of 142 dancers at their games only 26 came from within a 50-mile radius of San Francisco. By comparison, 26 came from British Columbia, over 1,000 miles up the coast. There has been an upsurge of interest since then and greatly increased participation.

The First World War made little difference to the Caledonian Club's Highland games, which were held as usual, but the Second World War was quite different. The games were cancelled for the duration; there were only a few social dances, Highland dancing and an occasional concert. Financial returns from post-war games were sometimes disappointing and it was not until the games moved to Santa Rosa that significant improvements could be seen. Those who attended have very happy memories of the games at Rosa, and the increased attendances and financial considerations resulted in the games moving to Pleasanton in 1994.

Jim Jardine has provided a tremendous amount of information for this chapter, including copies of old newspapers and old club documents, for which I am grateful. The following are his quotes on the Club's input to international Highland games of the present and becoming a major 'player' in the worldwide circuit that now exists. Jim wrote in the 2003 games programme:

> We certainly owe our biggest debt for the existence of the Heavy Events Games of the current high standards to the combined efforts of Past Chief (P/C) Malcolm Ramsay, our Athletic Chairman Emeritus, from the Caledonian Club and David Webster OBE, our announcer and the originator of the World Highland Games Heavy Events Championship, for bringing all this about. If it were not for David Webster's lifelong interest and promulgator of Scottish Games throughout the world, we would never have seen the World Championship contests we did in 1999, 2001 and 2002 (and 2006). David's first trip here in 1971 with a troupe of Scottish performers laid the foundation. If it weren't for the vision of Malcolm Ramsay when he saw the quality of David's athletic troupe and Malcolm's organizational abilities and dedication for almost quarter of a century to follow, we wouldn't have what has come to be called the US Invitational Championship.

> The century-old Caledonian Club was first enhanced in 1972 when Scotsmen James McBeath and Charlie Simpson came to throw at the Santa Rosa Games, bringing the Scottish implements and teaching the locals how it was done. The resulting competition became so good that in 1975 it came to be known as the US Championships. P/C Ramsay managed these Games from their inception in 1975 until 1989.

The games in October 1971, mentioned by Jim Jardine, were part of the worldwide 'British Days' series, which took a selected Highland games

Back row: *Charlie Simpson, Dave (Darth Vader) Prowse, Ian Campbell, Bill Anderson. Front row: John Ross, Charlie Allan, Clayton Thomson. Pomona, South California, 1980.*

Dave Brown, USA, has performed with distinction in Several World Championships. New Hampshire.

American heavies have been highest placed in the new millenium.

team to places in Sweden, Japan, Australia, America and beyond. There were many others, including dancers and pipers, in the group.

Held in the Golden Gate Park in San Francisco, guests of honour included Her Royal Highness Princess Alexandra and husband, The Honourable Angus Ogilvy, and Malcolm Ramsay. There were huge crowds and the personalities of the team won their hearts and minds. Likewise, the friendly, hospitable Americans charmed the visiting Highlanders and the bonds of kinship that were woven developed and strengthened over the years. The spin-off resulted in two-way visitation of games participants in Scotland and San Francisco and, in due course, all over America.

It all began with immigrants, then Dinnie and the Victorian champions, but the Caledonian Club of San Francisco and this new team added different elements, the most significant being the continuity of exchanges and the structuring of categories based on ability. The introduction of novice, amateur, women, age group masters and professional classes provided active participation for many and motivation to move up the ladder. This resulted in greatly increased numbers of participants and their supporters and raised the standards on the basis of 'the more milk the more cream'. Nowadays, America has more world-class talent in 2008 than anywhere else in the world. Currently, contenders being considered for world championships include more Americans than any other nation. These Americans have one thing in common: they have all competed and enhanced their reputations at the games of the Caledonian Club of San Francisco.

CHAPTER FOURTEEN

Olympic Inspiration in Paris

Highland and Olympic games

'Is not the whole glory of sport the pitting of manly strength and skill, one against the other?'

The quote above is from *Geordie*, a cult film from 1955 about a young Scottish Highland games athlete who eventually won an Olympic gold medal in hammer throwing.

It may be difficult for many to see any genuine connection with Highland games and Olympic games but there is indeed a very basic and important link that has largely been forgotten. Numerous writers have made comparisons and brief references to this matter. For example, Professor E. Norman Gardiner, the great researcher on the Olympics, commented in 1967 on the athletic contests described by Homer: 'The nearest parallel to them is to be found in the sports of the Highland Clans.'

Over the years, we have recorded the Highland games held at the Paris Exhibition in 1889. It was a historic event in many ways, being one of the earliest and biggest international Highland games, and it included the very first physique team competition.

Wullie Baxter of Milngavie, the world's most prominent ethnic wrestling historian, did some research involving the famous Strathallan Highland Games, from which came some revealing and surprising information.

Wullie is President of the Federation International des Luttes Celtiques and President of the Federation of Indigenous Scottish Sports and Games, and often speaks at international conferences in these capacities. At a UNESCO conference in Kazakhstan to deal with the promotion and development of traditional sports and games, Wullie was asked to prepare a paper. In part of this presentation, he condensed his findings on the Highland and Olympic connection as follows:

Baron Pierre de Coubertin of France. Reviver of the Olympic Games.

Indeed the modern Olympic Games owes its very existence to a visit Pierre de Fridi, Baron de Coubertin made to the Paris Exhibition in 1889. There to his astonishment he saw a Highland games taking place. Every culture has its sporting competitions but Scottish Highland games are unique and De Coubertin saw wrestlers, strongmen, swordsmen, runners, high and long jump, hop step and jumpers, pole vault for height, musicians (bagpipers) and dancers all competing in one small area about the size of a football field.

De Coubertin's dream of reviving the Olympic Games had become jaded but he was immediately reinspired; he saw for the first time that his vision was practical. Soon after, in 1890, he travelled to England to visit Dr Brooke who had organised an annual Olympic Festival at Much Wenlock since 1850. The rest is history.

The Gathering of the Clans in Paris at the Paris Exhibition was a

Courtesy of Strathallan Games committee and W. Baxter.

❖ PARIS. ❖

A MONSTER

HIGHLAND ❖
❖ **GATHERING**

WILL BE HELD UNDER THE PERSONAL DIRECTION OF THE

STRATHALLAN GAMES COMMITTEE,

WITHIN

The Cour De Nestle, Paris.

(ADJOINING THE EXHIBITION)

On **THURSDAY** and **FRIDAY**,

17th and 18th OCTOBER, 1889.

Over £700 will be given in Prize-Money.

In addition, Gold Medallions d'Honneur will be given to
the Champions in each Event.

very special event that has been reported in different ways, not always sticking to the facts. The excellence of the occasion, with some 300 competitors, could not have been faulted. The problem was that French organisers had not understood the general appeal and high standard of the Highland games and gathering and simply slumped bare details of the games amid general information of the great Paris Exposition, of which it was part. By failing to properly advertise the Highland games in their own right, the organisers' neglect led to poor audiences and unfilled coffers.

The public and the special guests who did attend were enthralled. Amongst these was Baron de Coubertin, who was very enthusiastic and inspired by the spectacle. For some time, he had been promoting the idea of an international event for the nations of the world to meet in friendly competition in a wide variety of sports. The Olympic ideals of today were very much in his mind but he had never seen the concept in

The Scot is Kenneth McRae of Nairn c.1887.

Of noble descent, Launceston Elliot's relatives included the Earls of Minto, Viceroys of India and a Governor General of Canada. He was described as 'The finest man of English birth', which he disliked as he was born in India of Scottish ancestry.

action until he saw the Highland games in Paris. This experience strongly supported his theories and crystallised his thinking.

Seven years after witnessing the Highland games, De Coubertin's visions were realised and the Olympic Games of 1896 became the first of the modern Olympics.

The Scottish influence was significant and easily discernable in the Athens Olympics of 1896. There were competitions in throwing the hammer, putting the shot, throwing weights for distance and pole vaulting – all Scottish activities

Gilbert Elliot (1761–1814), 1st Earl of Minto and Viceroy of India.

Launceston Elliot, left, in the Olympic sprint. His father, Gilbert, accompanied him. Athens, 1896.

THE WORLD HISTORY OF HIGHLAND GAMES

popular at Highland games, as the Baron had seen in Paris.

In Britain's Olympic team, Launceston Elliot, a young strength athlete, won Britain's first gold medal. Elliot, in direct line of the Earl of Minto in southern Scotland, was keen on Highland games and, being a superb all-round sportsman, participated in several of the Olympic events in Athens, including sprinting, wrestling and rope-climbing, and took gold and silver medals in weight-lifting at the first modern Olympics.

The Paris Highland Games were run on traditional lines and the Strathallan Committee was largely responsible for the organisation. Of the 300 competitors, 60 were athletes, the best of these being Kenneth McRae of Nairn, George Johnstone of Aberdeen, Owen Duffy (who was born in Ireland but who later joined the Edinburgh police force) and Jimmy (Clogger) Currie of Ecclefechan. They were well supported by the Glasgow police force, with Superintendent Mackintosh and Captain Donald taking a personal interest in the proceedings.

Clogger Currie.

Gilbert Elliot, 1897–1914, 4th Earl of Minto, Viceroy of India, Governor General of Canada and Minister Plenipotentiary of Corsica.

Newspaper reports concerning the competitions were flattering: 'In every class of Highland sport the contestants have exhibited the very highest talent'. The arena had been used previously by Buffalo Bill's Circus and was ideal for spectators. There was, however,

From Highland games to Olympic Games. Athens Olympics Poster, 1894.

some criticism: the publicists did not know anything about Highland games and they were blamed for not having 'bold' advertising.

A feature was the presence of the British Ambassador, Lord Lylton, who had a guard of honour consisting of a detachment of Glasgow Police in full uniform. Not one of these well-built men was less than 6 feet 2 inches in height. On the previous evening, the policemen had a tug-of-war competition against a contingent of Mexicans from Buffalo Bill's Circus. The Scots nearly ran away with the rope and Colonel Cody expressed his admiration for the Glaswegians, saying that a score of them could pull down the Eiffel Tower! Their tug-of-war victory was all the more meritorious because there were only eight policemen against 12 Mexicans.

Owing to the importance of this meeting and being in an era where there has not been a great deal of readily available information, here are some of the results of the last day of competition.

Heavy hammer

First place	Kenneth McRae (Nairn)	88 feet 6 inches
Second place	A. McCulloch (Govan)	80 feet 8 inches
Third place	George Johnstone (Aberdeen)	80 feet 6 inches

Light stone

First place	Owen Duffy Edinburgh	44 feet 4 inches
Second place	Kenneth McRae	43 feet 9 inches
Third place	Donald Fraser	42 feet 10 inches

Light (16lb) hammer

First place	Kenneth McRae	115 feet 4 inches
Second place	George Johnstone	113 feet 7 inches
Third place	A. McCulloch	103 feet 10 inches

There was also a physique contest, with 12 men selected from the Glasgow Police and 12 from the heavies. The heavies won, their team included the famous throwers and wrestlers, including 'Clogger' Currie, born in Dumfriesshire in 1847. A reporter complained that height and other measurements had not been taken into consideration, nor were there 'evolutions to bring out smartness of form or action'. He conceded that 'in truth both teams deserved a prize. Twenty-four such stalwart men are not often seen'.

The competitors did their job very well and one newspaper reported:

> A finer body of men has never been put together, and in every class of Highland sport, the contests have exhibited the very highest talents. It is a great pity that all their skill and energy met with little public recognition.

Coubertin also went to Princeton University, USA and watched students train for Physical Director George Goldie's Caledonian Games.

I am pleased that in this book we can give long-overdue credit to the Strathallan organisers, the competitors and the Baron's Olympic inspiration, and hope that readers will recognise the lasting but long forgotten value of the Paris Exhibition's Gathering of the Clans.

The Paris Highland Gathering, 1889.

THE WORLD HISTORY OF HIGHLAND GAMES

CHAPTER FIFTEEN

War Games

For many centuries, clan warriors, Scotland's private armies, the popular Highland regiments and Highland brigades have enjoyed Highland games, not just as preparation for war but also as a *substitute* for war. Until recently, the regiments existed under their own names – such as the Gordons, Seaforths, Argyll and Sutherland, Cameronians and Highland Light Infantry – and they all trained sportsmen, pipers and pipe bands, dancers and tug-o'-war teams. Their contribution to the customs and culture of Scotland was valued and should never be forgotten.

Following the Act of Proscription, the only way Scotsmen could wear the kilt openly and without fear of punishment was to join the British army. The first Scottish regiments

McIntosh,
Creek Indian Chief.

were formed after the 1689 Jacobite rebellion. They had a reputation of being fierce and fearless fighters and they soon became a valued part of the armed services. After the 1745 uprising, there were 20 Scottish regiments, which became very potent, colourful symbols of Scotland.

Many regiments had their own Highland games and these continued into our own time. They have taken our events around the world and an early example is during the American War of Independence (1776–83). On this occasion, 'the Jocks', as Scottish soldiers were often called, taught Creek Indians traditional Highland games. It was said that the Creeks outran the Scots, but the latter won the throwing events. Some may find this a little doubtful, but information from Joseph Hood,

Highland Brigade Games, Cairo 1883.

an American friend, indicates a very strong connection between the Scots and the Creeks.

Captain McIntosh, a Scottish army captain, and a full-blooded Creek woman had a son born around 1875. This boy mingled with Scottish Highlanders in Georgia and learned to speak a little Gaelic. Young McIntosh grew to be a 'tall, finely formed man' and, siding with the Americans, he earned great respect. He was exceedingly brave in battle and highly complimented by General Jackson. Eventually, although half Native American, he was promoted to major and then general.

A faction of the Creeks resented his actions and on 30 April 1825 he was attacked by a band of Indians, who set fire to his house. A one-sided battle ensued. When McIntosh ran out of ammunition, he was shot and badly wounded. As he struggled to rise, an Ocfuskee Indian plunged a knife up to the hilt into his heart. If the Scottish soldiers integrated with the Creeks and produced such men, the earlier claim to having taught the Native Americans Highland games seems quite reasonable.

The 'heavies' of the McHardys were well known over the centuries as the greatest ever Highland games family, and John McHardy (1801–82) was one of the most interesting. In a remarkable career, he fought sea battles with pirates, the French and Spanish; became an admiral in the British Navy; and finished his working life as a police chief constable. McHardy, who knew at first hand all about wars and games, inherited land in Florida and, having sold it, lived for a short time with a tribe of Seminols, headed by their chief, Nomartha. He was very popular, learning fast and then teaching. Before he left in 1823, his Native American friends had a special ceremony in which he was made a tribal chief of the Seminoles. It is not unlikely that he would

have taught them the traditional Highland activities that the McHardys loved so much. Links with Native Americans are still strong and in recent years, Andrew Hobson and his sisters, proud of their Navajo upbringing, have made a great impact on Highland games circuits in America, Scotland and Ireland. All three, including the women, have competed at a high level in heavy events.

Scotland's Highland Brigades have produced many excellent competition pipers and more than a few fine heavies, the earliest of these, to my knowledge, being big Sam MacDonald (1762–1802), whose height has been quoted as low as 6 feet 10 inches and as tall as 7 feet 4 inches. Sergeant Sam and his pet, a mountain deer, were popular wherever they went. He was immensely strong and many stories are told of his escapades. The soldier's uncommon size and strength attracted a great deal of attention and for a time he appeared in the Opera House in Haymarket, London. Around the 1780s he was 'porter' to the prince, who later became King George IV. Sam was quite a character and served in the army, from the 3rd Sutherland Fencibles (1772) to the 93rd Regiment (the Sutherland Highlanders), until he died in Guernsey in 1802.

Big Sam MacDonald (1762–1802) of Lairg. Caricature by John Kay (1742–1826).

Over the centuries, soldiers from Scottish regiments have

competed in Highland games, and in 1844 the event originally called Montreal Highland Games was temporarily changed to the 'Montreal Olympics'. The 93rd Highlanders were outstanding throughout the competition, particularly Sergeant McGillivray, who won hammer throwing and shot putting.

There have been many army pipers in Highland games prize lists and the School of Piping at Edinburgh Castle made an enormous contribution in maintaining a high level of instruction.

An aspect of piping that is now almost forgotten is the piper's place in battle. In bygone days, when going to war often meant hand-to-hand combat, the pipers would go 'over the top' and into the thick of the fray, playing their pipes to inspire and motivate their companions.

Army piper of the 74th Highlanders, later known as the Highland Infantry. Watercolour by Henry O'Neill (1798–1880).

The war cries of the Scots and the skirl of the pipes once caused the Duke of Wellington to exclaim 'I don't know what they do to the enemy but they certainly terrify me!'

There have been many examples of pipers continuing to play the pipes even if they are badly wounded. One of the best examples of a piper's bravery was at the battle of Dargai Heights, in north-west Pakistan, on 20 October 1897. Piper Findlater, of the gallant Gordon Highlanders, was wounded on one foot and also on the opposite ankle. He fell to the ground but immediately picked up his damaged pipes and carried on playing from where he left off, despite what must have been very painful wounds. He was awarded the highest honour, the Victoria Cross, for his heroism in battle.

This is all well known in north-east Scotland.

Piper Findlater VC (1872–1942) Gordon Highlanders.

At least two songs were written about the incident and *Comin' fae Dargai* was still popular during the Second World War.

Another song gave graphic detail:

> Wounded sore in that gallant rush of
> Highlanders, brave and strong,
> He fell to the ground but soon he is up with a
> blast of national song.
> The bullets shower around yet louder the music
> swells...

After the war, heroic Findlater was fêted at Highland games, playing the pipes and acting as judge. As time passed, he fell upon hard times, receiving little sympathy from his employers. George Frederick Findlater vc died of a heart attack on 4 March 1942 but his memory lives on and his Victoria Cross is proudly displayed in the Gordon Highlanders' Museum in Aberdeen.

In fighting forces throughout the world there have long been physical tests to select elite warriors. Scotland and Iceland have had stone-lifting tests for their warriors. The Vikings used a series of heavy stones to determine the seating positions of the men in the longboats to give optimum use of their respective strengths. Those lifting the largest stones sat in the middle of the boat and the next in strength to the front and rear of the strongest. The weaker men sat at the extremities by the bow and stern.

In Glen Lyon, Scotland, there were Fienne or Fiana, the elite warriors. These were not Fingals or Irish men, but the aristocracy of Pictish kings. They used two of the events seen at Highland games as selection criteria for suitability for fighting service.

Before the days of British army regiments, the clan system provided virtually ready-made fighting forces, and when it suited the powers-that-be they were used to the full. Before the clans there is considerable evidence to indicate that the stone forts in Glen Lyon were built by the Picts around 500 AD and remained so until 843, when Kenneth MacAlpin (Cináed mac Ailpín), 34th King of Dalriada, became the first King of the Picts and Scots.

To be accepted, the Fienne (elite warriors) had to lift a conical stone and place it on a platform. For many centuries, one of the best-known *clach nearts* (stones of strength) lay in the

Highland Brigade Games, Egypt, 1883.

THE WORLD HISTORY OF HIGHLAND GAMES

Dr Bill Crawford and the Fienne Stone in Glen Lyon.

Back in 1681, John Campbell was awarded a number of titles, including Viscount of Tay and Paintland and also Lord Glenorchie. He coveted estates in Caithness and when he was selecting recruits to fight in the north, prior to acceptance, he tested their power and agility. The basic

Verden. The location for these games is a city in Lower Saxony, Germany.

test was to leap over a double plaid while wearing full fighting apparel. A double plaid measured 4 feet 9 inches. A test like this, combined with lifting a manhood stone, would certainly separate the men from the boys. Activities such as tug o' war and wrestling were, and to an extent still are, other aspects of training and competition in inter-clan and armed services competitions.

historic Glen Lyon, 'the glen of the crooked stones'. At the time of writing, there is some speculation on the future of this important relic. A local farmer has removed the stone from its previous position. It is hoped that the problem can be resolved amicably to have the testing stone restored to its traditional resting place, continuing its challenge to strongmen worldwide.

The traditional *clach cuid fir*, lifting the manhood stone, was certainly a challenging selection procedure. Manhood stones are so called because youths would prove they had reached manhood by lifting the stone on to a wall or a barrel at waist height. If they were successful they could claim to be a man and were entitled to wear an eagle's feather in their bonnet. This could be the origin of the saying 'a feather in your cap' when someone has done something praiseworthy.

Ancient warriors, Scottish mercenaries in Europe, post-rebellion recruits and modern soldiers have undergone tests of strength, choreographed dances and composed fine pipe tunes, regardless of where they have been stationed. Their celebrations of sporting and cultural endeavour

The 51st Highland Division was one of Scotland's crack regiments and there is a popular Scottish Country dance called 'The Reel of the 51st'.

Kilted Foot Race. Highland Brigade in Cairo, 1883.

Army Highland Games, Aldershot, 1874.

Argyll and Sutherland Highlanders parade to the Highland games.

have been well documented and there is no doubt of their great contribution in maintaining and developing various aspects of Highland games.

There is a wealth of further information in this sphere and it is worthy of much more investigation and dissemination.

Soldiers in camp at Wimbledon, England, throwing the hammer.

THE WORLD HISTORY OF HIGHLAND GAMES

CHAPTER SIXTEEN

Pipers and Piping

Sculptures from the earliest times have depicted the playing of bagpipes. In the past, all clan chiefs had bards who would celebrate the brave deeds and special occasions of the people in song and verse. They would commit to memory the names and dates of all past chiefs and, in the absence of books, they became the historians of the clan. Before battle, they would pass among the men with exhortation and encouragement, holding forth on honour and duty and the disgrace of cowardly retreat.

In the 6th century, three Gaelic clans under Fergus Mac Erc went to war, and the battle noise drowned out the voice of the bard. Since then, pipers have used the sound of the great Highland bagpipe to inspire and motivate warriors. This tradition continued for centuries and there are numerous examples of the outstanding bravery of pipers who were honoured for the part they played. The adoption of the great Highland bagpipe as the official musical instrument of Scottish regiments is important in helping to perpetuate this type of music. Strangely, although warfare is now very different from that experienced in earlier times, the pipes are still a major instrument of choice. In the outpourings of grief after 9/11 with the devastating destruction of New York's World Trade Centre, the bagpipes were on call at most of the funerals. The presence of a piper at funerals has been customary from very early times.

A few hours after a battle, a sad lament on the same instrument can bring tears to the eyes of the toughest of men. For hundreds of years, the bagpipes have been considered indispensable for most special occasions. From weddings to funerals, the pipes have expressed gladness or sadness. Having said that, it is at the Highland games and similar competitions that the highest standard of piping is to be found. This is the best setting to hear the *ceol mor*,[1] the classic music of the bagpipes, also called the *piobaireachd* (or pibroch, pronounced 'peeb-roch'). Rather than classic pibrochs, the general public usually prefer reels, jigs, stately strathspeys, stirring marches and well-known airs. In pipers' parlance, this lighter music is known as *ceol beag*, the little music.

Cameron Highlander. Pipes and pipers are very versatile. Their music can raise the spirits and inspire Scots in battle, and also terrify their enemies.

There have been bagpipes in other countries but they have been held in highest esteem in Scotland and Ireland. The clan piper was very close to the chieftain, sharing their food and drink. This started a tradition for pipers, the thirstiest of men, who were quite willing to take anybody's drink and not confine their favours to chiefs alone!

Piping competitions have been instrumental (excuse the pun) in encouraging talented pipers to practise religiously and hone their skills to reach the highest of standards and pass on historic compositions from one generation to the next.

In this context we must include the extraordinary phenomenon of the hereditary piper. Briefly, for centuries Highland lairds and clan chiefs had pipers who did a similar job to the bards and seanachies and these pipers passed on their knowledge, techniques and compositions from father to son for many generations. Back in 1771, Tobias Smollett wrote a very candid, perhaps tongue-in-cheek piece, about a hereditary piper of Dougal Campbell of Argyll. It gave a good idea of pipers' duties and showed how protective they were of their positions. This is a shortened version of what he said about the laird and his piper:

> He finds it impossible to abolish the ancients customs of his family. His piper, for example, who is an hereditary officer of the household, will not part with the least particle of his privileges. He has a right to wear the kilt, or ancient Highland dress, with

William Ross. Queen's piper, 1884.

Old print of McArthur, hereditary piper to Ranald Macdonald of Staffa.

the purse, pistol and dirk – a broad yellow ribbon, fixed to the chanter-pipe and is thrown over the shoulder, and trails along the ground, while he performs the functions of the minstrelsy. He plays before the laird every Sunday in this way to the kirk, which he circles three times, performing the family march, which implies defiance to all the enemies of the clan; and every morning he plays a full hour by the clock, in the great hall marching backwards and forwards all the time, with a solemn pace, attended by the lairds kinsmen, who seem much delighted with the music. In this exercises he indulges them with a number of pibrochs or airs, suited to the different passions which he would either excite or assuage.

Angus was the earliest documented McArthur. In 1733, he was piper to the Lord of the Isles:

> Mr Campbell has an invincible antipathy to the sound of the Highland bagpipe, which sings in the nose with a most alarming twang, and, indeed, is quite intolerable to ears of common sensibility when aggravated by the echo of a vaulted hall. He therefore begged the piper to have some mercy upon him, and dispense with this part of the morning service. A consultation of the clan being held on this occasion, it was unanimously agreed that the laird's request could not be granted without a dangerous encroachment upon the customs of the family. The piper declared that he could not give up for a moment the privilege he derived from his ancestors; nor would the laird's relations forego an entertainment which they valued above all others. There was no remedy; Mr Campbell, being obliged to acquiesce, is fain to stop his ears with cotton, to fortify his head with three or four nightcaps, and every morning retire into the penetralia of his habitation, in order to avoid this diurnal annoyance.

THE WORLD HISTORY OF HIGHLAND GAMES

Unlike the above and held in great respect, the best examples of hereditary pipers are the MacCrimmons, hereditary pipers to the MacLeods of Skye since the mid-1600s. One of the most enthralling aspects of my research into Highland games was the investigation of the hereditary pipers of clan chiefs in ancient times. More than a decade ago, there was what seemed to be an attempt to debunk the eminent MacCrimmons. Living members of this ancient piping family were very hurt by those negative comments, particularly by one incredible unwarranted attack, as there are detailed records of the MacCrimmon pipers over the centuries.

At the end of the 15th century, Alasdair MacLeod granted lands at Borreraig to the MacCrimmons, who founded a piping college and trained many great pipers there. Clan chiefs were proud of their pipers and treated them like gentlemen. The best pipers had their own servant to look after them and carry their pipes. There is a tremendous number of fascinating stories told about hereditary pipers, especially the MacCrimmons, and although there may be some doubt about the authenticity of some of these legends, it can be proved conclusively, by well-researched documentation, that the MacCrimmon pipers existed, and still do exist today.

Following the publication of an earlier book, I had the good fortune to be contacted by Malcolm MacCrimmon, the ninth hereditary piper to the MacLeods of Dunvegan. Now living in Winnipeg, Canada, he provided me with an artistic family tree.

However, it has to be said that even well-meaning writers have perpetuated inaccuracies by passing on legends. These tales have become part of life's rich tartan tapestry. These are more than outweighed by more valuable contributions, such as the rare and most comprehensive account

The MacCrimmon family tree and details, by Malcolm R. MacCrimmon and Iain N. MacCrimmon

by George C.B. Poulter, published in 1936, a copy of which I have in my personal library. There are also the writings of Fred MacLeod and the detailed, extensive and interesting publication by R.B. Campbell. The latter points out some 'historical' shortcomings and anomalies in a measured and almost kindly manner.

The piping legacy of the MacCrimmons for some three centuries was traced by Poulter until 1820, and stopped when Donald MacCrimmon emigrated to Canada and settled in Ontario. However, Poulter did not know then that a boy christened Malcolm Roderick MacCrimmon was born in Edmonton, Alberta, in 1918. This was the grandson of a well-known railroad contractor, an earlier Malcolm MacCrimmon, famous for opening up Alberta and adjacent areas of Canada via the new railways.

The tales of 'the old people', his piping forebears, fascinated Malcolm Roderick MacCrimmon, and as he grew up his main interests in life became practising the bagpipes and researching his ancestors. Their story is a fascinating one but let us digress for just a moment to briefly review some earlier days of the instrument and its players.

Royal and competition piper Robert Brown, Balmoral.

There are many references to bagpipes and pipers from the 11th century onwards, and by the 16th century it was a poor clan that did not have its own piper. Chieftains' hereditary pipers covered several generations.

The MacLeods have lived at Dunvegan Castle on Skye since 1225 and their hereditary pipers, the MacCrimmons, were the best known and the most talented. In the 1590s, Alasdair MacLeod granted lands at Borreraig to the MacCrimmons. They lived in one end of their long two-storied farmhouse, and at the other end they established a college of piping that had a profound effect on the world of music.

Many of these masters are still remembered and described at length in the books mentioned above and in my previous writings. Adding to those tales of the very early MacCrimmons, or MacCrummens, I must also point out the entry of 24 August 1815 in Sir Walter Scott's diary:

> MacLeod's hereditary piper is called MacCrimmon, a Lieutenant in the Army, and a most capital piper, possessing about 200 tunes, most of which will probably die with him, as he declines to have any of his sons instructed in the art.

This piper played every day at dinner and maintained his minstrel's privilege by putting on his bonnet before playing. The valued retainer described by Sir Walter was Donald Ruadh MacCrimmon of Borreraig, born in 1773. He was gazetted Lieutenant in the Caledonian Volunteers in North America on 24 October 1778. Donald fought in several skirmishes but by 1799 he had returned to play his beloved music on his native Skye. He was referred to as Captain MacCrimmon, the eighth hereditary piper, but nine years on he was back in the army, commissioned as Lieutenant in the 10th Royal Veteran Battalion on 6 April 1808. There are numerous references to him until the time of his death in London on 31 July 1825.

A key figure in a later branch of the family tree is Donald MacCrimmon, born in 1788. When his wife, Catherine, died in 1819, he decided to emigrate to Canada, and with his five-year-old son Roderick, he walked from Glenelg to Greenock to catch a ship to the New World. Donald settled in Woodville, Ontario, where he obtained a Crown grant. By working exceedingly hard, he cleared Glen Woodville of heavy hardwood trees and successfully farmed the land until he died on 13 February 1863.

When young Roderick grew up in Canada he married a Skye lassie, Sarah Murchison, and their son Malcolm, born on 27 March 1851, went to Manitoba in 1872 and freighted supplies from the USA to Canada. This led, in turn, to railroad construction and pioneering efforts that earned him lasting fame. In 1882 he married again, to Flora, a young lady who had been born on the Scottish island of Mull, and very interestingly she was a MacArthur, the piping rivals of the MacCrimmons.

Their grandson, Malcolm Roderick MacCrimmon, born in 1918, was the person referred to in the opening of this piping section. With genes from MacArthurs and MacCrimmons and imagination fuelled by legend and folklore, it is not surprising that his piping improved by degrees and he was accepted into Edmonton Boys' Pipe Band, the North Vancouver Pipe Band and the Seaforth Highlanders. When war became imminent, Malcolm enlisted in the Calgary Highlanders, and was posted overseas in their pipe band. In due course, he was highly delighted to obtain a transfer to the Scots Guards and had the unique distinction of being the only soldier transferred from a Canadian to a British Regiment in the Second World War. The highlight of this posting was studying under Pipe Major William Ross at the Army School of Piping in Edinburgh Castle.

Always steeped in the past as well as planning for the future, Malcolm had long corresponded with Sir Reginald MacLeod of MacLeod, Chief of the clan, and while on leave during the war a life-long ambition was achieved – he went over the sea to Skye. In Dunvegan Castle he had an audience with Dame Flora MacLeod, the 28th Chief of the clan, and on this auspicious occasion, the hereditary appointment was reinstated and Malcolm MacCrimmon became the MacLeods' 9th Hereditary Piper.

The story does not quite end there. Malcolm returned to Canada after the war, married and started a family. He called his daughter Flora after his clan chief and he was equally proud of his two sons, Padruid and Iain Norman MacCrimmon. It was the latter who carried on the family tradition and starting

Famous painting of a McCrimmon piper by R. R. McIan (1803–56).

playing the chanter at the age of eight, then enrolled in Edmonton Boys' Pipe Band. He studied under some highly respected piping tutors, famous wherever pipes are played, including John McLellan, the then Chief Instructor at the Army School of Piping in Edinburgh Castle. As a competitive piper, Iain proved his worth by taking many top awards in north-west USA and western Canada. He also served as a much-respected pipe major for two Grade One professional bands. There was another irresistible urge from the creative MacCrimmon blood surging through his veins: he was desperately keen to compose his own pipe music, so in 1978, with some reluctance, he retired from pipe band competitions to concentrate on his own compositions.

This proved most successful and after he had written four books of his own tunes, his music had been on 20 recordings by established pipe bands. Some are recognised as popular classics, played at world championships and recorded for posterity and widespread sale.

Thirty-seven years after Malcolm MacCrimmon became hereditary piper, he retired in favour of his son and John MacLeod of MacLeod, 29th Chief of the clan, personally confirmed the appointment of Iain MacCrimmon as the 10th Hereditary Piper.

Since then, Iain has fulfilled many official duties in Skye and elsewhere. At the age of 40, he found his bloodlines tugging hard for his heart and he took his Scottish wife, Charlotte, and his family to live in Scotland and perpetuate his favoured cultural activities in their native land. The full circle

Iain McCrimmon, 10th Hereditary Piper to the McLeods.

had been completed. Credit should also be given to the MacLeods of MacLeod for their far-sighted sponsorship of the arts from the barbaric times of old until this high-tech age with so many competing claims for attention.

There are many other such pipers and mentors worthy of mention, such as Donald Gorm MacDonald of the Isles, who bestowed lands of Hunglatter, Skye, on the MacArthurs, his much-respected hereditary pipers. They previously had a school of piping on Ulva, an island off Mull, which of course was based on the tuition of the MacCrimmons. Early MacArthurs include Angus, Neil and Iain Ban, the latter's son.

The great Angus Macpherson (1877–1976) came from a long line of pipers including James, outlawed after the '45, and lived in a cave with the then Cluny Macpherson.

Charles McArthur (b. 1706) studied under the remarkable Patrick Og McCrimmon and became almost as good as his tutor. At the age of 75, he competed at the first Falkirk Tryst and took second place, the winner being Patrick McGregor.

Malcolm (Calum) MacPherson, depicted in the photograph at the MacPherson Museum, was another great piper and tutor. His two most noted pupils were his sons Angus and John MacDonald of Inverness, who won some of the highest awards in piping.

I was previously privileged to meet

Calum MacPherson.

Calum's son, Angus Macpherson MBE (1877–1976), who seemed to prefer his surname spelt without a capital 'P'. Just as with at least three of his forebears, he competed with success at Highland games and he judged at Braemar Games for more than 50 years. When he was in his late 90s, he told me of his life and position as the hereditary piper: 'I was initiated into the mysteries of piobaireachd by the peat fire at Badenoch, my tutor being my father, Malcolm.' Angus believed that such a hereditary environment provided inspiration to transfer a piper's musical soul to his fingers. The Pipers' Hollow at Dunvegan, he said, was where the MacCrimmons composed and played some of the finest *piobaireachd* the world has ever known. Their own music echoed back to them from the surrounding rocks like silent judges and they were able to hear and correct imperfections to their music. The composers, it was said, would stay in the hollow without food and water until they had finished composition. There has been speculation that this regime (starvation and thirst) may have induced a state of creative hallucination that added to their genius.

John MacDonald has often been referred to as the 'King of Pipers' and his qualifications support this view. He grew up amongst competition pipers, including two uncles and Sandy, his father, who gave him his first lessons. Donald Cameron, Champion of Champions at the Northern

THE WORLD HISTORY OF HIGHLAND GAMES

Piper MacDonald for the Duke of Fife.

Meeting, who died in 1868, had trained Sandy, but John was also taught by Calum Piobaire (MacPherson). Largely as a result of such expert guidance, John MacDonald won Northern Meeting 'Clasps' in 1903, 1908, 1924, 1927, 1929, 1933 and 1934.

John was a great analyst and interpreter of pipe music, although no doubt he would scorn such terms, but because of his knowledge he could perhaps be the most important saviour of the classic music as played by the old masters. He lived at a time when academic upstarts with comparatively little experience, and even less practical ability, attempted to take over piping and denied giving professional pipers a voice in deliberations. MacDonald acted fearlessly, spoke out against these people and boycotted their activities. Many of the great pipers he had tutored supported his views and, being held in high respect, others joined them. They continued with the old methods and compositions as they had long been played, thus saving for posterity the classic pibrochs as played over the centuries.

Amongst the many famous pipers taught by

Pipe Major John Macdonald of Inverness. Honorary Piper to King George V, Edward VIII and George VI.

John was Pipe Major Robert (Bob) Nicol of the Royal estate at Balmoral and of the 2nd Battalion Gordon Highlanders, being in active service during the Second World War. Bob was a piper from the age of seven and

became an all-time great of the piping world. He loved competing at Highland games, where he proved his superiority time and again at the most important games. He was a master of the *piobaireachd* and took prizes galore in marches, reels, strathspeys, jigs; indeed, all events. Pipe Major Nicol was a man of tradition; he was taught the *canntaireachd* and taught his pupils in this method. He felt it a duty to be true to the origins of the art as taught by the earliest masters, so it is not surprising that his favourite pibroch was *Lament for the Children*.

Pipe Major R.B. Nicol (1905–78) competing at Braemar.

When his competition days were over, he travelled far and wide as a teacher, judge at games and, of course, simply playing the tunes he loved. In his declining years he stayed in a cottage on the Birkhall estate, Balmoral, and when he died in 1978, traffic stopped in the main street in Balmoral as he was ceremonially piped to his resting place at Durris Kirkyard, close to where he was born. As far as I am concerned, it has been adequately proven that there has been a tremendous dynasty and that clan chiefs sent their pipers to be taught by the MacCrimmons. Their peers and their descendants have highly praised the musical heritage they left behind. I acknowledge exaggerations and errors, but the style, idiosyncrasies and traditions of ancient pipers such as the MacCrimmons and MacArthurs are still in evidence at Highland games today. We are fortunate that this legacy still enriches and will continue to enrich those who are genuinely interested in Scottish culture.

Many of the prize-winners and composers at the most important competitions have come from the western Highlands and Islands, and still do – although naturally, as the world changes, we do find a wider spread of talent and exposure. This has been emphasised by the *Mull of Kintyre* reaching *Top of the Pops* in the 1970s and the widespread popularity of the pipe tune *Highland Cathedral*, composed by two Germans. We wonder what the ancient MacCrimmons would think of that.

A few favourites from my library are listed below.

A History of the Clan MacCrimmon		
G.C.B. Poulter, FSA Scot	1938	
The MacCrimmons of Skye		
Fred T. MacLeod, FSA (Scot.)	1933	
A Highlander looks back		
Angus MacPherson	1956	
The MacCrimmon Pipers of Skye		
Robert Bruce Campbell	2000	
Highland Days		
Seton Gordon	1963	
The Highlanders of Scotland		
Kenneth MacLeay	1872	
Costumes of the Clans of the Scottish Highlands		
McIan and Logan	1845	

Pipe Majors MacDonald and Reid at the McCrimmon Cairn.

Major competition winners

The Northern Meeting, Inverness

1887	Alex Fletcher
1888	William Boa MacRae
1889	Pipe Major John MacKay
1890	John MacDonald
1891	Colin Thomson
1892	Pipe Major John Cameron
1893	Pipe Major Donald Mathieson
1894	Pipe Major Donald Campbell
1895	Murdo MacKenzie
1896	Alex MacKenzie
1897	William Campbell
1898	Murdo MacKenzie
1899	David C. Mather
1900	William Meldrum
1901	William MacLean
1902	James A. Center
1903	Donald MacKay
1904	Corporal William Ross
1905	George S. MacLennan
1906	George S. Allan
1907	Torquil MacLeod
1908	Pipe Major Thomas Clarke
1909	Pipe Major Mackie
1910	William Laurie
1911	George Yardley
1912	Donald L. MacKenzie
1913	Pipe Major J.M. Lawrie

First World War

1919	Pipe Major William Gray
1920	John MacPherson
1921	Pipe Major Robert Reid
1922	Pipe Major Donald Chisholm
1923	Angus MacPherson
1924	Allan M. Calder
1925	John Wilson
1926	John MacDonald
1927	Malcolm R. MacPherson
1928	Robert U. Brown
1929	David Ross
1930	Robert B. Nicol

1931	Donald MacLean
1932	Pipe Major Charles Smith
1933	Pipe Major James B. Robertson
1934	Corporal Peter Bain
1935	Piper J. MacGrady
1936	Philip Melville
1937	Hugh C.R. Macrae
1938	Archibald MacNab

Second World War

1946	Roderick MacDonald
1947	Pipe Major Donald MacLeod
1948	Donald P. MacGillivray
1949	Corporal Andrew Pitkeathly
1950	John D. Burgess
1951	Pipe Major Ronald MacCallum
1952	Pipe Major Robert MacKay
1953	Pipe Major Donald MacLean
1954	Donald MacPherson
1955	William M. MacDonald
1956	Captain D.R. MacLennan
1957	Iain MacFadyen
1958	Lewis Turrell
1959	RSM John A. MacLellan
1960	John McDougall
1961	Pipe Major Donald Morrison
1962	Duncan J. MacFadyen
1963	Kenneth MacDonald
1964	Hector MacFadyen
1965	William MacDonald
1966	John MacFadyen
1967	Hugh A. MacCallum
1968	John Wilson
1969	Corporal I. Morrison
1970	Andrew Wright
1971	James MacIntosh
1972	Dr John MacAskill
1973	Jack Taylor
1974	PM James MacGregor
1975	Murray Henderson
1976	Angus MacLellan
1977	William J.R. Livingstone
1978	Dr William Wotherspoon
1979	Donald Bain

1980	Tom Speirs
1981	Jack Lee
1982	Colin Roy MacLellan
1983	Pipe Major Gavin N.M. Stoddart
1984	Allan MacDonald
1985	James McGillivray
1986	Roderick J. MacLeod
1987	Michael Cusack
1988	Dr Angus MacDonald
1989	William MacCallum
1990	Greg Wilson
1991	Alfred Morrison
1992	Angus MacColl
1993	Bruce Woodley
1994	Corporal Gordon Walker
1995	Robert Wallace
1996	Wilson Brown
1997	Duncan MacGillivray
1998	Stuart Shedden
1999	Major John Cairns
2000	Stuart Liddell
2001	Niall Matheson
2002	Bruce Gandy
2003	Chris Armstrong
2004	Alasdair Gillies

In 2005 *the competition moved to Aviemore*

2005	Donald MacPhee
2006	Alastair Dunn
2007	Iain Speirs

World Pipe Band Championships – Grade One

From 1906 to 1946, the Cowal Gatherings 'Argyll Shield' was recognised as being for the World Championships. Award winners are listed in *Scottish Highland Games* by David Webster (1973).

Listed below are names of the *winning bands* since 1947, the host town and pipe majors.

Winning Band	Host Town	Pipe Major
1947		
Bowhill Colliery	Edinburgh	C. Sutherland
1948		
Shotts and Dykehead Caledonia	Glasgow	T. MacAllister

Fergus Drum Major.

Drum Major Ian Morrison, Lonach Highlanders pipe band.

Winning Band	Host Town	Pipe Major
1949		
Glasgow Police	Edinburgh	J. MacDonald
1950		
Edinburgh Police	Dundee	D. S. Ramsey
1951		
Glasgow Police	Edinburgh	J. MacDonald
1952		
Shotts and Dykehead Caledonia	Ayr	T. MacAllister
1953		
Clan MacRae	Edinburgh	A. MacLeod
1954		
Edinburgh Police	Aberdeen	D.S. Ramsey
1955		
Muirhead and Sons	Stirling	J. Smith
1956		
Muirhead and Sons	Belfast	J. Smith
1957		
Shotts and Dykehead Caledonia	Paisley	J.K. MacAllister
1958		
Shotts and Dykehead Caledonia	Aberdeen	J.K. MacAllister

Winning Band	Host Town	Pipe Major
1959		
Shotts and Dykehead Caledonia	Kirkcaldy	J.K. MacAllister
1960		
Shotts and Dykehead Caledonia	Inverness	J.K. MacAllister
1961		
Muirhead and Sons	Edinburgh	J. Smith
1962		
277 Btn Argyll and Sutherland Highlanders	Belfast	J. Weatherstone
1963		
Edinburgh Police	Dumfries	I. McLeod
1964		
Edinburgh Police	Ayr	I. McLeod
1965		
Muirhead and Sons	Forfar	R. Hardie
1966		
Muirhead and Sons	Inverness	R. Hardie
1967		
Muirhead and Sons	Oban	R. Hardie

Winning Band	Host Town	Pipe Major
1968		
Muirhead and Sons	Grangemouth	R. Hardie
1969		
Muirhead and Sons	Perth	R. Hardie
1970		
Shotts and Dykehead Caledonia	Aberdeen	T. MacAllister
1971		
Edinburgh Police	Lanark	I. McLeod
1972		
Edinburgh Police	Hawick	I. McLeod
1973		
Shotts and Dykehead Caledonia	Ayr	T. MacAllister
1974		
Shotts and Dykehead Caledonia	Stirling	T. MacAllister
1975		
Lothian and Borders Police	Corby	I. McLeod
1976		
Strathclyde Police	Hawick	I. MacLellan BEM
1977		
Dysart and Dundonald	Aberdeen	R. Shepherd
1978		
Dysart and Dundonald	Lanark	R. Shepherd
1979		
Strathclyde Police	Nottingham	I. MacLellan BEM
1980		
Shotts and Dykehead Caledonia	Glasgow	T. MacAllister
1981		
Strathclyde Police	Aberdeen	I. MacLellan BEM
1982		
Strathclyde Police	Glenrothes	I. MacLellan BEM
1983		
Strathclyde Police	Glasgow	I. MacLellan BEM
1984		
Strathclyde Police	Glasgow	I. MacLellan BEM
1985		
Strathclyde Police	Hamilton	I. MacLellan BEM
1986		
Strathclyde Police	Glasgow	I. MacLellan BEM
1987		
78 Fraser Highlanders Canada	Glasgow	W. Livingston
1988		
Strathclyde Police	Glasgow	I. MacLellan BEM
1989		
Strathclyde Police	Glasgow	I. MacLellan BEM
1990		
Strathclyde Police	Glasgow	I. MacLellan BEM
1991		
Strathclyde Police	Glasgow	I. MacLellan BEM
1992		
Field Marshal Montgomery	Glasgow	R. Parkes

Winning Band	Host Town	Pipe Major
1993		
Field Marshal Montgomery	Glasgow	R. Parkes
1994		
Shotts and Dykehead Caledonia	Glasgow	R. Mathieson
1995		
Simon Fraser University Canada	Glasgow	T. Lee
1996		
Simon Fraser University Canada	Glasgow	T. Lee
1997		
Shotts and Dykehead Caledonia	Glasgow	R. Mathieson
1998		
Victoria Police, Australia	Glasgow	N. Russell
1999		
Simon Fraser University Canada	Glasgow	T. Lee
2000		
Shotts and Dykehead Caledonia	Glasgow	R. Mathieson
2001		
Simon Fraser University Canada	Glasgow	T. Lee
2002		
Field Marshall Montgomery NI	Glasgow	R. Parkes
2003		
Shotts and Dykehead Caledonia	Glasgow	★
2004		
Field Marshall Montgomerie	Glasgow	★
2005		
Shotts and Dykehead Caledonia	Glasgow	★
2006		
Field Marshall Montgomerie	Glasgow	★
2007		
Field Marshall Montgomerie	Glasgow	★
2008		
Field Marshall Montgomerie	Glasgow	★
2009		
Simon Fraser University Canada	Glasgow	★
2010		
St Laurence O'Toole, Ireland	Glasgow	★

★ (as of 2003 name of pipe major is no longer provided.)

[1] *Ceol mor*; phonetically, 'kale more', meaning 'big music'.

This painting by R. Mclan shows the popular sword dance, the Gillie Callum. If before a battle a clansman doing this war dance stepped on the swords it was considered a bad omen.

THE WORLD HISTORY OF HIGHLAND GAMES

CHAPTER SEVENTEEN

Scotland's Superb Dances and Dancers

Scottish dances are probably the best-known national dances in the world. At an international dancing festival in South Africa, Highland dancing was judged to be the most sophisticated and skilful ethnic dancing of all the many nations participating in the event.

The most familiar movements are probably those relating to the Highland fling. As Scots travel the world wearing their kilts, people will lift their arms in the air and put one foot up to the opposite knee and jump about in a parody of this dance.

It is important to recognise that there are two distinct kinds of Scottish dancing: Highland dancing, as seen in competitions at the games, and Scottish country dancing, the social dancing of Scotland. There are also competitions in the latter, although it is mainly socially orientated, but it is probably this competitive element in both disciplines that produces the high standard of dancing seen widely in Scotland. I leave out of this equation the mad but entertaining 'Strip the Willow' and eightsome reels that are frequently encountered at Scottish weddings.

It is extremely fortunate that Scotland has such a wealth of dances that are very widely practised. Bearing in mind the vast number of Highland games throughout the world, *no other country can equal Scotland in this respect* and I urge the powers-that-be not to be complacent, for all this could be lost in this rapidly changing modern world in which children and young people prefer computer games to physical activities. We had already lost a large part of a wonderful Scottish

dancing heritage when John Calvin, John Knox and other mid-16th-century reformers did their utmost in their preaching to discourage all forms of dancing. The Kirk introduced very oppressive legislation including fines, public humiliation and excommunication. Penalties varied in different areas. In Aberdeen in 1562 the first was humiliation before the congregation, a second offence earned a ducking before the public and three-time offenders were banished completely from the town.

Dancing and piping were specific targets, especially at weddings, where there were further profanities with 'drinking loose speeches, singing of licentious songs and profane minstrelling'. Funerals in those days were less scrutinised and might have been more fun

A detail of dancing at the Penny Wedding by Sir David Wilkie.

Dancers at Crystal Palace Highland Games.

than weddings! There could well have been an eleventh Commandment: 'Thou must not enjoy thyself.'

In the 1700s, religious views were a little less narrow minded, but by then some of the old favourite dances were lost for all time. Fortunately, a few were still practised in remote districts but just when things were going well again, there came the '45 Rebellion and the resulting ban of all things Scottish, including dancing and piping. Piping was no longer an integral part of weddings and funerals and any kind of Scottish dancing or piping at weddings risked a fine in the first instance and being called before the Kirk Session. While local hypocritical Holy Willies were often openly ignored as a gesture of defiance, frequent offenders risked the draconian measures of the government, who thought nothing of sending people to the colonies for minor offences. As a result,

It is said that that girls and young women do not participate enough in physical activity. It is certainly not so in Highland games circles. This mass dance was done at Inverness Highland Games in 2006.

Scotland almost became a music and dance Sahara. The pendulum then swung the other way, as can be seen, and these activities flourished once more, first at home and then abroad.

Now there are signs that things are changing again in Scotland and efforts must be made to maintain the high standards achieved by hard work and dedication over a long period of time.

I find it amazing and extremely disappointing that a Scottish Parliament would exclude dancing from a study of Scottish Highland games, given the enormous value of the activity from cultural, tourism and health-related points of view. The governmental study that excluded dancing and piping reported that participation levels in Highland games were low. Yet there are numerous Highland dancing competitions at Highland games that can attract around 900 competitors to a single gathering. Not many governing bodies could match this. Low participation indeed!

It is irrelevant whether or not Highland dancing is a sport. It is a healthy, energetic, entertaining activity for boys and girls, men and women. It brings large numbers to Scotland and is an integral part of Highland games, Scotland's largest widespread tourist attraction. I think that most would agree that the brief of any such survey

THE WORLD HISTORY OF HIGHLAND GAMES

Highland Games are now very dependent on sponsors and appreciate the support they give.

should not omit the important elements of Highland dancing and piping.

Local governments, if not national ones, have long assisted in maintaining games-associated traditions. Aberdeen town council, for example, supported Francis Peacock, an 18th-century dancing teacher who helped perpetuate old dances and steps. As well as being a noted teacher, Francis recorded his work in book form, which greatly benefited future generations. Peacock's Close, off the Castlegate in Aberdeen, is a fitting reminder of this oft-quoted teacher.

Turning to the lengthy background of Scotland's dances, it must be said that, as in other Highland games events, it is often difficult to separate fact from fable. Many early dances have not survived simply because there was no formal structure to record and perpetuate this element of

our heritage. The harpists and seanachies may have done a good job in recording major events, the highs and the lows of the lairds and communities, but leisure and recreational activities were very low on their agendas.

It has been widely explained that the Gillie Callum, or sword dance, owes its origination to an incident at the battle of Dunsinane in 1054. There, it is said, the future King Malcolm III slew one of Macbeth's chiefs then placed his sword over that of his vanquished opponent and danced in exultation over them. It is a colourful story but for the reasons given, researchers have found but

Lonach c. 1903.

Bobby Watson (centre) who became a dancing champion.

few valid references more than 175 years old. However, the tune 'Gillie Callum' mocks the tax gatherers of King Malcolm Canmore who reigned from 1058 to 1093. There are many different spelling for the old Gaelic words, for example, academics spell Callum as Chaluim, and nowadays we use the name Calum or Malcolm.

For years I have been telling of the traditional origins of the Highland fling but it irked me that I could not recall the names I had been given of the persons credited with the introduction of this most famous Highland dance. In the finishing stages of my research, I eventually found a battered old book with the story. Perhaps other Highlanders may also have a claim but here is the story as I found it.

Long ago in the great Mar forest, Alistair MacDuff lived in a crude cottage he had built without assistance from others. Although advancing in years, Alistair was a great piper and at his very best had played at Scone Palace, where he had accompanied his clan chief to the coronation of a Scottish king. Alistair passed his skill on to many others and few could equal his skills as a piper, tutor and composer. His most dedicated student

Dancing at Balmoral servants' Highland Games.

was his 11-year-old grandson, Ian, the apple of his eye. Old MacDuff, now 70, loved to instil in his pupils the spirit of pipe tunes and how to interpret the music to convey moods of the moment. One autumn day on the banks of the Dee, Alistair was playing on his chanter and Ian was spotting fish in the clear shimmering water of the river, when a rustle drew their attention. It was a handsome stag, lithe and strong, leaping sure-footedly from rock to rock with beauty and grace.

The old man enthused about the agility and elegance of the animal, declaring that nobody could duplicate the easy, flowing natural rhythm of the deer. The laddie protested that he could 'loup' like the deer and, matching his words, he raised his arms in the air like the antlers of a deer and put his finger to thumb to form the face of a stag then proceeded to jump lithely from stone to stone, poetry in motion. Alistair picked up his chanter and played as he had never played before and Ian came before him dancing, with arms still raised as he 'hooched' in exultation. The pair replicated the dance many times as autumn changed to winter and at Deeside ceilidhs their dual contribution was much appreciated. By the time Alistair was laid to rest, Ian MacDuff had become a fine piper but was even better known for his exquisite dance. His 'fling', as it became known, was famous and copied many times. In due course, he too taught his children to play the pipes and to catch the spirit of the dance by reminding them of the majestic monarch of the glen that inspired the first Highland Fling.

It has been pointed out that the 'Fling' is performed in a very small area (the size of a targe or shield) and that it is easy for the travelling teachers, known as 'dancies', to teach standard steps to several pupils at the same time. While dancies naturally preferred to have several pupils working at one time in a barn or loft, they would

Army dancer complete with full plaid.

The 1st Seaforth Highlanders demonstrate the Reel o' Tulloch.

also teach in the room of a house. The Highland Fling, with many relatively simple steps and a range of arm movements, was a very appropriate dance to practise many skills in limited space; hence this dance became very well known.

The beautiful, graceful *Seann Triubhas* (literally meaning 'old trousers') is widely believed to be linked with the wearing of trousers after the banning of the kilt. The double-shaking action of the feet is said to indicate a desire to shake off the restraints placed upon Highlanders. The dance begins in a slow tempo and then speeds up in the last steps to a fitting climax.

The Hullachan, more correctly the Strathspey and Reel o' Tulloch, is a lively foursome, although in competitions dancers are scored as individuals. The dancers weave round each other in figure-of-eight patterns like those described by Roman invaders many centuries ago when they tried, but failed, to conquer Scotland. It is said that the dance has origins in Tulloch or Tullich, the Deeside clachan that gives the dance the second part of its name. The minister was late one winter Sabbath and his parishioners kept warm by doing wee dances, stamping their feet and waving their arms. There is a version of the tale explaining that the dancers weaved in and out, in figures of eight, in the aisle between the two blocks of pews.

'Wilt thou go to the barracks, Johnnie?'

I have made the point that various traditional dances and throwing events existed before being brought together to form a programme of Highland games as we know them today. I have also pointed out that the north-east of Scotland was the stronghold of such developments. I am therefore delighted to present some very interesting old, and little publicised, information as further proof of these beliefs.

Long ago, Bonny Jean, the Duchess of Gordon, raised the Gordon Highlanders with her own unique recruiting strategy. She rode around Aberdeen and district on a beautiful white horse, presenting a spectacular picture. On seeing any able-bodied young man, she called her catchphrase 'Wilt thou go to the barracks, Johnnie?' She then offered a shilling from between her lips and many braw lads could not resist a kiss from this beautiful noblewoman. Her kiss sealed the contract and the Gordon Highlanders became a very active and famous regiment. A dance was composed in honour of the Duchess and 'Barrack's Johnnie' is still a popular competition dance at modern Highland games.

Bonny Jean's son was George, the Marquis of Huntly, who once rode over 100 miles from his home to the Northern Meeting in Inverness, the venue for the 2007 World Highland Games Championships. The Marquis changed horses eight times in the seven-hour journey and his enthusiasm made him the most popular man of the meeting.

Dancing experts point out a French influence in some of the figures, speculating that these are probably from the court of Mary, Queen of Scots, who spent some years in France. The pirouette and the finishing French-style *entrechat* are specific examples of this characteristic. If this is the true origin, it is a marvel that such dance movements survived through many trials and tribulations over the centuries.

There was a turning point when laws were ignored and dancing took place at the Highland Society competitions in Falkirk. There, Highland

In the early 1930s, when wearing of medals was commonplace. They were sometimes called the 'Tartan Terrors'.

dancing was originally done by pipers when they were having a much-needed break in a three-day programme. By 1787, trained Highland dancing enthusiasts who were not pipers took over at Falkirk and gradually prizes were introduced for the best dancers.

When competitions were held in Edinburgh, they were held indoors. A letter to a magazine in 1817 reflected the narrow-minded attitudes that still existed. It begins by criticising stage lighting as it makes the dancers look like black-legged Highland sheep, but went on to say:

> The exposed limbs of the dancers are sometimes exhibited to view in a manner altogether super-fluous and highly offensive to any lady of correct taste and feeling – and not a little so, to some of the other sex, who may not perhaps be entitled to express themselves according to their true sensations on the subject.

When Highland games in their present form were formalised in and after 1819, it is perhaps this attitude that caused the dancing competitions to be open to men only. In the latter part of the 19th century, soldiers of Highland regiments formed a significant proportion of well-trained dancers at the games. Queen Victoria frequently referred to Highland dancing and exhibitions, always by male dancers. The many pictures depicting these occasions show only men, often in fairly wild gyrations. The formal balls were usually the only exception since these were very social events.

This situation lasted for a long time but attitudes changed, probably with the tremendous contribution of women to the war efforts in the two world wars. Between 1914 and 1918, women did all kinds of jobs previously done only by men, and in the ammunition factories, imperative in that kind of warfare, women pushed back the boundaries in many different ways. It can be seen that by 1948, when regular world Highland

Dancing in torchlight for the Prince of Wales, son of Queen Victoria, at Mount Lodge.

dancing championships were held at Cowal, women more than held their own with their male counterparts.

The next major change came in 1952, when the Aboyne Games Committee introduced a costume for women dancers and introduced a very feminine competitive dance, Flora MacDonald's Fancy. The Aboyne dress, as it is still known, was based on the traditional dress of Highland women of bygone days. This was a loose-fitting tartan skirt giving ample freedom of movement, a light-coloured, loose-sleeved blouse and a close-fitting bodice.

Flora MacDonald's Fancy, which came from the Western Isles, was popularised by my dynamic

Dancing history was made in 1976 when female dancers were accepted for the first time in dancing competitions at Braemar.

old acquaintance Mrs Isobel 'Tibbie' Cramb of Aberdeen. She was taught this by an old lady from Peterhead who was descended from an itinerant dancie in the Buchan area. Tibbie was a collector of old dances and the Hill Manuscripts of 1841 was her greatest discovery. She did some great detective work to trace the relatives who finally unearthed this old book that described dances of the past. The owners had thought that it was a worthless 'jotter', and they had previously used the blank pages to keep telephone numbers.

D.G. McLennan reinstated Highland Lilt and Highland Laddie, two women's dances that were popular over a century ago. He was taught these by John McNeil, a well-known Edinburgh dance teacher. The Duke of Edinburgh naval connections led the Braemar Games committee to add the entertaining Sailor's Hornpipe to the Braemar programme to honour the Duke's marriage to Queen Elizabeth.

The Great Dancers

In the past, I have written a good deal about great dancers such as Johnny Pirie, Willie Sutherland, J.L. McKenzie and Bobby Watson, but in spite of this I cannot ignore them now for no games book would be complete without at least a brief review of these colourful characters.

Johnny Pirie was the first truly great Highland dancer. He was undefeated in some dances and a conservative estimate of his winnings at games was over 600 championship medals and £5,000. This was an enormous sum in those days but he earned much more by teaching at the highest level, being teacher in residence for two weeks at a time in Haddo House for the Earl and Countess of Aberdeen.

Johnny's mother loved dancing, and although, in the 1880s women were not allowed to compete, she watched the games with Johnny, her wee bairn. It was said that George Johnstone, the popular heavy, noticed that, although he was just a toddler, the little boy had a good sense of rhythm and would copy the dancers to the sound of the pipes. With considerable parental encouragement, Johnstone regularly carried the lad to 'Dancie' Duncan's loft at Portlethen, the idea being to present a novelty number at the end of the season dance. The item was a great success and the regular lessons paid off the following year when wee Johnny won two third prizes at Portlethen Highland Games.

John Pirie (b. 1876) in 1893.

A newspaper of July 1893 in my collection gives a slightly different story. It says John was first taught by John McLeod, an old and enthusiastic terpsichorean at the Bridge of Dee. Pirie, this newspaper said, made his first bid for honours at Bourtiebush at the age of seven, and won two third prizes. It also says that an abscess in his leg kept him out of competition until 1887, when he won a medal, then went on to great success from that point. He even danced before the Queen in 1890.

Myra Miller-Richardson's pupils. Champion dancers often go on to become good teachers and maintain traditions.

The alternative account says that Angus Gibson, who had bravely piped at the Indian Mutiny, was piper for the competition and he was amazed that such a small boy could earn 30/- (£1.50) for two dances – it was more than a farm labourer earned in a week.

One connoisseur, describing Pirie at the peak of his powers, enthused: 'While most Highland dancers rise from the board to execute their aerial movements, John only comes down now and then to touch the board!' The artistry of this champion should not be interpreted as 'jumping'. There are dancers who achieve good elevation with a jump but lack the artistry of the champion and, without this artistic interpretation, it becomes of little value.

The Piries (my relatives) moved to Aberdeen, then Johnny, George, Margaret and Barbara (Babs) formed a professional dancing act, 'The Pirie Family', that toured the country with a stage show, *The Gathering of the Clans*.

When Johnny's competition career was over, he concentrated more on teaching. Amongst his many pupils were champions such as Mary Aitken, J.L. McKenzie, Bobby Watson and many more, sounding like a 'Who's who' of Highland

THE WORLD HISTORY OF HIGHLAND GAMES

dancing. Johnny retired in 1931 but lived on until he was 72 years old.

After Pirie were there were stalwarts such as William and D.G. McLennan, the Cuthbertson brothers and Willie Sutherland of Thurso, probably Pirie's main rival.

A colourful character, he was a tailor by trade and, like the tailors of those days, habitually sat down with his legs crossed. At Haddo House, previously one of the best in Aberdeenshire, one very impressed spectator exclaimed, 'Man, look how well balanced Sutherland is on his legs. You would think his moustache was evenly parted to a hair'. After these the Lowes came on the scene, and George Lowe's articles contain useful historical information.

The McKenzies moved to Aberdeen and eventually in 1952, 'J.L.' won the world's Highland dancing championship and retained it for three years. His wide contribution to dancing earned him an MBE, but he died in 1991 at the age of 86.

Another fine competitor and teacher in Aberdeen was the irrepressible Bobby Watson. While McKenzie was somewhat shy and stern, Bobby was an extrovert, always ready for a laugh, and his dancing reflected his personality, particularly in dances such as the hornpipe and Irish jig. He would even dance a Seann Truibhas when accompanying himself on the bagpipes!

Bobby was born in 1914 as war broke out, and his father was killed in the fray. His mother, known as Madam Watson, opened a dancing school in the Green, Aberdeen, and attracted 400 pupils. Bobby was not one of them; his mother sent him to Johnny Pirie for instruction, as Bobby's mischievous nature disrupted her classes and he did not like being taught by his mother.

Under Pirie's stern tuition, the youngster's dancing developed rapidly and he was soon winning local competitions. In due course he won the Junior World Championships at Cowal. He reckoned that with the many eliminating heats in those days, he had to do as many as 32 dances in one day.

He accepted an invitation to appear at the Tivoli Theatre in Aberdeen and showed his versatility in performing many different forms of dance and also in playing bagpipes, fiddle and accordion. Soon he was appearing all over Britain and overseas. During this time, he met an attractive dancer, Mavis Clare, and they went on to marry.

During the Second World War, Bobby was in the Royal Air Force and Mavis belonged to the Civil Defence. Back home in 1947, he and Mavis opened a successful dancing school but he continued to compete at Highland games. This much-valued side of his life came to an end when he severed his Achilles tendon. However, a new opportunity made him more popular than ever. Bobby Watson became a television personality participating in popular shows such as *The Kilt is my Delight* and *The White Heather Club*. It is estimated that Bobby was involved in over 500 television programmes.

Bobby was always immaculate, had a great sense of humour and a fund of funny stories.

J.L. McKenzie (left) was an unforgettable champion in the old tradition. He was a country lad living on his father's farm near Turriff in North East Scotland and was taught dancing in barns and lofts by the old itinerant dancing teachers known as 'dancies'. Bobby Watson is on the right.

People travelled far to be taught by him and I can recall groups of Highland dancers from Sweden taking a personal interest in his well-being as he grew older. They took turns of tidying his garden as their colleagues were given his valued advice. He died on 9 November 1997.

Today's Competitors

More recently, there have been great competitors, including Gordon Yates, Victor Wesley and Billy Forsyth, the latter making a massive contribution as an administrator. As the years go by, the girls and women have greatly outnumbered the boys and men. Reflecting this, I recall, with great pleasure, the teaching of Mary Aitken and Jean Milligan and the dancing of Stirling's Catriona Buchanan, Betty Jessiman, who was the best of many fine North East competitors, and Wilma Tolmie of Dundee; of the overseas dancers I first favoured Lynne Dickson, but standards continue to rise. There are also great teachers, such as Jean Swanston and Myra Miller Richardson, who have been stalwarts over the years, first as competitors, then as ambassadors of Highland dancing on overseas tours, and now as dancing teachers and competition organisers. Jean's sons became excellent athletes like her husband John, and Myra's daughter Jayne and granddaughter Kira Ewing, have followed in her footsteps.

Victor Wesley and young Nicola Webster were taught by Jean Mackie at her dancing school in Springboig, Glasgow, the Webster household being next door. Nicola spoke of a big boy that was very, very good at Highland dancing, little knowing that this youngster would win the 1961 West of Scotland Boys Championship and Adult World Championships in 1968, 1969 and 1972. Previously, the great J.L. McKenzie of Aberdeen was the only man to achieve such a distinction. In 1970, Victor won a two-year scholarship to

Deryck Mitchelson.

study classical ballet in America and went on to win many other championships at Highland games on both sides of the Atlantic. Victor Wesley was, for a time, one of the most controversial critics of the Official Board of Highland Dancing. He believed that there should be freedom of choice, allowing dancers affiliated to various organisations to compete in world championships. He thought that judging was over-regulated and while strict standardisation might be warranted in early levels of competition, elite dancers should be allowed more scope for artistic interpretation of the dances. Officials and

Christine Lacey.

Gareth and Ailsa Mitchelson.

a lovely girl who was always very popular when appearing at international games, won hundreds of prizes over the years.

Young Gareth has been dancing as long as he can remember and has strong memories of competing from the age of nine and winning a pre-championship at 11 years of age. With perseverance and the inevitable ups and downs of this intensively competitive activity, he reached world championship standard, first placing in the finals when he was 16 years old. At 17 he was runner-up and in 1985 he became world champion. In total, he won outright a record of *four* world senior titles. There was a great era of strong world championship competition between Gareth and his brother Deryck, who won three world titles, first in 1991, 1994 and 1995, and Gregor Bowman, first in 1986, 1990, 1992, 1997 and 1998.

The Mitchelson brothers won seven world championships between 1985 and 1995, an all-time world record. By 1998, Gregor Bowman won a record *five* wins – then came Colleen Rintamaki of Canada, who won an uninterrupted run of five world championships, an all-time record.

Canadian dancers have been very successful at the World Championships held at Cowal Highland Gatherings and Colleen Rintamaki (b. 1980) is probably the most-praised adult competitor of the current millennium. She began Highland dancing at the age of four and started teaching dancing at age 18. This Ontario favourite was trained by Joy Tolev and inspired by the stylish Gene Kelly, whose unforgettable performance of *Singin' in the Rain* is still relished by those lucky enough to have seen it. She loves

Gregor Bowman.

administrators have not always welcomed his outspoken enthusiasm but none would deny his undoubted talents as a dancer. Victor became a judge at the Royal Braemar Gathering.

In the 21st century, we are still witnessing the passing down of a dancing heritage, with wonderful dancers like the Mitchelsons being prime examples.

Wilma Tolmie was one of the great Highland dancers of the 1960s, winning the World Championships of 1965, taking over the top spot from Billy Forsyth, who was World Champion in 1963 and 1964. Wilma married Pipe Major George Mitchelson and their three children, Deryck, Gareth and Ailsa, would watch her as she won competitions all over Scotland. True to Highland games tradition, they too began dancing at an early age and all won many championships. Ailsa,

Colleen Rintamaki of Canada.

Grace Davidson (Kilwinning),
Junior World Champion.

1955	Catriona Buchanan, Stirling
1956	Sheena McDonald, Thornliebank
1957	Sheena McDonald, Thorniliebank
1958	Sheena McDonald, Thornliebank
1959	Gordon Yates, Tarves
1960	Flora Stuart Grubb, Australia
1961	Betty Jessiman, Huntly
1962	Sandra Bald, Kirkcaldy
1963	Billy Forsyth, Bridge of Allan
1964	Billy Forsyth, Bridge of Allan
1965	Wilma Tolmie, Dundee
1966	Sandra Wright, New Zealand
1967	Irene McKenzie, Grangemouth
1968	Victor Wesley, Glasgow
1969	Victor Wesley, Glasgow
1969	Victor Wesley, Glasgow
1970	Lynne Dickson, Australia
1971	Rosemary McGuire, Banknock
1972	Victor Wesley, Glasgow
1973	Hugh D. Bigney, USA
1974	Aileen Robertson, Ayr
1975	Linda Rankin, Prestwick
1976	Aileen Robertson, Ayr
1977	Linda Rankin, Prestwick
1978	Sandra Kennedy, Bearsden
1979	Christine Lacey, Alexandria
1980	Christine Lacey, Alexandria
1981	Ailsa Simpson, Barrhead
1982	Christine Lacey, Alexandria
1983	Helen Fitzpatrick, Stenhousemuir
1984	Lesley E. Bowman, Dundee
1985	Gareth Mitchelson, Monifieth

choreographed Highland dancing and would like to see more such competitions.

From this overview of a very fascinating component of Highland games, we can see that the best traditions in this respected and time-honoured discipline are being perpetuated and indeed, developed, by Scotland's wonderful dancers and teachers.

World Highland Dancing champions (Cowal Games)

1949	Margaret Simpson, Stirling
1950	Margaret Simpson, Stirling
1951	J.L. McKenzie, Aberdeen
1952	J.L. McKenzie, Aberdeen
1953	J.L. McKenzie, Aberdeen
1954	Catriona Buchanan, Stirling

Aileen Robertson, Junior World Champion, 1972; Adult World Champion, 1974 and 1976. Four times British Champion.

Glenys Gray of New Zealand in 1986.

1986	Gregor Bowman, Dundee
1987	Gareth Mitchelson, Monifieth
1988	Gareth Mitchelson, Monifeith
1989	Gareth Mitchelson, Monifieth
1990	Gregor Bowman, Dundee
1991	Deryck Mitchelson, Monifieth
1992	Gregor Bowman, Dundee
1993	Jacqueline Smith, Ontario
1994	Deryck Mitchelson, Monifieth
1995	Deryck Mitchelson, Monifieth
1996	Jacqueline Smith, Ontario
1997	Gregor Bowman, Dundee
1998	Gregor Bowman, Dundee
1999	Colleen Rintamaki, Ontario
2000	Colleen Rintamaki, Ontario
2001	Colleen Rjintamaki, Ontario
2002	Colleen Rintamaki, Ontario
2003	Colleen Rintamaki, Ontario
2004	Tony Cargill, Arbroath
2005	Erin Rose, Ontario
2006	David Wilton, Forfar
2007	David Wilton, Forfar
2008	David Wilton, Forfar

Victor Wesley.

Billy Forsyth and Charlie Mills.

These images are from postcards, probably around 100 years ago.

CHAPTER EIGHTEEN

'An Ancient, Manly and Friendly Game'

In researching Highland games, I have noted numerous references to 'kiting'. These reports had nothing to do with flying kites but referred to the sport of quoits. In this sport, heavy metal rings are thrown for accuracy rather than for distance. It is certainly an ancient game, with definitive information going back to the 14th century, when it was one of the named sports banned at that time.

William Stewart (1829–1900).

A few heavies did throw 'kites' (quoits) as a form of recreation. William Stewart (1829–1900) of Perthshire, for example, was a well-known thrower who competed regularly and successfully in quoiting contests.

Quoits are thrown at a pin in a small area of clay, and scores are given to those landing nearest to the pin. This is the same principle as in lawn bowls, curling and other popular Scottish sports and it is possible quoiting was derived from horseshoe throwing, or perhaps even discus throwing.

Like other traditional Scottish sports, strength is an important asset. Quoits vary in weight, with regional and local differences, from as little as 1lb, but 23lb quoits have been used by the stronger competitors. The distance thrown also varies considerably, but it appears that

This man throwing quoits is from an old postcard published more than 100 years ago.

distances of 54–66 feet are most common.

In addition to strength, muscular endurance is also required in lengthy tournaments where hundreds of throws may have to be made without a loss of form. One of the longest events on record took place in Ayrshire in 1834, when contestants threw quoits for six hours.

Pub landlords would often set up quoiting rinks beside their premises to attract business, and in the distant past there was, almost inevitably, heavy drinking and some gambling.

The two world wars resulted in the decline, and almost extinction, of the sport. Hostilities, however significant, were just part of the problem. Quoiting was largely a rural sport and a decline was seen with the drift to the cities and later the huge decrease in rural workers. I recall, with pleasure, regularly watching dozens of men quoiting alongside the local pub at Garlogie, some ten miles from Aberdeen. The host and organiser was Robbie Shepherd, father of the radio personality and games commentator of the same name.

There are still around a dozen quoits clubs in Scotland but the sport seems to have dropped out of all Highland games programmes.

Luss Highland Games 1887.

THE WORLD HISTORY OF HIGHLAND GAMES

CHAPTER NINETEEN

Great Scott! A Speedie Competitor and a Big Mac

Although light field events were included in very early games, there was less information than in other aspects of Highland games. In Edwardian times that changed considerably. At that time, the three Scott Brothers – Bryce, Tom and W. Morris – were hailed as super athletes in Ayrshire, Scotland. The most famous of the trio was Bryce Scott of Kilmarnock, who became a premier Highland games athlete from 1903 until 1922. As he was very active and popular in the jumps (high, long, pole and triple jumps), looking at these light field events through his eyes gives a clear picture of the characters, the conditions and the standards of the first two decades of that century.

Bryce Scott won a great many prizes at Highland games and no doubt would have enhanced his reputation further still had there not been a world war. Nevertheless, he set long-standing records that lasted until the 1950s when his cousins, Tom and Jay Scott of Inchmurrin, came along to set new standards and add to what became an athletic dynasty. This dynasty was further enhanced when Tom's son, Dougal, became a very competent prize winner in light events.

Bryce was more than just a talented jumper and pole vaulter. He was also a fine writer and, being vitally interested in heavy events as well as his own specialities, he collected a remarkable number of newspaper cuttings giving the results of Highland games. He also recorded all his own performances alongside the placing and measurements of his rivals. The well-set-out pages with very neat writing give an accurate overview of Scottish Highland games in the post-Victorian and immediate post-war eras.

Fortunately, his direct descendant, also Bryce Scott, kept the invaluable collection, which contributed immensely to this book. I am deeply appreciative of the Scotts' contribution to my research of Highland games.

It is easy to understand Bryce Scott's passion for Highland games but few could convey this as well as the man himself. He had been living in England for some time and went to visit some friends in Aberdeen. He could not resist a trip to Deeside, and as he stood in the shadow of steep snow-clad Lochnagar, he recalled the processions of Highlanders at Lonach, Aboyne and Braemar:

> The Scots blood leapt in a' my veins as I fought again my battles on the green sward of the games arena to the accompaniment of the pibroch.

Young Bryce Scott.

Scott decided to have his memories and records published and his recollections of travels and personalities were featured in a long-forgotten newspaper series. His informative contributions were very worthwhile, giving an understanding of Highland games athletes over two decades of war and peace.

He was born at Laggish, a sheep farm in Ayrshire, not far from the border with Galloway.

As a boy, he roamed the moors, jumping every burn (stream) and bog he encountered. He saw challenges everywhere and gradually improved from jumping over the narrow parts to leaping to wherever there was a decent run up and safe landing.

When his schooldays were over, he departed from his home with 'a bible and a blessing' and in Kilmarnock served his apprenticeship as an engineer.

When he returned home for a holiday, Bryce took his recently acquired jumping shoes and athletic kit. His brother Tom was his first sporting opponent and although he had just finished a hard day's work in the hayfield, Tom had no hesitation in accepting his brother's challenge in long jumping. Tom rolled up his trouser legs, removed his shoes and jumped in bare feet, which had been their usual practice. Bryce, in proper clothing and new shoes, exceeded his brother's mark. Tom, in a last despairing effort, cast aside his trousers and, wearing nothing but his shirt, took an extra long run – but it was not to be. The shorts, shoes and no doubt the confidence they gave him allowed Bryce to beat 'lovable Tom', as he called his brother.

At the age of 21, Tom was 5 feet 11 inches and 12.5 stone in weight. Until the outbreak of war, he competed mainly at the Galloway Games, although sometimes he would compete further from home. He did no specialised training, believing that tending the sheep on the hills and physical farm work were adequate for his needs. Considering this casual approach, his figures were impressive: hop, hop and leap (no misprint), 46 feet 6 inches; long jump, 21 feet 6 inches; high jump, 5 feet 10 inches; pole vault, 9 feet; and 16lb hammer, around 90 feet. Sadly, Tom died of wounds in the Great War. 'He was a singularly loveable character,' said Bryce.

Bryce's first big competition was at Dunoon's Cowal Games, which is still a major event. He packed his gear into a neat bundle, wrapped in brown paper and tied with string. He saw a man with an athletic physique and claimed he knew he was a competitor because he was big and he carried a bag! His guess was correct – it was Neil Nicolson, the oldest of the famous athletic family from the Kyles of Bute. Neil, seeing that Bryce was a novice, invited him to join him in the arena and made the young man feel at ease. Bryce repaid him by beating him in both flat jumps.

Scott's first outing of 1904 was at Galston in

Hitherto unknown pole vault statistics with mentions of well-known names.

1912. Tom Scott, Alex Finnie and Murdo Fraser. Note the popular way for working men to wear a scarf in bygone days.

THE WORLD HISTORY OF HIGHLAND GAMES

Ayrshire, still a popular venue 100 years later. It was held at Cessnock Castle, the Scottish seat of the Duke of Portland. Here, he tied with Nicolson with a moderate hop, hop and jump of 42 feet 8 inches. Charles Gillies beat Bryce by 5 inches with a long jump of 19 feet 10 inches. George Merchant from Lumphanan, in the north-east, won the vault with 10 feet.

It must always be remembered that these performances were made in primitive conditions, often without sand pits and proper equipment. In preparation for the Border games, which some-times included a *standing* high jump, Bryce Scott trained by jumping over string fixed to natural, rustic uprights. This did not stop him from beating the best in the Borders at Jedburgh, his standing jump of 4 feet 6 inches beating A. Dickenson of Morebattle. Scott also did a stand-ing hop, hop and jump of 30 feet 2 inches and running flat jumps of 44 feet 10 inches and 21 feet 5 inches *on hard ground*.

Some friendly rivalry existed between the heavies and the leapers. The famous heavy Charlie McLean teased Bryce Scott, telling him he had to win a first at Bridge of Allan before he would be worth considering as an athlete. This motivated young Scott, for Bridge of Allan was the venue for Strathallan Highland Games, long considered the national champi-onships. The result was that he did win a first, indeed he took two firsts, with a good long jump of 20 feet 1 inch and 44 feet 10 inches in a fair hop, hop and leap, as it was called in a newspaper article.

The different conditions of those days have already been men-tioned but Bryce Scott's venture to

Charles McLean.

a North East gathering illustrates another aspect of the life of an athlete 100 years ago. With a dearth of events in the south-west, Scott headed for Dunecht Games, some 14 miles from Aberdeen. He set out from Glasgow Central railway station at 4.20am on the morning of the games. He had probably stayed in the station overnight as there was no public transport at that time and he would not have had access to a car to take him from Kilmarnock to Glasgow. In Aberdeen, professing knowledge of this mode of transport, he hired a pony and trap and with a dancer, G.J. Melvin from Arbroath, and another competitor, they took turns of the reins in the 14-mile journey to Dunecht.

The officials had not heard of Bryce Scott but George Johnstone, the well-known Aberdeen heavy, explained to the organisers that Bryce was anxious to catch a train back to Glasgow and it would help if the times of some events could be brought forward. George was a much-respected figure and they were glad to oblige. Having won with 41 feet 5 inches and 20 feet 6 inches, Scott hurried back, changed, harnessed the nag and hastened back to Aberdeen faster than animal rights protestors would have liked. The trio caught the train with seconds to spare, thus saving them a night sleeping rough.

Bryce Scott competed against all the leading jumpers on the Scottish games circuit for 20 years and provided a bountiful supply of information about these men. In 1909, young Mack Thom from Dumfries had powerful legs that made up for his lack of height, and he did 45 feet 7 inches in the triple jump. During the same season, most of the best assembled at the 'Brig' (Bridge of Allan), where Mackay Macgregor held the Strathallan Games. The best jumps there in 1909 included John Speedie's excellent record high jump of 6 feet and triple jump of 47 feet 4 inches. Hugh McAskill (or M'Caskill) did a long jump of 21 feet 4 inches. Like Scott, these men competed in all the jumps and most also competed in the pole vault. One of the men most admired by the jumpers was John McKenzie, who not only competed in the jumps but won the pole vault with 10 feet 5 inches and created the sensation of the day when, competing with the heavies between his jumps, he defeated the legendary A.A. Cameron in throwing the heavy hammer.

A week after those Strathallan Games in 1909, the 'new kid on the block', Mack Thom, did a long jump of 20 feet 5 inches. Bryce had a 'hat trick', scoring his three wins with 20 feet 10 inches in the long jump, beating Alex Finnie in the pole vault, and placing first in the high jump. This winner was, as always, full of praise for his opponents and on this occasion was particularly complimentary when praising N. Little of Annan, who cleared 5 feet 2 inches in the high jump, *even though he had only one leg.* He used a stilt in the run-up but dropped it before making his effort, springing from the ground to come down on the other side on the same foot as the take off on the other side. It was a truly magnificent feat.

Scott continued to improve and kept on winning and placing high in the jumping events in spite of rising standards and stiff competition from athletes such as Speedie, Corbett and McFarlane and, of course, the two very

versatile stars, John McKenzie and later Walter Knox of Canada.

There was a particularly happy day in September 1909, when the three Scott brothers competed in the athletic events run in connection with the Girvan Cattle Show. This was very near their own home so they were well known and popular with the crowd. Between them, they won all the jumping events and local spectators were ecstatic when they placed first, second and third in the long jump. Bryce W. Scott did 20 feet 11 inches, Tom Scott did 20 feet 5 inches, and W. Morris Scott did 19 feet 10 inches. Considering the lack of jumping pits, these were excellent competitors. There was great enthusiasm when Tom and Bryce were battling it out in the high jump. A local sheep farmer shouted to Tom for all to hear that if Tom beat Bryce in this event, he would give him a lamb. Tom cleared 5 feet 8 inches to take first prize and the lamb as a bonus. Maybe, just maybe, Bryce would relax a little to obtain something extra for the family. Although there was never any mention of it in the Scott chronicles, there was a good deal of syndication in the light events. We know quite definitely that this was common between the two world wars. Competitors would form a small group to share expenses and prize money.

The Scott brothers generated good publicity, and one newspaper reported:

The exhibition of leaping by the Scott brothers was undoubtedly one of the chief attractions at the sports. The (pipe) band in particular seemed to be very appreciative and when one of the trio cleared 5 feet 7 inches in the high jump the band struck up 'Scots Wha Hae'.

From John James Miller's book Scottish Sports and how to excel in them, *1908.*

James Morrison.

Alex Finnie.

THE WORLD HISTORY OF HIGHLAND GAMES

There was a constant influx of new talent and in 1911 Walter Knox, an incredible all-round athlete, arrived on the Highland games scene. Knox established many new records and it is indicative of Bryce Scott's ability when we see that he would sometimes beat this remarkable newcomer. Always a great sportsman, Scott was generous in his praise of his new opponent. He greatly admired Knox and the Canadian reciprocated. The two were well matched and Scott was successful in persuading some games committees to specially feature their rivalry, pay their travelling expenses and perhaps put up a special prize for the winner.

Walter Knox, Canada.

Crieff Highland Games was one of the venues accepting the suggestion and advertised a 'Great International Championship'. A week before the contest, Knox sustained a sprained ankle, but rather than let down the committee he strapped up the injury and competed without complaint. His jumps were not up to his usual standard but he still managed to do a *standing* triple jump of 30 feet 11 inches, standing high jump of 4 feet 9 inches, standing long jump of 9 feet 11 inches, running long jump of 21 feet and a pole vault of 11 feet. An amazing performance for an injured athlete, but it was not enough to beat Bryce Scott.

Walter, however, wanted to give the crowd its money's worth, and although in pain with his ankle badly swollen by this time, he asked the stands to be raised. Spectators were interested and amused when a joiner was brought in to make the stands higher as they had already reached their limit. Once the extra uprights had been added, Knox asked for the lath to be raised to 11 feet 7 inches, which he cleared, to loud and sustained applause. The winner, Bryce Scott,

in paying tribute to his worthy opponent, spoke of the Canadian's astonishing grit, determination and skill.

The two athletic stars corresponded with each other even after Knox returned to his homeland at the end of the season. There were many great battles between the top men during the following summer and the results at Strathblane in 1912 accurately reflect the situation, with one significant anomaly. Mackay Macgregor provided a handsome medal to be awarded to the winner of the leaping events. The award was to be over four events, which made it difficult for Knox to win and so it proved to be. Points were awarded as follows: first place, 7 points; second place, 5 points; third place, 3 points; and fourth place, 1 point. R.E. Scott won with 19 points, Speedie won 16 points, McCaskill won 11 points and Knox won 10 points.

One of Speedie's shoes burst in the high jump and he had to continue with a borrowed shoe, which unfortunately was for his take-off foot. This could have made all the difference between him winning and taking second place. 'Truly, the fates were unkind to John Speedie,' Bryce Scott commented. In spite of all this, Walter Knox had his moment of glory when he broke the record in the pole vault, clearing 11 feet 1 inch.

Shortly after, Bryce Scott achieved one of his ambitions by breaking the Aboyne long jump record set by Adam Bower of Old Meldrum in 1888. The record stood at 21 feet and at 11am, Bryce, complaining of being sleepy after the long trip from South Ayrshire, jumped 20 feet 6 inches, 20 feet 11 inches and finally did 21 feet 10 inches for a new record.

Scott was not so lucky when he and Knox

were attacking the pole vault record at Aboyne in 1912. Both badly injured their ankles and instead of going on to compete at Braemar they had to 'hirple' home, Bryce using a broken hammer shaft as a walking stick to take some weight off his painful injury. Always looking at the bright side, he pointed out that A.A. Cameron had broken the hammer shaft and he had acquired a nice souvenir of this great heavy.

Bryce Scott's injury had repercussions. His ankle had not properly healed by the start of the 1913 season and he began to have thoughts about the necessity of retiring from competition. Happy memories pulled him towards the games arenas, the Fields of Dreams, and his friendships with athletes, officials, pipers and dancers were too strong for him to break off lightly. There was one small consolation. It was not his 'taking off' foot that was injured, otherwise his athletic career would have been well and truly over. On 20 June 1913, he tested himself at the Lanarkshire Constabulary events at Broomhill Park, Airdrie. Strangely enough, he found his opponents were almost all of the same men who had started their careers about the same time as him over ten years earlier. The quartet of jumpers were John McKenzie, Donald Corbett, John A. Speedie and, of course, Bryce Scott. Mac and Bryce tied with 10 feet 6 inches in the vault. Speedie and Corbett tied at 10 feet 3 inches. Speedie won the high jump at 5 feet 9 inches and Scott was second with 5 feet 7 inches. Corbett was third

George Merchant was a spectacular pole-vaulter, whose style looked very dangerous. He would rise above the pole then throw it away when his feet were well above his head and back still to the crossbar. It always made

George Merchant.

spectators gasp. Merchant was ideally built for this technique. He had a well-built and strong upper body and light but powerful legs. At only 5 feet 4 inches and 9-stone body weight, he was described as a pocket Hercules. George was one of the best athletes of this period. His records lasted for many years and in later years the great John McKenzie and Finley Cramb used the same vaulting techniques as he did. He won at Aboyne for 10 years in succession between 1895 and 1904. His 10 feet 9½ inches pole vault record at Aboyne in 1900 was done with a heavy unyielding hickory pole and stood until 1908, when John McKenzie and Donald Corbett used light and flexible bamboo poles to beat it.

Although best known for his pole vaults, he was a very competent all-rounder. He could jump 3–6 inches above his own height and also win prizes in various jumping events, sprints, hurdles, obstacle and sack races. Depending on the other competitors, he would sometimes compete in shot putting, where he was good for his size.

There was one interesting occasion when George Merchant did not win the pole vault, being beaten by J. Bell of Langholm, a pole *climber* rather than a pole-vaulter. This was before the climbing technique was banned. The trouble was that these 'climbers' would plant their pole and swing up but if the balance was not right they would slide down and make another, sometimes several more, attempts. It became very annoying and monotonous for the crowd and worse still for the competitors waiting their turn. Merchant 'lost the place'; he became angry and made a few unprintable comments, which were heartily endorsed by many others. His focus gone, he had to take second place to Bell.

THE WORLD HISTORY OF HIGHLAND GAMES

ANCHOR LINE
TWIN SCREW STEAMER
CAMERONIA.
June 29° 1913

Dear friend Bryce,
a few lines to let you know
I am back to the land of
the heather. or expect to be
awork from today and am
going to the first games after
that date. my address will

Knox of Canada sailed to Scotland each year to compete until the war when it was then too dangerous. This extract indicates the spirit of camaraderie that existed.

By 1910, John McKenzie was improving in the heavy events and at Galston Highland Games he won prizes for caber tossing, putting the stone and hammer throwing as well as the pole vault and high jump. The quality of his caber toss can be judged by the fact that after Mac had won the caber, it was cut three more times before anybody else could succeed.

Spectators love to watch a good all-rounder who can compete with distinction in light as well as heavy events. Jay Scott of Inchmurrin during the late 1950s and, more recently, John Freebairn and Charlie Allan were the most notable competitors in this regard, but in pre-Great War days it was John McKenzie. The officials were not very keen on all-rounders. They gave the impression that they thought it demeaned their discipline. John McKenzie often got the rough edge of one particular judge's tongue but it did not stop him from taking prizes in light events, heavy events and even dancing, all on the same day.

One day, big John, in a rush to pack his bag, had overlooked his kilt, but did not realise this until he had reached the games field. There was a panic as he raced around looking for assistance, which was readily given. When he appeared to throw the hammer he presented himself in a kilt, but close inspection would have revealed that it was a large lady's tartan skirt with some expertly added pleats. The judges did not detect the difference, perhaps as McKenzie was always rushing to throw and hastening back to the jumps.

Accident! Vaulting at Partick Police Sports, 1910

John Speedie, Donald Corbett and Bryce Scott were asked to give a pole vaulting exhibition as a highlight in the programme. The item progressed well, although it had been observed that the crossbar was thicker and heavier than usual. It turned out that it was also much stronger.

The height of the bar was 10 feet 5 inches. When Corbett attempted this, he did not have enough speed in his approach to allow him to swing right over the bar. He released and pushed away the pole but his outstretched arms and torso went down on the crossbar, which was quite unyielding. This caused his body to rotate under the bar and he came down flat on his back, completely unconscious. Sandy Duncan, trainer for Partick Thistle Football Club and a top professional pedestrian of the late Victorian era, rushed to his aid and resuscitated poor Donald. It put a sudden end to the exhibition and it is told that Chief Constable Cameron vented his wrath on those responsible for providing this equipment. It could have been much worse. With modern-day equipment, this sort of thing would not have happened.

These men were tough. Just four days later at the Glasgow Police Annual Sports, Corbett was back in action, winning the high jump and vault (10 feet 8 inches), and in an exhibition vault outside the competition he did 10 feet 10 inches.

Bryce Scott takes 1st equal at Aboyne Games 1922. Pole vaulting without a pit and without a 'box' to place the pole were commonplace.

Pre-war years

It has been said that there were games at Bridge of Allan since the late 1840s or early 1850s, but I have not been able to substantiate such an early date for these splendid gatherings.

In the early days of Strathallan Games, the Bridge of Allan was known as the Queen of Scottish Spas. The gathering at this charming watering place attracted a fashionable crowd and it rapidly gained a very good reputation. It is interesting to note that in early years the programme included horse racing, archery and jumping events for women as well as men. The press recorded that these were popular events.

Walter Knox went to Shotts first in early July in 1911 and he rapidly became one of the outstanding Highland games personalities.

He most certainly added interest to the jumping and vaulting events. Like John McKenzie, he would also compete in putting the stone when there was the possibility of a prize.

Knox's ankle injury in 1912, mentioned earlier, did not interfere too much with his programme. Late in the season, it was still giving him trouble and he campaigned for sand pits to be provided at Highland games. The Aboyne Committee always liked to meet the needs of the athletes but were unwilling to cut a hole in their treasured turf and decided that two bed mattresses would be better than a sand pit. This was a mistake and the mattresses were never produced again. Walter Knox and Bryce both encountered the same problem. They both landed partly on one mattress and twisted their ankles as they dropped from heights in excess of 10 feet. Scott was first to be injured and was carried to the

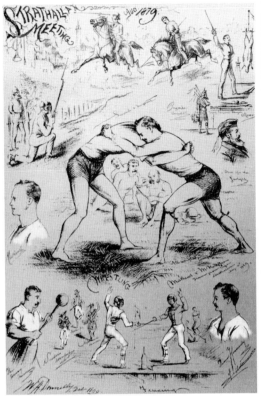

Strathallan Highland Games in 1883.

dressing tent. While he was bathing the injured ankle, John McKenzie came into the tent carrying

Long jumper Bryce Scott (left) wrote to his son on the back of this photograph. 'In 1919 your old dad was 39 years old and did 22 feet on hard turf. In 1932 George Masson (right) was 20 years old and did 20 feet and had a landing pit.'

Walter Knox on his back, Knox having done exactly the same thing in clearing 11 feet 1½ inches for a new Aboyne record.

Bryce Scott's ankle was slow to heal and again he felt his career might be over, but his comments reveal his motivation and dedication: 'Friendships made with officials, athletes, pipers and dancers as well, were too strong to break off lightly. To retire meant far more than one cared to admit.'

In June 1913, he was back competing with his contemporaries, placing equal first with John Mackenzie, doing 10 feet 6 inches in the vault and 5 feet 7 inches in the high jump to take second place to Speedie. Donald Corbett was third. They, and a growing band of rivals, had a good and successful season in 1913 but the clouds of war were gathering.

A few days before the outbreak of war they all met up at Bridge of Allan for the famous Strathallan Games. Jimmy Ferries of Aberdeen won the hop, step and leap with 44 feet 8 inches, Scott was second and Donald and Ewan Kennedy, brothers from Fort William, followed in that order. Scott moved up to first in the long leap (20 feet 6 inches); Ferries and Ewan Kennedy followed. John Mackenzie won the pole vault with 10 feet 7 inches, which Scott failed. Donald Corbett was third. Charlie McLean, one of the heavies who frequently entered light events, was fourth. Scott took the high jump with 5 feet 8 inches; A. Macpherson of Blackford, Corbett and Ewan Kennedy followed.

They did not meet in such competition again for at least four years. War was declared. The skirl of the bagpipes now called men to war instead of games. Most athletes immediately answered this call to arms and just as quickly, many paid the ultimate price. They said it was the war to end all wars. Sadly, it was not.

F.R. Cramb and J.K. Speedie.

Peace

After a five-year break, many annual games resumed, but some of the more remote committees in small hard-hit areas decided against resuming. At the games there was some surprise and great joy when surviving athletes were reunited. Good-natured joking about grey hairs and lost body weight were tinged with deep sorrow on hearing of losses of former competitors and relatives. Those who had read the reports of John Mackenzie's death were delighted to know that Captain John had actually survived, although was badly wounded. Soon things settled down and the athletes focused on the present and the job in hand. They were back in business. On the resumption of the games in 1919, I have noticed that newspaper results would often give the armed service rank of the athletes, such as Captain J. McKenzie, Captain Cramb MC, indicating he had won the Military Cross in action.

The tough times and ups and downs of the games are well illustrated by the experiences of a group of athletes who competed in the first post-war Aboyne Games. Things were looking up, for instead of spending a night in a railway station before the games and returning the same day, one four-man syndicate got together and booked overnight accommodation in Aberdeen. Arriving in Aberdeen the evening before the games, tired and hungry, the four stayed in a double-bedded room. There were others in the same 'digs' and the group then consisted of heavies John Nicolson, Alex Finnie and James Graham, and jumpers John Speedie and Bryce Scott. After supper the athletes decided to go to see Valentine Macdonald, also known as 'Big Mac', a very jovial heavy who was also a publican in the Granite City. They were assured that his pub was quite nearby but they found that it was quite a distance and by the time they got there the pub doors were locked. One went round the back of the pub and saw there was still a light on upstairs, indicating that Big Mac was not yet in bed. As the group made their way round, the light went out. Rather than risk the wrath of the big man, they wearily tramped all the way back to their lodgings.

The very dedicated, and by this time long-faced, Bryce Scott hastened to bed, but with animated conversations on all sides, sleep was out of the question. The 'crack was guid', and Alex Finnie, the life and soul of the party, told the leapers that this was the best preparation they could have and he could expect to break some records next day. Scott was not so convinced but he still enjoyed the camaraderie until the wee sma' oors of the morning.

Next day, a decidedly stiff Bryce Scott took a long time to limber up and, precisely at 11am, for this was the meticulously timed Aboyne Games, the long leap commenced. Speedie and W.S. Reid of Aberdeen took the lead with 20 feet 2 inches. With only one jump left, Scott, now well limbered up, and mentally motivated, made an all-out effort. He reached 22 feet to win the event – and the Aboyne record he had craved for many years.

First to congratulate him was Finnie, who

proudly proclaimed that had it not been for his last-minute preparation, Bryce would never have produced such a jump. Later in the day, John Speedie won the high jump but the previous night's late session and the long walk was blamed for his inability to break the Aboyne record. Finnie kept out of the way, which was just as well as Scott injured his ankle and was unable to compete before royalty at Braemar the following day. He did have the consolation of winning the pole vault, the only event in which he competed. Speedie won the high jump easily.

In 1919, Speedie and Mackenzie were still prominent. The Kennedy brothers improved their ranking and newcomers such as Ritchie Tough and J. Cameron of Dalmeny appeared on the prize lists. The latter was about the best pole vaulter of the season but not yet quite up to previous standard. He won at Thornton with a vault of 10 feet, which was too much for veterans Speedie, Mackenzie and Scott, who had announced his retiral but continued to regularly attend the games as a spectator until 1922. He always carried his spikes just in case there was a possibility of a prize! It was the last time that the three friendly rivals met in competition and there was a touch of poetic justice when all three finished equal.

Between 1904 and 1922, Speedie and Scott competed against each other 158 times. Speedie won 113 times and Scott won 126. The remainder were ties. Big John Mackenzie won more prizes in total as he also competed in heavy events and always gave the specialist jumpers stern competition in their favourite events.

Fittingly, Bryce Scott ended his fine athletic career at Braemar by winning in the pole vault, beating all the hungry young newcomers. He still used a stiff, wooden pole but by this time he had fitted an aluminium tip with three small prongs to prevent it from slipping. Four days after competing at Braemar, he took up a new appointment in Yorkshire.

Duncan Macgregor of Dunoon became a physical education teacher at Aberdeen Grammar School, and, with Ewan Kennedy of Fort William, he was the last of the old guard, but a new crop of light field events competitors were now getting into their stride. Many of them were from the north-east of Scotland, where the games continued to thrive. In the flat jumps during the 1920s, there was G.J. Cameron, P. Hector, J. Mair, R. Shand, J. Macpherson, J. Ross, F. Tait and J. Esson. Best known were Aberdeen's W. Livingstone, G. Middleton and C.J. Cameron of Elgin.

Middleton long jumped 21 feet 4 inches at Rothienorman and 20 feet 11 inches at Braemar in 1923, and 22 feet at 'Rothie' and 20 feet 8 inches at Braemar in 1924. J. Ross did some fine jumps, doing 22 feet 9 inches in 1925 at Mintlaw to surpass his 21 feet 7 inches two years earlier. P. Hector was more of a runner than a jumper but won numerous long jumps, scoring between 21 feet and 22 feet.

Livingstone came into his own in the mid-1920s, winning many victories in the long jump and hop step and jump. He won first place in the triple jump at Aboyne and also at Braemar on successive days in 1927.

The north-east of Scotland provided most leading high jumpers during the 1920s. These included W. Chalmers, J. Cooper, A. Cruikshank, W. George, P. Hector, J. Masson, G. Middleton, W. Smith, F. Tait and the young Adams of Aberdeen. Further north, W. Fraser of Conan Bridge and George Grant of Nairn were tops.

More southerly high jumpers at the games included G.J. Ralph, J. Edwards and James Black of Kinlochleven. In 1927, the latter became the man of the moment when he cleared 5 feet 8 inches at Alva, 5 feet 9 inches at Inveraray and 5 feet 10 inches at Callander.

Pole vault results did not improve significantly in the 1920s and a variety of styles were still very much in evidence. Some vaulters cleared the cross-bar with their backs towards it; others followed Donald Corbett's style of turning to face the bar as it was crossed. In those far-off days, since there was no box in which to 'plant' the pole, there were various views on exactly where the pole should be placed prior to the swing. This type of equipment was used until the late 1950s and even later by isolated competitors. In only one matter was there uniformity, because sandpits were the exception not the rule, athletes tried to land *feet first*, on their toes, with their knees slightly bent and their arms extended for balance.

Looking back, it can be seen that, for a number of years, Bryce Scott was the best all-rounder in the light field events. Archie Campbell dubbed Bryce as 'the Flying Scotsman' and stated categorically that Scott was the long jump Scottish champion from 1906 to 1921. His record of 22 feet at Aboyne stood from 1919 until equalled, but not beaten by, George Masson of Aberdeen in 1932.

Tom Scott, seen with son Dougal, still lives on the island of Inchmurrin.

There were two significant differences: Masson was aged 21 while Scott was 39 when he made the record, and George Masson leapt into a prepared sand pit while Bryce Scott jumped from grass to grass.

One day in late May 1932, the Scott family of Laggish, Barrhill, Ayrshire, were sitting at lunch when their father, David F. Scott, walked in and proudly informed them that he had bought Inchmurrin, the largest island in Loch Lomond. To say they were astonished is an understatement. Two weeks later, when it was publicly announced, it created an even bigger stir, for the island was to be used as a base for a world-record attempt on the motorboat speed record.

Inchmurrin is a lovely island amongst some of the most wonderful scenery to be found in the world. Until two years before the sale it had been the property of the Duke of Montrose and was used as a deer park. At the south-west are the ruins of the castle of the ancient Earls of Lennox, whose family included Lord Darnley, husband of Mary, Queen of Scots. The island was visited by James IV in 1506 and by James VI in 1585 and in 1617 after the Union of the Crowns. This is the briefest of histories, to give a flavour of the island's connections with nobility and royalty.

THE WORLD HISTORY OF HIGHLAND GAMES

Fabulous Jay Scott of Inchmurrin. Scottish Champion, 1956 and 1957 and Scotland's best all-rounder.

David's sons, Tom and Jay Scott, were brought up on the island and became the 'nobility' of Highland games, being Scotland's best all-rounders, thus adding most significantly to the athletic Scott dynasty begun by their cousins, Bryce and Tom Scott.

Tom and Jay were very active immediately after the Second World War; Tom turning professional in 1947 and Jay in 1948. Tom could high jump 6 feet 2½ inches and Jay did one inch more for a Scottish record in Scottish conditions with a minimum of sand. Because of this, the two Scotts high jumped scissors style, landing on the feet each time. They were at their best around 1955–60. In the later years, Tom stayed at home looking after business interests on the island, while Jay travelled more, at home and abroad.

Jay Scott was an extremely versatile athlete and a truly charismatic man who charmed the crowds with his personality and performances. Although he was the Scottish heavy events champion in 1958, he also won sprints, middle distances, a record hop, hop and jump of 51 feet 11 inches, hop step and jump of 48 feet 10 inches, and, of course, long and high jumps. His presence did much to enhance the games and he travelled far and wide as a popular member of the first group of itinerant international heavies.

Others in this adventurous athletic band who travelled the world included the great Bill Anderson, who beat all comers, Olympian shot putter Arthur Rowe, 6 feet 7 inches Dave 'Darth Vader' Prowse, Jock McColl of Luss, Loch Lomond, Sandy Sutherland of Alness and Louis McInnes of Oban.

Wrestling at Luss Games, Loch Lomond, c.1904.

THE WORLD HISTORY OF HIGHLAND GAMES

CHAPTER TWENTY

Wrestling at Highland Games

Wrestling has been practised all over the world since ancient times and the sport has long been prominent amongst the Celtic nations. Not surprisingly, wrestling was included in Ireland's Tailteann Games, an annual celebration that continued for many hundreds of years, having a lifespan longer than the ancient Olympic games. Wrestling was one of the sports that the Gaels brought with them when they crossed from Ireland to Argyll, and the earliest evidence of wrestling in Scotland can be seen on carved stones. One of the oldest Celtic crosses in existence shows two beastly characters in the 'backhold' position, which gives the name to the ethnic style still popular in Scotland. At Glenferness House, near Nairn in the north-east of the country, the backhold style is seen again on the Prince's Stone. Loose-hold wrestling is in evidence on the Tulibole Stone, now housed in the National Museum of Scotland in Edinburgh. Both these important Scottish stones date from around the 8th and 9th centuries.

Wrestling in front of the Royal Pavilion at the annual Braemar Games, 1955. Ed Anderson referees.

Such evidence, carved in stone, became very scarce when statutes were put in place, specifically 'forbidding under the highest ecclesiastical censures having wrestling matches or sports in churches or cemeteries'. A similar statute prohibited 'dances or lascivious games'.

National heroes such as William Wallace and King Robert the Bruce were both known to be competent wrestlers. Their extraordinary physical as well as mental superiority fascinated James I. On hearing of a very old noble woman of the Erskine family who was extremely knowledgeable on such matters, he decided to visit her. She occupied the Castle of Kinnoul and had known the greatest men in the land. She was very well informed about Wallace and Bruce so when King James interviewed her at length, the lady, now blind, was asked many questions so James could build up a physical comparison of the two heroes.

'Robert,' she responded, 'was a man beautiful and of fine appearance. His strength was so great that he could easily have overcome any mortal man of his time, save one – Sir William Wallace! But in so far as he excelled other men, he was excelled by Wallace, both in stature and in bodily strength; for, in wrestling, Wallace could have overthrown two such men as Robert. And he was comely as well as strong, and full of the beauty of wisdom.'

There are a great many early references to wrestling in Scotland, particularly in the backhold style. This style was even more popular in the north English counties of Cumberland and Westmorland, where there were very fine prizes at large tournaments. The English professionals 'invaded' Scottish games with a good deal of success, to such an extent that the backhold style became known on both sides of the border as 'Cumberland and Westmorland' wrestling. Fortunately, the ethnic name was not forgotten

William Wallace's statue in Aberdeen.

Alex Munro, Helmsdale, Sutherland. He accepted the challenges of overseas wrestlers.

and in 1891 Leon Ville in Paris wrote of Scottish backhold wrestling: '...having the appearance of dancing with only three or four attacks'.

Wrestling was included in very early, formalised Highland games. In the Borders, the famous poet James Hogg, the Ettrick Shepherd, and Professor John Wilson (known as 'Christopher North') were both wrestling enthusiasts and, along with Sir Walter Scott, they included backhold wrestling in St Ronan's Games, which have continued for over 180 years. The earliest wrestlers there are mentioned in our descriptions of the Border games (Chapter 2).

Many of Donald Dinnie's 11,000 prizes at Highland games events were won in over 2,000 wrestling matches all over the world. He travelled throughout Britain, America, Canada, New Zealand and South Africa, taking on all comers, especially targeting national champions in various wrestling styles. He was particularly good in back-hold bouts. Scotland had some great wrestlers who excelled in the first golden age of the sport, the decade from around 1898 to 1908, when the Russian Lion, George Hackenschmidt, was supreme and set new standards. Hackenschmidt wrote that Alex Munro and A.A. Cameron were amongst the strongest and best wrestlers he had ever met.

Other great Scottish wrestlers, such as Frank Crozier and the Bain brothers, competed with

Jimmy Esson, Aberdeen.

distinction in genuine international wrestling competition and authentic world championships, such as that won by Jimmy Esson of Aberdeen in 1908. This win made Esson famous in the sporting world and photographs of him appeared in British, French and Russian magazines before the outbreak of the First World War. Notable visiting wrestlers to the games include John Lemm of Switzerland; Maurice Deriaz of France; Englishmen Matt and George Steadman, George Louden, Charlie Green, Hexham Clark, Dougie Clark; and John Threlfal of Garstang.

Japanese wrestlers Tarro Miyake, Eida and Kanaya arrived on the 1905 Highland games circuit with mixed results. They were joined by a fourth at Mintlaw Games. Local farmer John V.

Frank Crozier was of Jamaican extraction and trained at the Govan Police Gym. He wrestled at Highland games but became famous when he won the World's Middleweight Championship in freestyle wrestling. He was officially recognised as being the first black champion in this sport.

Gray of Old Don accepted their challenge. The ju-jitsu (now judo) champion was not at all intimidated by Gray's 16 stone (224lb, over 100kg) muscular physique, indicating that 'the bigger they are, the harder they fall'. A reporter present at the games said that Gray grabbed the Japanese 'like a dog with a ferret' and within 30 seconds Gray

had his squirming opponent well and truly pinned.

Fine Scottish Highland games wrestlers who were active around 100 years ago include James Scott of Canonbie and heavies such as Duncan C. Ross, Alex Finnie, John McKenzie, James Morrison, G.M. Ross, Jock Nicolson, Jack Parr of Aberdeen,

John Lemm, Swiss mountain guide.

Jimmy 'Clogger' Currie and George Johnstone, to name but a few. The latter two were, at various times, considered Scotland's best wrestlers. From the late 1920s and early 1930s, Jim Anderson and George Clark were top traditional heavies and also successful professional wrestlers.

Nowadays, very few traditional heavies enter wrestling events, for reasons that will be explained. In recent times, heavyweight Rab McNamara of East Kilbride has been unbeaten for many years and outside the games he has won two European championships and ten world championships. 'Big Rab' also beat a Japanese Sumo wrestler, Shuei Mainoumi, rated fifth in the world, who toured different countries, challenging national champions in televised bouts. In a three-fall bout, Rab took the first throw in four seconds and the other two in about the same amount of time. The wrestling lasted a total of 15 seconds, excluding rests between falls.

Jim Anderson, Dundee.

Glasgow's Rab Clark is another great technical backhold wrestler, who has won world titles in the lighter weight classes. Wullie Baxter, acknowledged as the world authority on ethnic wrestling, has praised Rab Clark as 'technically the best backhold wrestler of the 20th century'. Wullie is the most active organiser of wrestling events at Highland games at home and abroad. His competitions are usually steeped in tradition. A piper plays a gathering call and the competitors, wherever they are, make their way to the arena. There, the rules, etiquette and traditions are scrupulously maintained. Regardless of the weather, the hardy contestants give 100 per cent effort.

Unfortunately, wrestling is not as widespread at the games as it was in the past. There are several reasons for this. One is that the traditional heavies seldom enter these events as they would be competing against specialists and they fear injuries when participating in this hotly contested

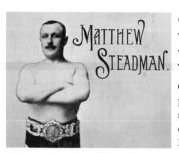

Matt was a favourite English wrestler at Scottish Highland games.

combat sport. Likewise, backhold wrestlers are not happy because of what they call 'political repression'. Their fearless spokesman said:

Governments of all political persuasions use international sporting success to justify or distract from government policies. Local and national governments also exacerbate the threat to indigenous sports because of neglect. In many countries (and Scotland is a good example), all traditional sports are officially distained in the quests for the poisoned chalice of Olympic success.

Traditional wrestling is worthy of inclusion in every Highland games. It would be sad to see it follow in the way of other sports now extinct from our programmes. I personally believe that the future of the sport is assured, as long as there are enthusiasts like Wullie Baxter to lend a guiding hand, but the trouble is that there are not too many 'bonny fechters' like him around.

George Steadman, (1846–1904) won many prizes at Highland games.

Rab Clark of Glasgow is one of Scotland's best ever wrestlers.

THE WORLD HISTORY OF HIGHLAND GAMES

CHAPTER TWENTY ONE

The Heavy Events

Putting the stone is one of the oldest sporting strength events. It requires only a suitable stone from a field or river, a mark at the throwing point and markers to show where the stone lands. Putting the stone is not exclusive to Scotland but it is widely recognised as an ancient traditional Scottish sport. Until metrification throughout Britain, the common measure of weight was 14lb (1 stone). For all weighing of goods, a stone was standardised as 14lb, so this is what was used in the putt. At Braemar in particular there has been, and still is, a standing putt of 28lb (2 stones) in weight. It is believed that the weight of 16lb was used only for competition after a plentiful supply of shots (ie cannon balls) became available from Highland battle fields. To ensure uniformity, the weight of 16lb became recognised as the standard weight for putting. River stones continued to be used at traditional professional games in preference to iron shots, but it is accepted that the standard weight is 16lb. There

Bill Anderson putting the stone. Doug Fales, Canada.

was also a Scottish measure of 22lb, but that died out as a standard domestic and agricultural measure and now we find a lack of uniformity. Putting stones now usually vary between 22lb and 24lb. In Europe, the 10kg weight of stone remains the most common (this is 22lb, happily the traditional weight).

In bygone days, not all throwers were 'heavies'. Some smaller and lighter men excelled in putting the stone and could usually hold their own except against larger champions. Charles McLean was only 5 feet 9 inches in height and weighed 12½ stone (168lb, 76.3kg). McLean was very strong for his size and also won many prizes for caber tossing. One of the good overseas throwers at Highland games was John D. McPherson of Canada. He was of similar weight to Charlie McLean and his putting performances were also on a par.

McLean's put of 45 feet 10 inches with the 16lb at Aboyne beat Donald Dinnie's 30-year-long Aboyne record. Of course, when using a 22lb stone, the heavier men could surpass those lighter, and A.A. Cameron's put of 39 feet 5 inches at Aboyne surpassed all his rivals' puts until that time. Armchair experts as late as 1930 said that it would never be beaten. It is always dangerous to make such suggestions and of course the 'prophets' were proved wrong.

We use the Aboyne records for comparison, as Aboyne has long used the same weights on its very level Green of Charleston. In addition, it always has experienced judges and keeps meticulous records.

This event developed from a simple standing put behind the trig, followed by a shift or hop across the designated throwing area. America's great thrower, Parry O'Brian, improved on this by standing at the rear of the area with his back towards the trig. He then moved at speed towards the trig and turned his upper body vigorously as he extended for the delivery of the stone. The best stone putter ever seen at Highland games was Brian (Barney) Oldfield, who competed at numerous games in America and broke heavy and light stone records at Braemar in 1973, when he put the 16lb stone a distance of 63 feet 2 inches – a record that has never been broken to this day. At 6 feet 5 inches tall and 19 stone (266lb) in weight, he was a very fine figure of a man. He introduced a new style of putting that has been copied throughout the world and used by all the top throwers. In the Oldfield style, the whole body is rotated in a spinning movement as the thrower moves across the area to gather great momentum before finishing the putt. It has never been adequately publicised that he practised and introduced this technique after studying Scottish athletes throwing the 28lb weight at Santa Rosa, California.

Oldfield said: 'The Santa Rosa Games were great, especially when the Scottish athletes came over and started showing us the ropes. I was a track and field guy and I learned my rotational technique from the Scotties.' As far as I know, track-and-field historians have never recorded this important development's link with Highland games.

In the new millennium, the best stone putting at world heavy events championships was 60 feet, by Petur Gudmundsson, the Icelandic champion and contender at two Olympic games. He put 60 feet in the rotational style, a standing put of 50 feet 6 inches with a 21lb stone, and over 40 feet 3 inches with a 26lb stone.

Throwing Weights for Distance

Throwing the 28lb and 56lb weights for distance are popular events and often show very different results, in spite of the fact that they are the same type of throws. In throwing the 28lb weight, a thrower with good technique is a joy to behold. The nimble footwork, quick turns and final, very dynamic, effort combine to show us poetry in motion. The whirl of the kilt in this event gives photographers some of the best sporting images ever seen.

Throwing the 56lb requires tremendous strength and heavier men have an advantage, but co-ordination is also very important. If the thrower is not careful, the acceleration and velocity transferred to the weight can take on a life of its own. This can upset the thrower's technique and very often 'foul' (disallowed) throws are registered because the athlete stepped beyond the limits of the throwing area.

Bruce Aitken throwing a 28lb weight.

THE WORLD HISTORY OF HIGHLAND GAMES

Originally, putting the stone and throwing the weights for distance were all done in the standing style. Some latitude was allowed in weight-throwing in the late 1890s and throwers were not disqualified if there were some foot movements. The man responsible for introducing the rotational style of weight-throwing was Alexander Cheyne of Monlettie, in the Buchan area of north-east Scotland. At the start of his career, in post-First World War years, he used the pendulum swing (like everybody else in those days) but he followed through vigorously, bringing his rear foot up the trig as he threw. This was first seen at New Byth Highland Games, in Aberdeenshire. This was copied by others and before long, in the 1920s, A.W. Campbell developed this quarter-turn of the body into a half-turn and as others caught up, so he moved on and did a full turn, throwing a distance of 25 feet with a solid block of 56lb, without any chain attached. He and his colleagues went on from there, doing one and a half turns in 7.5 feet and a double turn in 9 feet. The well-known

28lb weight for distance. Doug Fales, Canada.

athlete and reporter on Highland games, John J. Miller, wrote:

> Archie Campbell has the most perfect style of weight throwing I ever saw. If A.A. Cameron had his style and finish he could, with his superior strength, easily make records of 40 feet with 56 and 70 feet with 28lb. Campbell the innovator lived to see standards soar. He wrote 'I had never seen more than 23 feet being thrown with a block 56lb but 23 feet would not win a prize at a Sunday school picnic with 56lb. now.'

Jim Maitland threw the 56lb weight 36 feet 4 inches and years later, in the 1930s, George Clark went on to exceed this. For some time, Francis Brebner was the best Scottish thrower in this event and Geoff Capes was England's best. In world-class events there have been throws over 90 feet with the 28lb weight.

The world records at the time of writing are: 28lb, 94 feet 6.5 inches by Matt Sandford; and 56lb, 49 feet 8 inches by Eric Frasure. These, of course, are with manufactured throwing weights with handle and chain, the length overall being a maximum of 18 feet.

Although great strength is a tremendous advantage and must be acquired, good technique is also essential in order to excel in these sports. Many would-be throwers simply try to duplicate the positions used by the champions and try to copy their movements. There is nothing wrong with this but there are some fundamental factors that need to be addressed. Good timing is a factor not generally emphasised and many performances would be greatly improved if the final, explosive effort can be timed to perfection. This applies to all throws.

The most productive sequence of movement is very logical and easy to understand but it is more difficult to master. The large strong muscles must be used first in order to overcome inertia without losing good body positions. Then, when these muscles are moving into their inner range (ie their shortest length) for maximum effort, the smaller and faster muscle groups (eg shoulders, arms and calves) are strongly activated. The big muscle groups are in the centre of the body and the last joints to be extended (eg the ankles and the wrists in the put) are at the body's extremities. So it can be seen that the movement flows outwards from the centre of the body.

Another thing that must be understood, and does not contradict the above in any way, is that *power comes from the ground*. The turns are for acceleration and to create forward momentum, so throwers should keep their feet near the ground rather than leap into the air as they turn. In the final effort the feet must drive into the ground, and the whole body will extend dynamically to produce a forward and upward trajectory of the implement. Good, well-coached throwers demonstrate all these points.

Keith Tice tossing the caber. Doug Fales, Canada.

Tossing the Caber

Caber tossing is one of the most distinctive Scottish sports. It requires considerable athletic ability, with balance, co-ordination and, naturally, strength being high on the list of physical requirements. Although generally accepted as the most popular and spectacular in the heavies' battery of tests, it has not always been included in all Highland games. In the coastal areas of the North East, where trees were once in short supply, several important games did not feature the big stick. The main reasons given for this are not only the lack of suitable cabers but also elements of safety.

Cabers vary enormously in size and while it is easy to ascertain the length of cabers, the facilities to weigh a caber are not generally available at Highland games. The result is that the weight is often exaggerated. The tales of long cabers weighing 200 weight (224lb; 102kg) or more are not to be believed.

Cabers of 16–18 feet can be turned by most modern Highland games athletes of good standing, and it helps if there is a good taper. If the top end of the caber is thick and the bottom end thin, the caber has a high centre of gravity and will turn easier than a caber that is thick all the way down. There is a simple formula to work out the suitability of cabers for various levels of competition but this is not widely used.

The average person has little knowledge of what size of caber it is possible to toss. In the mid-1970s I arranged for the gift of a caber to be sent to the Caledonian Club of San Francisco, as some time over the years caber tossing had been dropped from its schedule. We went to a forest and selected a very long, straight and trimmed tree and asked that 10 feet be cut from the top end of the tree and the next 20 feet be the caber to be sent to America. The instructions were written to pass to the woodsmen, who were to strip the bark from the thin end of the caber before sending it to the American address given.

I received a very strange message from California sent by Charlie Simpson, a Highland policeman and fine heavy athlete, who had gone to give an exhibition of throwing events. In discussing it with him afterwards, it transpired

THE WORLD HISTORY OF HIGHLAND GAMES

A high throw is necessary to turn the caber. Hans Lolkema (Netherlands) shows how it is done.

that the woodsmen had measured from the wrong end of the tree. They cut the caber from the thickest (lower) end of the tree, which was absolutely impossible to turn. The first Californians to see the caber argued about whether it was humanly possible for even a Highlander to toss this gigantic log.

Unlike the other Scottish throws, cabers are not tossed for distance. Throws are judged by how *straight* they are thrown. The thrower tries to turn the caber 'head over heels' in a perfectly straight line, the so-called 'clock face' method of judging. Assistants set the caber upright with the smaller end on the ground. The judge stands behind the caber tosser who, unassisted, lifts the caber so that it rests on his shoulder and the side of his neck. When balanced, he runs, gathering speed, then stops suddenly and as the caber comes off his shoulder and neck, he gives it a huge heave to toss it on to its heavy end and overturn it directly away from the line of throw. The judge should keep directly aligned with the athlete, who, having tossed the caber, remains in the same place. If the end of the caber, the athlete and the judge are all directly in line, it is a perfect throw, which may be equalled but cannot be beaten. This is where the 'clock face' term comes in. The perfect throw is 12 o'clock. If the caber reached vertical and fell directly to the left that would be rated as 9 o'clock. If the same to the right it would be 3 o'clock. In a good competition, the best throws would be nearly straight and most international judges give scores of 11 o'clock (slightly left) or half-past one (slightly more to the right). Some of the old school of Scottish judges believe it to be more accurate to score in minutes only, so instead of saying 9 o'clock they would say quarter to twelve. They believe that this is more accurate and easier to assess.

Occasionally a thrower will 'slew' the small end of the caber, making it go a bit round rather than over the perpendicular. This is called a 'fifer' and it is not permitted by competent judges.

The best caber tossers over the ages have been, in chronological order: John Tait, Donald Dinnie, A.A. Cameron, Jock Nicholson, Sergeant Major Starkey, Ed Anderson, George Clark, Bill Anderson and Grant Anderson. The international throwers then came along and Jim McGoldrick (USA) was supreme and may have been the best ever. Grant Anderson is another contender for that honour. Most recently, Doug MacDonald (Canada) has been the best in the world. Of the current crop, Gregor Edmunds (Scotland) is top, especially if it is a very large caber. With a long skinny caber, Carl Braun was hard to beat during the 1990s.

Throwing the Hammer

Throwing the hammer was originally done with an ordinary, thick-handled sledge hammer of about 3-feet length. Competitors standing sideways to the trig would swing the hammer backwards and forwards before releasing it. This was called a pendulum swing. Donald Dinnie suffered arm injuries throughout his career and after the first of these he stood with his back towards the stop-board and, using his uninjured arm only, swung the hammer in a full circle round his head, thus introducing the 'round the head' type of hammer throwing. Of course, two hands were used after recovering from his injury.

There have been many good hammer throwers who were quite light yet did some good throws. Finlay R. Cramb (12 stone, 168lb, 167½kg) and John McKenzie (13 stone 7lb, 182lb, 83kg) are good examples.

The first great hammer thrower of the mid 1920s was Jim Maitland of Deskford, Cullen, who did 121 feet 3 inches at Aboyne in 1926.

Grant Anderson throwing the hammer.
Doug Fales, Canada.

Gordon Martin of Scotland throwing the hammer at the Fergus Games.

Sean Betz, World Champion 2008, releasing the hammer.

The Aboyne hammer actually weighed 16½ lb and A.A. Cameron's best with this same hammer, on the same ground, was 117 feet 6 inches.

Around 1928–29, A.W. Campbell, the very knowledgeable Buchan farmer, advocated spiked boots with 2-inch heels for hammer throwing, but soon after, as recorded elsewhere in this book, the first to use 'bayonet'-type spikes projecting from the front of his boots was A.J. Stuart of Glenlivet.

Although those from other countries now often beat Scottish athletes, the Scots continue to hold their own in throwing the hammer. Bill Anderson, Grant Anderson, Stephen King and Bruce Aitken have all broken world records. Alistair Gunn and the two Gordons, Forbes and Martin, have been fine hammer throwers at significantly lighter body weights than those previously mentioned. Bruce Aiken of Auchenblae holds the 16lb world record with 156 feet 8½ inches.

Matt Sandford of Melbourne, Australia, broke the Scots' dominance in 1998 by throwing a 22lb hammer a distance of 129 feet 10½ inches. The American records are: 16lb – 150 feet 9 inches by Ryan Vierra; and 22lb – 124 feet 7½ inches by Eric Frasure.

Throwing 56lb for Height

Throwing a 56lb weight for height is an ancient Scottish traditional strength sport. I had been inclined to think that because it requires special equipment it would be a fairly modern innovation,

Throwing the 56lb weight for height.
Doug Fales, Canada.

but this is not the case. References have been found in sporting papers and books dating back to Napoleonic times and there is no doubt that it existed before then.

Sometimes called 'weight over bar', when properly presented it is definitely one of the most spectacular and popular Highland games events.

It was an ancient farming sport and as is so often the case, it is in North East Scotland that we find early evidence of an expert in such throwing events. It was originally practised informally throwing a 56lb weight over branches of trees and in farmyards where an object, such as a barrel top, was suspended from the pulley of hay lofts and gradually raised, as is done today, to eliminate contestants until only the winner is left.

Robert Barclay Allardice (1779–1854) was widely known as Captain Barclay. His father was a Member of Parliament; the family had noble titles and owned the large Ury House and estate that can still be seen on the outskirts of Stonehaven.

A sporting magazine in 1807 reported that Barclay did some strongman feat and then gave a demonstration of throwing a 56lb weight for distance and height. It is the *earliest documented account* which I have found that gives a weight for height thrower's name and measurements of the throw.

In a standing, straight-arm pendulum swing, he sent the weight 25 feet in distance and then threw the 56lb 15 feet high. It was a very fine performance. Interestingly, it is mentioned that 'he threw without turning, in true Scottish style'. Captain Barclay was probably the best known sporting officer and gentleman of the Regency period (1811–20). He trained several leading bare-knuckle fighters, including Tom Cribb for his historic match against Molineux. The Captain was also famous for his pedestrian feats, including walking 1,000 miles in 1,000 hours for 1,000 guineas. He was described as 'one of the strongest men of his time'.

When Scotland's Sports Hall of Fame was opened at the National Museum of Scotland in 2002, Captain Barclay was one of the first inductees. *Boxiana* by Pierce Egan, published 1813, the book most coveted by boxing collectors, was dedicated to Barclay, the peer of British sportsmen.

The best exponents in living memory of throwing the 56lb weight for height event were, in chronological order: Ed Anderson; George Clark; Henry Gray; Grant Anderson (the first to exceed 16 feet); Bill Kazmeier of the USA; Mark Higgins of England; Ben Plucknet of the USA

(18 feet 3½ inches); Manfred Hoeberl of Austria; and jovial Wout Zjilstra of the Netherlands, whose record at 18 feet 8.4 inches. This was finally exceeded by Mike Zolkiewicz, USA, who achieved 18 feet 9 inches. Most of these are very tall and heavy men. Currently, Kyrylo Chuprynin of the Ukraine has been breaking Highland games records in Scotland.

In the last few years, Americans have been throwing with a spin but this is officially outlawed in Scotland, Canada, Australia, Germany, Holland and France. Throws with spinning are also not allowed in the world championships.

Captain Robert Barclay from Hercules, a Russian magazine, c.1913.

Popular Wout Zjilstra of Freisland, the Netherlands, one of the world's best ever throwers in 'weight over bar'.

Bill Kazmeier at Braemar.

THE WORLD HISTORY OF HIGHLAND GAMES

CHAPTER TWENTY TWO

Heavies Who Made History

The Taits

The Tait family have had a long history in Scotland. In 1527, George Tait was captain of Brodick Castle on the island of Arran when it was besieged. He was murdered in a revenge killing in 1528. Fortunately, through the ages, later Taits channelled their aggression and energies into a variety of sports at Highland games. Over 150 years ago, a shepherd, John Tait of Glendoch, Crawfordjohn in Lanarkshire, had seven sons. Three of these sons became Highland games champions: John, born in 1831; Gavin, born in 1834; and William, born in 1841. These men were 6 feet in height and had fine physiques.

*John Tait
1831–96.*

John, the oldest of the trio mentioned above, became the Scottish Champion by virtue of his wins against all comers from the Northern Meeting in Inverness to the Glasgow Gathering at College Green. He became head keeper to the Duke of Hamilton, serving him for 30 years, and in 1878, when the Prince of Wales (later King Edward) visited the estate, John masterminded the daily hunts. On the second day, in four hours of hunting, the prince and nine others bagged 968 rabbits, 134 pheasants, 65 hares, 14 woodcocks, one partridge, five deer and seven sundries. The bag established a record, which was correctly documented and recorded. It also reports that 'the Prince complimented Mr Tait on the splendid show of game'.

John trained William in heavy events in order to become a full-time athlete, and when William was good enough, John retired instead of competing against his younger brother for the title. He did, however, come out of retirement to oppose the American, Thomas Rice (also known as Thomas Jarmey) in hammer throwing (see Chapter 7).

William first became proficient in running and jumping and then in heavy events. He was an all-round champion until 1860, his spikes caught on a top bar when he was hurdling. He had a bad fall and a broken leg. The badly set bone left one leg one-and-a-half inches shorter than the other. Thereafter, he could only do heavy events but was badly handicapped. He was the Scottish heavy champion in 1855–56, before Dinnie came on the scene.

In 1870, William Tait competed at Aboyne Highland Games, generally agreed by athletes as being the best games, a long-held opinion lasting until the 1960s and possibly beyond. William placed third in putting the 16lb stone, beating the noted John McHardy into fourth place. Although the great Donald Dinnie was not present that year, there was a good line-up of heavies including John George, who won the light and heavy stones events, heavy hammer and tossing the caber. Other competitors included William Bremner, Charles McHardy, J.C. McHardy, John Moir, Alex Grant, George Mearns and W. McCombie Smith, who managed a third in the light hammer. When his days as a full-time athlete were over, William again followed in John's footsteps, becoming gamekeeper to the Duke of Hamilton. William died at Malvern Wells, Worcestershire, at the age of 58.

At 5 feet 11 inches, Gavin was the

*Gavin Tait
1834–1921.*

shortest of the brothers and as his right hand was maimed early in life, he confined his efforts to running, hurdling and jumping. In the early 1860s he was virtually unrivalled, winning the sprint, longer distance, hurdles and long jump for two years in succession at Inverness and so, like his two brothers, he was barred at that venue, and likewise at other games. He won at Glasgow, Edinburgh, Bridge of Allan and Dunkeld, then extended his activities to England and was one of the first Scots to win major athletic events, including those at the Crystal Palace and the Royal Oak Running Ground at Manchester. The Prime Minister of the time, Benjamin Disraeli, presented him with one of his prizes.

For a while, Gavin lived in England, but he returned to Scotland in the early 1880s. All the Tait medals, owned by Gavin, were displayed at the Ratloch Hotel in Larkhall. He emigrated to Canada and in 1921 a newspaper reported his death at Kelvingrove, Blacknook, Nova Scotia,

William Tait 1841–99 succeeded his brother John as Scotland's champion heavy of 1854–55.

aged 82. The Tait family records indicate that Gavin was born in 1834, so there are some anomalies. Kathy McSkimming, great-granddaughter of William, provided much of this information. She told me that Gavin's granddaughter, Catherine Tait, was a successful Highland dancer who won many awards, including the World Championship at the age of 17. She said this was in 1942 when the competition was held at the Usher Hall in Edinburgh, before the championships were hosted at Cowal.

William Tait's son competed at local Highland games until one day when unyoking a horse, a heavy load fell on his leg and the athlete's limb broke in several places.

In the fourth generation of sporting Taits there was a professional sprinter who won the famous Powerhall New Year sprint and later he became a fine boxer. William Tait's grandson, a farmer in Loanhead, Midlothian, said that, 'present day descendents of this famous family are still deeply and actively interested in sport'.

CHAPTER TWENTY THREE

Donald Dinnie

Donald Dinnie was the first sporting superstar. He gained this status by being a superb all-rounder in light and heavy sports alike, issuing wrestling challenges open to all comers, regardless of weight, and very seldom did he lose.

Donald had considerable business acumen and was the first athlete to benefit from sponsorship and endorsements on a large scale as he travelled to the furthest parts of the world for nearly 50 years (in the days when ships were still the means of transport for long-distance journeys). On land, he would ride a horse from town to town and transport his equipment with horse-drawn carriages. His career was much longer than all others in this sphere, being a professional from his earliest competitions at the age of 15. He was still giving strongman shows and competing with veterans, now called 'masters', 50 years later. In Scotland he competed in as many as possible of the 200 Highland games during the summer, entering between seven and 10 disciplines at each games, except in the north-east games, during which he could add many more disciplines to his list by entering local competitions in the mornings and open events in the afternoons. Later, adding on hundreds of overseas events, he won an incredible 11,000 competitions and a treasure trove of medals and trophies. Many of these were for records set in the individual disciplines. He won, for example, some 2,000 hammer throwing competitions and 2,000 wrestling matches.

In the many hundreds of photographs in newspapers and magazines, not one shows Donald wearing trousers. He always wore a kilt, even on horseback – he was a *very* proud Scot.

Above: *Dinnie. A rare photo of him wearing a belt of medals, now in the museum in Aberdeen with other fine Dinnie memorabilia.*
Below: *Dinnie with 'Medalic' Breastplate.*
Bottom left: *This image was on the front page of* Health and Strength *magazine over 100 years ago.*

Donald was born in 1837 at Aboyne in the north-east of Scotland. His father was a highly intelligent master-builder and stone mason, and was comparatively well off. He was also a poet, naturalist, Latin scholar and writer of at least five books. It is understood that many of his beautiful historical artefacts were gifted to the National Museum of Scotland in Edinburgh. In such an environment, he had a fine start in life. Donald inherited some of his father's skills and qualities, being able to read and write Latin, and he earned a fortune, in his

Dinnie with medals on plaid and cross-belt.

case from Highland games and wrestling. He was very careful with money, and his services did not come cheap.

Once, when the Royal party arrived late at Braemar and the caber tossing had already finished, he refused to toss the caber again unless he was paid two pounds (a week's wages in those days). 'I pay my taxes,' he said. It was pointed out that it was an honour to perform for the Prince of Wales (later King Edward). Dinnie's response was: 'I dinna gie a damn. I pay my taxes, and I'll tak'nae less'. The other athletes tried and failed, for the programme was well advanced and they were becoming fatigued. Finally, Donald rushed forward and turned it with ease to resounding applause.

The Prince of Wales was very interested. 'Who is that winning all the prizes?' he asked. An official replied 'Sir, it is Donald Dinnie of

Donald Dinnie 1837–1916. An original image by David Webster.

Deeside.' 'Deesidedly!' punned the Prince.

But did Donald get his money? We will never know.

Despite this parsimonious outlook, when he earned a large income overseas, Donald regularly sent money back to his relatives in Scotland. Contrary to some reports, he did not die a pauper, but he did lose a lot of his investments in a financial crash in Australia, where he lived and worked for many years. At Highland games, he would compete in as many events as possible. The heavy events, including wrestling, were his priority, followed by the high jump, pole vault, sprints and even hurdles.

He won around 500 running and hurdling events. He also won some prizes for shooting and quoiting, which were included in various 19th-century Highland games. Sometimes, in his first years at the games, he would compete in Highland dancing. His son Cuthbert also competed and won prizes for dancing while his youngest daughter, Eva, performed Highland dancing on the professional stage. Another of his sons, Edwin (b. 1877 in Aberdeen), was a professional strongman and joined Donald for a series of Highland games in South Africa in 1897. He inherited a significant number of his father's awards, including one of his breast-plates of medals.

From a historical perspective, the following dates are important.

In 1853, Donald had his first professional back-hold wrestling match at a feeing market in Kincardine O'Neil and competed at Fordoun Games, winning in the hammer, stone, caber, sprint and high jump events. He was only 15 years old. From 1858 to 1868, he worked as a stone mason and took three or four months off to compete on the games circuit. In 1867, he introduced the round-the-head style of hammer throwing and the use of a longer hammer, although the latter was not widely adopted until 1890.

During 1868 Dinnie made his best put: 49 feet 6 inches with a 16lb 2-oz stone at Lord Charles Kerr's bowling green in Kinoull, Perthshire. Soon after this, while horse-riding at speed, his steed passed too closely to a gate post and Dinnie's left knee was badly injured.

The Caledonian Club of New York invited him to the USA in 1870. He completed another tour of the USA and Canada in 1872, this time with James Fleming, which was fortunate as Dinnie sustained a severe injury to his hand and shoulder while pole-vaulting at Buffalo Games. This greatly impeded him in other events, but Fleming successfully upheld Scotland's honours much of the time. Donald Dinnie's third and final tour of these countries was in 1882–83, and he went on to New Zealand in December 1883 and to Tasmania and Australia in March 1884.

Dinnie's globetrotting lifestyle, his open challenges in various parts of the world and his charisma made him a sporting legend. When converted to present-day public price indices, his total earnings would have totalled more than one million pounds.

He is still remembered with admiration and his biography was published in 1999. Donald was inducted into the Scottish Sports Hall of Fame and in 2004 his memory was honoured at the World Highland Games Championship in New Hampstead, USA, when the current champions wore his likeness with pride. May he never be forgotten.

Left: *Dinnie c.1884. Right, Dinnie at Rothienorman Games, 1905. Design by Duncan W.D. Ford, 1912.*

George H. Johnstone with Scottish Championship belt, now in the West Highland Museum at Fort William.

Kenneth McRae.

THE WORLD HISTORY OF HIGHLAND GAMES

CHAPTER TWENTY FOUR

The Heavy Brigade

George Davidson, born in 1854 in Drumoak, a small village in Kincardine O'Neil, was quite a shy person in daily life but was a versatile athlete and entertainer and assumed an air of confidence and competence in the games arena, circus ring and stage performances. As a teenager, he competed at local games and in his 20s he moved further from home to compete against Donald Dinnie, Kenneth McRae and other first-class athletes.

George Davidson, born Drumoak, 1854.

A professional strongman act inspired him and he decided that he was more suited to such an activity. He trained hard with standard weights used on the farm for weighing crops and soon, with the exception of Donald Dinnie, he became the best weightlifter in Scotland. He was the best in Britain in his speciality of repetition lifting of block 56lb weights. Dinnie and Davidson devised a strength act and successfully toured all over Britain during the winter season, during which no Highland games took place. However, there was another Highland games athlete who could beat George Davidson, and who was almost as strong.

George Hardy Johnstone was born in 1864 in Portlethan, a small fishing village in Kincardine-shire near Aberdeen. He was 6 feet 1 inch in height and 15 stone (210lb, 95kg) in weight in his mid-20s but added some 10 kg as his career progressed. At the age of 16, he won a long-distance race but almost immediately moved on to heavy events at Banchory Games. George Davidson beat him easily in all events but in 1887 he reversed the situation at the Newcastle Exhibition with a convincing win over Davidson.

He was a powerful man and at one time, like Davidson, he joined Donald Dinnie in a strongman act. Johnstone was champion after Dinnie, Davidson and McRae. James Morrison was his main opponent and the two were very equal. George was the best heavy in the last decade of the 19th century but was beaten by Morrison in 1901. Johnstone regained the Scottish championship in 1902 but it was his last national title.

An intelligent and likeable man, George Johnstone made friends wherever he went. Although he was the best in that era, he was always unassuming and his throwing was described as being 'artistic', especially in hammer-throwing, in which he excelled. He had a strong, sturdy physique and for several years he was the best Scottish wrestler. In throwing the hammer, he was probably the first thrower to bring one foot out of its position at the end of his third turn, thus giving extra impetus in the release. He held the world record with a throw of 120 feet. On one occasion, his foot went above but not over or on the trig. He glowered at the judge, who had given him the thumbs-down signal but did not say anything. In his next throw he went as far back as he could behind the stop-board. 'Where are you going, Johnstone?' asked the judge as the athlete prepared to throw. 'I'm nae goin' to be fouled again,' he replied. With that, he gave a mighty throw that sent the hammer yards beyond the marks of his opponent's best throw.

One of the best throwers in the late 1880s was Kenneth McRae (b. 1850 at Beuly, Inverness-shire). He was a farm servant from the age of 8 until 18, then he worked in a whisky distillery.

He started competing in Highland games at 16 but was at his best when he was 30, then being 6 feet 3 inches in height and 15½ stone in weight. He was a fine hammer thrower. He used three, sometimes even four, preliminary swings and having delivered followed through with his right leg. Of course, this was long before blades in front of boots. McRae was Scottish Champion in 1887.

James Morrison, born 7 July 1874 in Drumore, Stirlingshire, had an even better physique than Johnstone, who was 10 years older. A Highland games reporter said Morrison was the closest athlete he had seen to the perfect Greek statue. He would have been amazed to see the athletes of today, who have better physiques than any previous generation as a result of their hard training and superior nutrition. By the turn of the century, there were a great many athletes competing at Highland games all over the country, but Johnstone and Morrison were the most popular of all.

Then along came Cameron, a gentle giant from Lochaber, who beat both these athletes without much effort at all. Alexander Anthony Cameron (also known as A.A. Cameron) had a relatively short reign as king of the heavies but he could beat all the opposition with comparative ease. This was not always the case. He was a very easy-going man and did not train properly, and he would not allow a competition to interrupt hard farm work.

He was a tall, lean, muscular man, who was power personified when he went into action. His records, however, were achieved by sheer strength rather than skill. Experts thought he was too relaxed and that, if he had had the motivation of Charlie McLean or John McKenzie, he would have established records that would have lasted for many years. Alexander Anthony was never upset if things did not go very well for him; he would smile, shrug his shoulders and chew a piece of straw. It was a habit he had acquired on the farm and if he could not find straw, a piece of grass was an acceptable substitute. It became a trademark characteristic. His sister Mary gave me a great deal of information, which was published in my previous book, *Scottish Highland Games*.

A.A. Cameron was also known as Muccomber, the name of his farm. From the turn of the century to the onset of the First World War, he was the outstanding thrower and beat many of Donald Dinnie's records. Other up-and-coming heavies such as John McKenzie and Charlie McLean challenged him in their own specialities, but in overall heavy event scores, Cameron was supreme – and he had an impressive world championship belt to prove it. This belt can still be seen in the Fort William Museum. Recently, I heard that a tune had been written in his honour, and on casually telling Wullie Baxter (the well known wrestling official), he said that his daughter, a talented musician, played such a tune as part of her repertoire. With a little research I found the full, correct name of the tune and a copy of the music. It is

A.A. Cameron 1877–1951 of Spean Bridge.

called 'Sandy Cameron, the Famous Athlete: A Pipe Strathspey'. It is a composition by the famed Scott Skinner, the King of Strathspeys, Scotland's most prolific composer, who was also a piping judge at Highland games. 'Sandy' Cameron's name has lived on for over a century in a fine piece of music played by classic musicians including Seylen Baxter, a professional cello player.

After retiring from the games, A.A. Cameron and his brother became successful sheep farmers. He lived in a famous house, featured in *The Flight of the Heron*, and later opened a hotel. He kept in touch with the Highland games circuit until he died in 1951 at the age of 74.

The Nicolsons

Highland games have had, and still have, an abundance of families of competitors whose cumulative abilities and fame are very significant. The Nicolsons, from the Kyles of Bute, were one such family. The most famous generation was active and successful for 60 years, from 1866 until around 1926.

Their grandfather had originally come from the Isle of Skye and when he migrated to Campbeltown one of his sons was 6 feet 3 inches in height, very tall for that era. Being very athletic as a young man, he annexed many prizes in his favourite events. He moved to Kyles of Bute and farmed at Tighnabruaich, where he married and had nine sons.

Highlanders of the north-east almost automatically become professionals at Highland games, but in the south-west the Nicolsons all started as amateurs and most of them later turned professional. The oldest brother, Neil, was a good all-rounder, high jumping 5 feet 7 inches without a landing pit; triple jumping 44 feet 6 inches; putting 40 feet with 16lb; and throwing the 16lb hammer 100 feet. He was also a competent back-

Sergeant Major Starkey, John Nicolson, Jim Maitland.

hold wrestler and a good sprinter. Next in line was Hugh, who won the 16lb put at Hampden Park in Glasgow in 1901 with a fine 43 feet 2½ inches. His greatest achievement was beating Alexander Anthony Cameron at Thornton in 1904, the only time the champion was beaten that season. Hugh put an 18lb shot 41 feet 9 inches at Alloa and at Dunoon did 47 feet 3 inches with 16lb for a Cowal record. He was also good with the hammers, specifically the amateur wire hammer and professional wooden-shafted hammer, and caber and backhold wrestling.

T.R. Nicolson, born in 1880, was the best international amateur heavy for many years and his hammer-throwing records were unbeaten for several decades. He began competing at the Buteshire Games in 1900, and a reporter in 1904 described Tom as 'the darling of the family, the finest amateur athlete that Scotland has ever produced'. In the 1909 championships, he did a fine 164 feet 8 inches and in 1912 took the title with 162 feet 2½ inches. His best ever was at Rangers sports when he did a genuine 169 feet 8 inches. He was not a one-event man; he also won prizes in the putt and wrestling. However, he was also a keen footballer, an enthusiastic golfer and a local hero on the shinty pitch. Tom was 5 feet 10½ inches in height and 12 stone 10 lb in weight, and was described as being beautifully proportioned.

From 1866 to 1875, unlimited runs were allowed in hammer throwing: in 1876 a 7 feet circle was introduced and in 1877 it became 9 feet. It has been said that John Flanagan introduced the thin wire and handled hammer but Rory McLennan and Thomas Jarmey used a similar implement in the mid-1860s. The professionals stuck with the original wooden-shafted sledge-hammer, but increased the length from 3 feet 6 inches to 4 feet and later to 4 feet 2 inches. For around 20 years in the era of the Nicolsons, not a single Englishman won the British Championships – the Scots and Irish dominated. John Flanagan was the only man in the world ahead of Tom Nicolson.

The Nicolsons were the backbone of the Kyles Athletic Shinty Club. They won the league title a record six times. John was the only brother who did not have a championship medal in the Shinty League Championship.

The war, however, interrupted their sporting careers. Malcolm and Celestine, amongst others, were soldiers and Malcolm, when away from the front line, became a good gymnast and physical training instructor. Celestine died of wounds on service with the Argyll and Sutherland Highlanders.

The youngest Nicolson, Andrew, was a member of the Glasgow police force and, like Tom, was a dedicated amateur, but it was John

(Jock) Nicolson who was best known to followers of the Highland games circuit. John Nicolson was 6 feet 1¼ inches in height and 17 stone in weight, and was, for some time, a member of the Partick police force in Glasgow. His first appearance as a professional was at the Cowal Gathering of 1908 in the local competitions, when he won the 16lb putt with 42 feet 1 inch and hammer with 103 feet 3 inches. Later, he made much better throws and at his best had wins over such greats as McKenzie, Starkey, Morrison, Graham, Cramb and, in their early days, Maitland, Ed Anderson and Clark.

Archie Campbell, a columnist known as 'the Buchan Farmer', wrote of Jock:

> He was champion in the lean years that succeeded the war but his distances with hammer and ball never reached first flight.

Nicolson was never beaten in backhold wrestling at a Highland games and in 1932 he won first prize at Gordon Castle. After a superb bout with George Clark, he had enough wind left to prance around like a schoolboy and indulge in a delightful game of football with a rival's bonnet.

Jock Nicolson was at his best between the end of the First World War and the mid-1920s. He was a judge at Braemar until 1957 and died in 1958. He competed for around 18 years, into the 1930s, and even today his photograph hangs in a Fifeshire pub. The Nicolsons were an extraordinary family of athletes and Jock was simply the best.

John McKenzie of Partick Police

Around 130 years ago, Glasgow police forces began recruiting from the ranks of Highland games. They seemed to have been particularly interested in heavies, including wrestlers and tug o' war pullers, but they also had some great pipers.

Many of Scotland's champions were policemen, particularly in the Govan and Partick precincts. This was not a short-term policy but one which continued for decades.

It was in 1902 that a 6-foot tall, blue-eyed, fair-haired young Highlander from Dingwall joined Partick Police. He was proportionately built at 80kg (187lb, 13 stone 6lb), and was one of the most versatile Scots competing in pre-war Highland games. John

John McKenzie.

McKenzie was born in 1879. He was splendid in light and heavy events, he boxed and wrestled and was one of the few heavies who would mount the dancing platform in open competition and win prizes. He was usually at or near the top of prize lists, but regardless of where he placed he remained genial and ready for a laugh.

This versatility and his very pleasant, outgoing personality made him probably the most popular competitor at Highland games in the first half of the 20th century.

Away from the games, he loved a round of golf, was an enthusiastic motorcyclist and dabbled in photography.

His abilities can be judged by these results in open competition. At Birnam Games in 1911, McKenzie threw a 17lb hammer a distance of 120 feet 10 inches for a new record. Most of the best throwers of that era competed with the same hammer and were well behind his mark. A.A. Cameron's best with this hammer was 113 feet. Pole vaulting was one of his favourites and his best was 11 feet 1 inch at Inverness, and in high jumping he did 5 feet 11 inches.

He was an excellent sprinter of

John McKenzie in full Highland costume.

Powderhall standard but the handicap system and the antics to beat the handicapper were not to his liking.

John McKenzie wrestled well in backhold style and also catch. He recognised that in each of these disciplines there were champions who could beat him, but in a combined heavy and light event competition, the only athlete who could come close to beating him was Walter Knox of Canada. If it was a full programme of seven heavy events and seven jumps, McKenzie would probably come out on top, but it would be close. Unfortunately for McKenzie, 14 event competitions were out of the question.

At the games he would often compete in two events at the same time, rushing from putting the stone to the high jump or from throwing the hammer to the pole vault.

In the same 'rushing here and rushing there' theme, it is known that one day with the aid of his speedy motorbike, he successfully competed in Methil Highland Games and the Police Sports at Kirkcaldy.

During the war, he rose to the rank of Captain and was in the thick of the battles. It was then reported that Captain John McKenzie had been killed in action – naturally upsetting his many fans and fellow competitors. It later transpired that he had been seriously wounded, but he had battled against the odds to make an almost a full recovery. Good natured and sociable, John McKenzie returned to the games circuit after the war, and although

John McKenzie, British all-round champion.

his best days on the greensward were over, he continued to laugh and joke with one and all.

A Turning Point

The First World War was a turning point in the lives of all Europeans of that generation. Everything was changed and would never be the same again. The feelings of grief and revulsion of the horrors of life in the trenches were passed on to the next two generations. The abrupt stoppage of everyday life was felt in all aspects of community life, Highland games included.

The season of 1913 was the last for five years, although quite a few games bravely continued in

A.A. Cameron, advancing in years, and Ed Anderson.

the summer of 1914. The great Strathallan Games were held just a few days before the outbreak of war. There were but a few isolated instances of Scottish gatherings during war years. Many pipers, dancers and athletes died or were seriously injured.

In 1917 there were efforts to raise morale with various sports but the response was mediocre. At one event there was to be a parade in fancy dress from the centre of town to the games field and, in spite of incentives and handsome prizes on offer, only one young girl turned up.

The games circuit did not get back in full swing until 1919. An important part of the proceedings at the various gatherings became a lone piper playing a lament for those who had fallen in battle. Thousands, with heads uncovered as a mark of respect, listened in absolute silence. Many games added a happier measure, adopted to restore the balance. After the lament, a cannon would be fired and then the bells would ring in local churches in a celebration of peace.

Now, a new batch of heavies came to the fore. 'Charlie McLean of Fort William was the don of heavy events', wrote one reporter. In the absence of big men with big throws, this lighter athlete was able to place ahead in overall points over Finnie of Dumfries and Melrose, a policeman from Partick in Glasgow; these two could only beat McLean with the hammers.

James Graham of Blair Drummond was slow in returning to training, he never fully recovered his previous form after being seriously injured in battle. The biggest ray of hope for the future of the heavies was Company Sergeant Major Robert K. Starkey of the Argyll and Sutherland Highlanders. He was born in Cambusburn in Perthshire, the third son of John William Starkey, who had 11 children. Bob worked in a limestone mine before joining Port Glasgow police force as a young man, but on the outbreak of war he immediately joined the Royal Artillery. While stationed at Cattrick Camp, a noted military depot, he became attached to the Welsh Fusiliers and then went to Germany attached to the Argylls. At this time, Bob Starkey was a regular prize winner in army athletics, being a physical training instructor with the Second Army Gymnastic School. Hostilities over, he took leave from his unit in Cologne, Germany, to take part in a few Highland games. Bob was tall, muscular and well proportioned.

Bob Starkey with Sir Iain Colquhoun.

He figured in the prize lists for the next decade.

Starkey did a 118 feet 6 inches throw with the 22lb hammer in 1924 and 74 feet 4 inches with 28lb at Pitlochry in 1925. Other throws were in proportion to these and he was outstanding at backhold wrestling.

On leaving the services, he became a whisky sales representative, his cheerful personality being ideal for such a job. Bob was an advisor for the Highland games scenes in the film *Geordie* and was an accomplished singer of Scots songs. He died at his home, Gateside in Stirling, and was buried at Bannockburn, where the great battle of 1314 took place.

Thornton Highland Games

I had heard some good reports of Thornton Highland Games, particularly from my good friend Al Murray, a noted weightlifter, strongman and the very first sports coach to be appointed by the British government. Al lived in Thornton in Fife and, to be honest, I thought that his enthusiasm was due to local pride and I certainly took with a pinch of salt the attendances which he claimed for this gathering. In fact, he was quite correct. Thornton was indeed one of the greatest of all games, and credit must be given where it is due. Looking back over the years, it seems strange that historians have never accumulated the incredible facts and figures about this gem of a games in the Kingdom of Fife.

Before the First World War, Thornton Games was described as 'the world's premier athletic meeting', and its appeal extended even beyond the confines of the United Kingdom.

Inaugurated in 1852, these games were held annually except during the wars. Delving deep into the origins, I discovered that unlike many other games that were based on the perpetuation of Scottish culture, Thornton Games had humble origins. It all began in 1851 with a light-hearted rivalry between two local worthies whose names have been forgotten with the passing of time. Thornton was little more than a village at that time but there was such great local interest in the exchanges between these two stalwarts that the Provost and Magistrates took a hand, constituted themselves into an organising committee, collected subscriptions and held the first Thornton Games in 1852.

As with the first Braemar gathering, the main item was a race. In this case, it was a 200-yard sprint between the aforesaid worthies, but each contestor had a wooden leg! Although their names are forgotten, they headed the first, rather unpretentious, programme, which rapidly developed into a mammoth Highland games of dignity and importance. The prize list was the key to their success and every great Scottish heavy sought to gain distinction at Lochty Bridge, where the games were held. Top liners such as Donald Dinnie and A.A. Cameron recognised that winning at Thornton gave prestige as well as money enough to fill their sporrans.

Thornton Games of 1913 gives a good indication of the leading lights in pre-war Scotland. In the jumps, entries included Walter Knox of Canada, Bryce W. Scott of Kilmarnock, J. McKenzie of Glasgow, John A. Speedie of Falkirk, J. Beattie of Aberdeen and another Scot, F.R. Cramb. The heavy brigade included A.A. Cameron, Charlie McLean, James Graham of Blair Drummond, John Nicolson and Bob Starkey.

Such talent brought crowds in the tens of thousands. Special train services had to be arranged and every train was packed and over-flowing. It was said that the people needed to be greased to squeeze them into the carriages! In 1913 there were around 50,000 spectators. Organisers today can only dream of having such crowds. In 1914, with war clouds speeding towards them, the crowd was down to 40,000 – still an amazing turnout. In 1919, an absolutely incredible number of 70,000 attended. I believe this is an all-time Scottish record. These are not figures given to me by over-enthusiastic officials – they are from official reports published in newspapers immediately after each of these games.

Edward Anderson, the Dundee Policeman.

George Clark of Fintry Grange competing at Aboyne

Ed Anderson and George Clark frequently competed at Thornton Games.

In the early 1930s, from John o' Groats to the Tweed, there were around 200 Highland games in Scotland. A regular Highland games newspaper correspondent listed the principal meetings of 1931 as Aberfoyle, Aboyne, Argyllshire, Breadalbane, Cowal, Crieff, Dundee Police Games, Inverness, Lanarkshire Police, Lochaber, Pitlochry, Saughton (Edinburgh) and Strathallan. I have listed these alphabetically as it is not known whether the original source tried to list them in order of merit. It is just possible that it was the latter, as two major gatherings, Cowal and Strathallan, were at the top of his list. However, the order of the remainder of the listing would not meet the main criteria in deciding an order of merit. It is also puzzling to note some strange omissions: Braemar is a very obvious example. I raised such topics with former athletes who competed in those days and it is felt that some athletes of the period may have influenced the situation. There was a long-standing attitude of 'inverted snobbery' amongst some Highland games participants who were fond of letting it be known that, as far as they were concerned, the presence of royalty meant little to them. From a sporting competitor's perspective, they preferred Aboyne but this was for reasons other than loyalty. As far as I can gather, the 'Braemar syndrome' was not anything personal against the Royals but very much due to the huge exodus leaving the games field after the Royals' departure, even although competitions were coming to a climax at that time.

Between the First and the Second World Wars, there were very mixed fortunes for Highland games and participants. The significant losses of competitors in every aspect of the games cannot be overlooked. There were marked developments in matters that affected the games, such as better transport and communication, but much worse socioeconomic changes. The drift to the cities was very noticeable in north-east Scotland, the main stronghold of Highland games, not just for heavies. Sport flourished, but the lifestyles of town dwellers were very different and not as healthy as in rural communities. Many sports enthusiasts became fans, but never seriously trained, and there was a new passion for spectating encouraged 'sports' such as greyhound racing with its associated betting. Scotland's love of Highland games, however, proved strong enough to overcome all obstacles, and age-old traditions remained as new champions emerged.

In the late 1920s, Ed Anderson of Dundee drew ahead of Starkey, and there were specialists such as the hammer thrower, Jim Maitland of Deskford. In 1924, Maitland introduced George Clark (1908–87) to the games. Both these men were from farming stock; George having been born and brought up on his father's farm of Fortry Grange in the county of Banff. This was a good era for the games, with many close competitions between Starkey, Maitland, Anderson and Clark. Ed Anderson was a well-respected man. He was a Dundee policeman who would diminish trouble firmly, but in a diplomatic manner rather than with aggression. He gradually rose to the rank of inspector and at every stage of his career he was very much admired by colleagues and public alike. He had a long career at the games, smoothly changing from being a competitor to a judge, officiating at Braemar in 1964 for the last time. He died in April 1966.

Meantime, during this period, a very young George Clark soon began to beat the old-timers in their favourite events. He, too, was a policeman of the old school and as he matured he became Anderson's firm friend. George diversified considerably and did very well as Scottish wrestling heavyweight champion and internationally acclaimed professional wrestler. He travelled extensively in Canada and the USA, taking on the best, and even had a tilt at the World Championship.

From 1929 to 1931, Ed Anderson and George Clark were very evenly matched. In 1931, Ed won at Crieff but George was not present. Clark performed better over the whole season.

In 1932, George Clark had largely taken over from Anderson and Maitland. Although George had a bad car accident in May 1933, he gradually recovered after several weeks' treatment, and decisively replaced Anderson as Scottish champion. Before the 1933 season ended, 'Clarkie', as he was known in the Aberdeen affectionate diminutive, had exceeded many of

The revival of Highland Games.

his personal bests and games records. Even his caber tossing improved to the stage that he could beat Ed, hitherto unbeatable with the big stick. Anderson was still best with the stones but in throwing 28lb and 56lb weights for distance, Clark had no equal. He was the first man to toss the Braemar Challenge caber (weighing around 120 lb and measuring 19 feet 2 inches in height). The sages of the games now bracketed him with A.A. Cameron and Donald Dinnie, declaring George the best heavy ever. He had all the attributes of an international athlete and, indeed, he realised his potential in this respect.

In the 1930s, after Clark and Anderson, the third place was often filled by G.E. Mitchell of Glasgow. Then, another Banffshire athlete, Alistair J. Stuart (often spelled 'Stewart') of Glenlivit, who had started competing in the late 1920s, rose towards the top of the ranking lists in 1933, winning more first places in hammer throwing than any other. This was particularly meritorious as Stuart was only 5 feet 8½ inches in height and 12 stone in weight. Overall, his performances dwarfed all other middleweights, including Jim H. Anderson (Ed's brother), F.R. Cramb and E.F. Bremner.

Many of Stuart's best throws could have gone unrecorded but some fine record-keepers realised that many would find it difficult to believe a man of his stature could do so well. They meticulously noted Stuart's exceptional throws (for that era), including the exact weight of the hammers. In Edinburgh, he threw a 15¾lb hammer 134 feet 5 inches, on this occasion beating George Clark by 11 feet. At Tomintoul, he hurled a 15¾lb hammer 133 feet. They were not recorded as Scottish records as the hammers were not the full 16lb, which was standard over the past three centuries. His all-time best throws are probably his 126 feet 5 inches exhibition throw at Oban

and his 125 feet 8 inches throw at Aboyne, which is totally level and with accurate implements. His 134 feet throw at Edinburgh was slightly downhill so was not accepted as a record.

It was reported that:

> The secret of Stuart's hammer throwing is a puzzle. Allied to a perfect style and delivery is a wonderful speed in swinging. In throwing a light hammer, standing style, he could take on the world and win.

I can throw some light on the situation for the puzzled reporter. Stuart had a 'secret weapon', which I have known about for years and mentioned in countless commentaries.

Based entirely on verbal information from Ronald Webster Snr and supported by Frankie Blair, a light events athlete in the 1930–50 era, I knew that A.J. Stuart was the innovator who introduced short bayonet-like spikes on the front of hammer boots. Recently, after much research, my faith in this theory was vindicated. In an account of the Strathpeffer Jubilee Highland Games, published before the performances mentioned above, I found this gem:

> A.J. Stewart is about 5 feet 9 inches and barely 12 stones; yet he can occasionally beat the best hammer men in Scotland. By means of as contraption of his own – an iron prong in the toe of his boot – his footing is made secure, and by perfect timing and delivery he got a distance of 96 feet with the 22lb hammer.

According to the earlier sources mentioned above, Alistair was tired of being in third place behind his arch rivals, and was conscious that there was a degree of instabilty before delivery, resulting from the momentum generated in his fast, dynamic swing. The 'prongs' (more correctly, 'blades') dug deep into the ground, giving him the necessary stability, which led to much greater distances. Naturally, after a while his arch rivals copied the blades and poor A.J. Stuart was once again beaten by his heavier opponents.

Years later, Alistair Stuart became a warder in Craiginches Prison, Torry, Aberdeen, then he owned and operated two of the best fish-and-chip shops in Aberdeen.

The next great hammer thrower to enter the field was a Ross-shire shopkeeper, J.L. McLellan of Alness (b. 1914). He increased the accepted world record throw to 129 feet 1½ inches and 103 feet 9½ inches with 22lb. George Clark continued his

Jack Hunter (6 feet 6 inches), Alex Thomson (5 feet 10 inches) of Aberdeen Spartan Club and Henry (Sandy) Gray (6 feet 4 inches).

winning ways throughout the 1930s and won overall prizes, although around 1937 he was often challenged by Robert (Bob) Shaw, who won local competitions at Braemar, and was listed as Scottish Champion in 1937.

Most of these men were very quickly in army uniform when the Second World War broke out. Clark must have been one of the first, for I met with him in Huddersfield, Yorkshire, in 1940, where he was given time off his duties with the Signals Regiment to accept a wrestling challenge. During his lengthy career, George Clark wrestled all over Britain and America, meeting world-class professionals, but Highland games always remained his favourite sport.

The war over, Clark, McLennan, Stuart and Shaw all returned to the games and soon they were joined by two massive young men: Henry (Sandy) Gray of Leochel-Cushnie, Alford, and Jack Hunter of Dunecht.

Henry was *at least* 6 feet 4 inches and was incredibly strong; Jack was *at the very least* 6 feet 6 inches. These were two of the most modest men to ever throw at Highland games. Neither carried any excess weight; they were very fine specimens of manhood. Jack Hunter held the Scottish Championship between 1950 and 1952, then in 1953 Ewen Cameron of Lochearnhead took the title.

Henry Gray reached his peak at this time and lifted the famous Inch dumbbell, the Dinnie Stones and the Scottish heavy events title. It was a good time for Henry, a deservedly popular man, who is still judging at Braemar.

At the very same time, across the Atlantic, there was conceived a development that became one of America's best-known Highland games. It would be hard to imagine a more interesting and beautiful setting. It also has a memorable, picturesque name.

Grandfather Mountain Highland Games

Set in beautiful scenery with a mountainous and forest background in MacRae's Meadows near Linville in the Appalachian Mountains, the Grandfather Mountain Highland Games were begun in 1956 by Mrs Agnes MacRae Morton (1897–1982) and Donald Francis MacDonald.

Linville, the nearest population centre, was founded by the McRae family in 1892. There in early 1950s, Mrs McRae Morton, one of the descendants of the founders, saw a newspaper article about the Highland Games. She took this to Donald McDonald of the *Charlotte News* asking if he would help her organise such an event. Donald obtained a copy of the Braemar Highland Games programme and the Grandfather Mountain Games were based on this. Sadly only two heavy events were included, putting the stone and tossing the caber. Social aspects have always been strongly featured with several ceilidhs, a Tartan Ball, and North America. Grandfather Mountain Games are now amongst the best-known in the United States.

They began with a modest programme of piping and dancing, and heavy events were relatively neglected until the early 1970s. The appearance of Bill Anderson in 1978 and the addition of a kilted mile race gave a boost to the proceedings and strengthened the appeal from a marketing point of view.

The cultural programme is another fine asset. These games now attract very large crowds and good American heavies such as Ryan Vierra, Dave Brown, Larry Brock and Mike Polkowski. Peter Gudmundsson, while living in America, also competed there and increased the putting the stone record. Former well-known athletes, including Ed Holcombe and Arnold Pope, judge the events.

Like other Highland games, there are wider cultural implications. Scottish Heritage USA is closely associated with the games. This non-profit organisation is dedicated to the exchange of people and ideas between Scotland and North America.

While plans were progressing in America for the first Grandfather Mountain Games, back in Scotland J.L. McLellan won 100 competitions in one season and finally achieved his ambition to win the Scottish championship. This inspired his young, very athletic neighbour, Alexander (Sandy) Sutherland, who asked McLennan to coach him. Big Jock did indeed train Sandy hard, and lo and behold, Sutherland took McLennan's crown. Some highly motivated newcomers, such as the always personable Jay Scott, Bill Anderson and Yorkshire's Arthur Rowe, then came onto the scene and records soared. These men were very good for Highland games – none better than the mighty Bill Anderson.

Grandfather Mountain, a wonderful setting for one of America's best known Highland Games.

A grand mountain top scene sent many years ago by Hugh Morton.

Scottish Country Dance, Celtic concerts, a parade of the tartans and a Sunday 'Kirkin' o' the Tartans. The Games are conducted as a charitable organisation with proceeds supporting educational scholarships. Like other Highland Games there are wide cultural implications. Scottish Heritage USA is closely associated with the Games and this non-profit organisation is dedicated to the exchange of people and ideas between Scotland

CHAPTER TWENTY FIVE

Icons of Highland Games

In the north-east of Scotland the tradition of Highland gatherings stretches back almost 1,000 years. It is therefore fitting that this corner of Britain should be the birthplace of Donald Dinnie (1837–1916) and Bill Anderson (b. 1937), two of the best known and most respected champions of all time.

Bill Anderson had a long, successful and interesting career that took him around the world, meeting the best athletes of many nations from the mid 1950s until around 1990. In 1959, he took over the Scottish Championship from the charismatic Jay Scott of Inchmurrin, and held the title until 1963, when it was taken over by the Yorkshire blacksmith, Arthur Rowe, a favourite

shot put contender at the 1960 Olympic Games in Rome. Bill and Arthur shared the Scottish title in 1964, starting a series of high-profile clashes of Titans that created great interest in the heavy events.

Bill outlasted Arthur but another great Olympian shot putter, Geoff Capes, was preparing to enter the fray, as was Commonwealth Games weightlifter Grant Anderson. Along with Bill, these men raised standards to new levels.

Bill Anderson won every major title, including five US Open Championships between 1976 and 1980, the Canadian Open Championship in 1977, the World Championship and the World Caber Tossing Championships. He has broken world

Bill Anderson MBE.

records, with his hammer throwing being particularly meritorious. The most remarkable record of all is winning the Scottish Championship 18 times between 1959 and 1987.

His participation at various Caledonian Club of San Francisco games in Santa Rosa earned him a legion of American fans. Bill was still winning championships at 40 years of age and his performances *after* this time exceeded recognised master records. The reason that many of these records have not been recognised is that Scottish handbooks, and many newspapers, only record the distance of *winning* throws. A number of very fine throws by Bill while in his early and mid-40s have been overlooked because, having placed second, they were not listed in the public domain. Many athletes would have protested, but not Bill Anderson. His long-lasting popularity is largely due to his impeccable demeanour. It would be difficult to find a finer sportsman, in the ethical sense. He proved to be a great role model for young people and in his world travels he was a superb ambassador for Scotland. I believe that his best authentic competition throws at over 40 and 50 years old should be ascertained, compared with existing records and then he should be given the credit he is due. The sporting rivalry between Bill Anderson and Arthur Rowe provided some of the best highlights of modern times and gave Highland games some much-needed publicity, dramatically boosting attendances. Now that Bill Anderson's athletic career is over, he continues to judge at major gatherings such as Braemar, and he has been a popular honoured guest at many Highland games worldwide. Bill was the guest of honour at the World Masters Championship of 2006 and World Championships of 2007, tokens of the respect in which he is held by games participants, organisers and the public alike.

From first-hand experience during decades

on the Scottish circuit, in competitions in England, Africa, Sweden, Japan, France and Hawaii, and on American and Australian tours – indeed in every continent of the world – Bill has never been seen to lose his temper, behave badly or act unreliably. He is, and always has been, a quiet, mannerly, gentle man, modest about his sporting fame and now happy in retirement with his wife and family. Bill Anderson passed his knowledge and skills on to his son Craig and his nephew Steve Anderson, both successful professional Highland games athletes (Craig having won the World Caber Tossing Championship in 1997).

Queen Elizabeth II, who over the years has presented many important trophies to Bill at the

Bill Anderson holds the caber.

THE WORLD HISTORY OF HIGHLAND GAMES

Bill Anderson MBE receives his Sports Hall of Fame award from Scotland's Minister of Sport. On the right is famous sports commentator Dougie Donnelly.

famous Braemar Gathering, honoured Bill by making him a Member of the British Empire, a coveted status reserved for those making a significant contribution to the British way of life.

His last major international competition was in Sydney, Australia, in 1988. For 32 years, he competed in approximately 30 competitions each year, performing in between five and seven different heavy events at each Highland games. It is estimated he won well over 5,000 prizes.

In 2007, Bill Anderson MBE was inducted into the Scottish Sports Hall of Fame, which is not just for Highland games but for *all* sports; indeed, Donald Dinnie is the only other games athlete honoured in this way. The ceremony took place at the National Museum of Scotland in Edinburgh, where the Hall of Fame is currently located. It was a fitting tribute to such an outstanding athlete.

During the 1970s, there was an influx of well-known amateur athletes into the professional

Left: *Sir Clement Freud, television personality, and Arthur Rowe with World caber tossing champion's trophy.*

ranks. There seemed to be two main reasons for this. Firstly, the Commonwealth Games were hosted by Scotland in 1970 and many amateurs waited until after this event before turning professional. Secondly, several top amateurs openly expressed disdain for the sporting drug culture which was becoming prevalent in track-and-field athletics, and they were delighted that action was being taken in the professional ranks against drug abuse.

In the late 1960s and early 1970s, as Senior Technical Representative of the Scottish Council of Physical Recreation, and then Division Head of the Scottish Sports Council, I was the most active campaigner against the rapidly spreading use of sporting drugs. Some sporting bodies with which I was closely connected took little notice but in 1970 I took steps that led to the introduction of drug testing and stringent measures with very severe penalties to discourage doping in Highland games. Success would not have been possible without the great support of Charlie Allan, the fine all-round games professional, and Dr George Browning of the Scottish Association of Sports Medicine, of which I was Secretary for some time.

Athletes such as Laurie Bryce, Douglas Edmunds and Grant Anderson very much appreciated drug-testing initiatives and were valued recruits in the professional circuit.

Douglas Edmunds had been Scottish amateur heavy events champion and the first amateur to put the shot over 50 feet, which he did with 51 feet 8 inches on 24 April 1965 in a Glasgow versus Edinburgh universities competition. A very consistent and versatile performer, between 1964 and 1970 he won Scottish National Championships in the discus three times, and was shot put champion five times. He also won two Scottish weightlifting championships and represented Zambia at the World Powerlifting Championships in the USA. He played rugby for Zambia during his three-year stint as a metallurgist in the copper mines.

I first heard of Douglas when Tony Chapman, National Athletics Coach for Scotland, praised Edmunds and McHugh, two incredibly strong schoolboys at St Joseph's School, Dumfries. As a result, I invited them to compete in the Scottish Junior Weightlifting Championship being held in Glasgow. Doug participated in this and won. He was a little less successful when he joined the international group competing in Sweden's 'Gotland Island Games'.

Turning professional, Douglas Edmunds won the world championships in caber tossing on two occasions between 1976 and 1978, and also took

Grant Anderson (b. 1945). Commonwealth Games weightlifting medallist and World Highland Games Champion 1980 and 1982.

the Braemar Championship on two occasions, being one of the few to turn the famous Braemar challenge caber. Douglas was contender for the World Heavy Events Championships in the USA, Africa and Scotland.

Born on 29 April 1944, Douglas grew to a height of 6 feet 2½ inches and went off the scale on most weighing machines, growing even larger over the years. From his earliest days in heavy sports, I have done all I could to encourage and assist him not only in Highland games but also as a strongman official. His son Gregor followed in his footsteps and even exceeded his father's performances.

One of Douglas's long-time friends is Dr Laurie Bryce, 6 feet 1½ inches and 252lb, a public school athletics champion who represented his country at the 1966 Commonwealth Games in Jamaica and again in 1970. While living in Auchtermuchty (it takes a Scot to say it properly!) and Perth, Laurie won many prizes as a Highland games professional before making career moves which first took him overseas and then to England. Fortunately, we had not seen the last of Laurie at the games. In 1995, he returned to throw with distinction in a most enjoyable international Highland games competition for Masters. In true Highland games tradition, he introduced his son Colin to the games circuit, who also became a fine thrower.

Grant Anderson of Dundee (b. 1945) was another amateur who turned professional during the same period. He was a champion weightlifter and a record holder in the 1960s and 1970s. During this time Grant was selected for the Commonwealth Games, winning a bronze medal for Scotland. He adapted his strength and skill to Highland games and became three-times champion of Scotland and placed first-equal with Geoff Capes in two other championships.

Grant finally won the World Championship in Highland games in 1980. He competed in many lands and his quiet but sociable demeanour made him popular with athletes and officials alike. Grant, 6 feet 4 inches and 286lb, was a hard man to beat. He won world championships, world caber championships, broke world records in throwing the 56lb weight for height – with many throws over 16 feet, and did 123 feet 8 inches with the 22lb hammer at Santa Rosa. Unofficially, he broke the world record with the 16lb hammer, throwing 151 feet 11 inches in the summer of 1985 at the Royal Agricultural Show in Bath, and did 151 feet 11 inches, slightly uphill, a few days later at Skipton Highland Games. He usually competed in about 40 top-class games each year, picking up many injuries and cumulative strains along the way. In spite of this, he was one of the busiest and remains one of the most successful professional athletes of all time.

After Arthur Rowe, the next outstanding Englishman was Geoff Capes, born 23 August

Mighty Geoff Capes, an all-time great.

1949. From being the village tearaway, he became a respected policeman and world-famous athlete. He was the biggest of a family of nine children, an imposing figure at 6 feet 5 inches and weighing upwards of 320lb. His brothers were all over 6 feet, as was his sister Christine and his mother. As a young all-round athlete, Geoff represented his county at basketball, soccer and cross-country running. He also won some amateur Highland games in parallel with his athletic career.

He was Britain's best-ever shot putter, Commonwealth Games Champion of 1974 and 1978, European Indoor Champion of 1974 and a triple Olympian – in 1972, 1976 and 1980. As an amateur, Geoff set 17 British records and represented his country in 67 internationals, which was more than any other sportsman. He was officially voted Britain's best-ever field events athlete.

Capes broke many records all over the world but he saved his best for Scotland. He was at his best in 1982–83, when he put the 16lb stone 65 feet 3 inches at Oxton and 53 feet 4 inches with 22lb at Crieff. At Tomintoul he threw the 56 feet over the bar at 16 feet 9 inches and at Drumtochty he did 91 feet 5 inches with the 28lb weight for distance. Amongst his major victories were world titles in Nigeria and Scotland and several Scottish championships.

He also won Britain's Strongest Man and World's Strongest Man titles in television events and became quite a folk hero of the 1980s. Long after his athletic days were over, Capes remained a very popular personality, in demand for television appearances and guest spots. In 2007, he was awarded a coveted Oscar Heidenstam Award for services to sport and physical culture. Geoff's protégé, big Mark Higgins (6 feet 9 inches and 364lb), was another great all-rounder from south of the border who added interest to the Scottish games scene.

Scotland was continuing to produce some first-class heavies and George Patience of Tain, Francis Brebner of Peterhead and Alistair Gunn of Halkirk immediately come to mind. Between them, they have scooped up most of the main awards in the last ten years of the 20th century. George was one of a trio of Commonwealth Games stars who became Highland games professionals after the games of 1986, along with Chris Black and Eric Irvine. All three were very welcome additions to the national and international circuits.

George Patience, born on the Black Isle, was, and still is, a fine figure of a man, at 6 feet 1 inch and 238lb. He was Scottish schools shot and discus champion and five-times Scottish discus champion before he reached the Commonwealth Games finals in 1986. He turned professional in 1988 but, being a very conscientious paramedic, he declined scores of international invitations over the years; this, along with many back injuries, slowed his progress. Despite this, George eventually won the World Championships in 1994, but he deserved many more titles and rewards. His son now competes in Highland games.

Another of this ilk is Francis Brebner, a good-living man from the north-east of Scotland. Francis lived and breathed Highland games. It was the most important thing in his life and he pursued his ambitions with enthusiasm, determination and dedication. His records and titles are many – world records in weight throwing, seven-times world caber champion, Scottish Champion and champion of games all over the world, even in Japan. Only the World Championship eluded him, but he did win second place. Had Francis been better at throwing the weight for height, he would definitely have won

Francis Brebner, Peterhead, won several world championships, including seven in tossing the caber.

Kevin Thom, a champion powerlifter who changed to Highland Games.

the world championship, but with big entries and world-class professional strongmen he dropped too many points in this event. The high regard in which he is held around the world was well illustrated when the world championships were held in Waipu, New Zealand, in 1995. Francis was invited to take part in a religious programme on radio and although he had never done anything like this before, he responded admirably.

Born on 27 November 1965, he is 5 feet 10 inches and at one stage weighed over 300lb, being tremendously broad and muscular. Francis has had competition puts of 54 feet 10 inches with 16lb at Airth in 1995, and 45 feet with the 22lb put at Aberdeen in 1996. He made world records of 47 feet 10 inches in the 56lb for distance and 94 feet 1 inch with 28lb for distance. He threw the 16lb hammer 149 feet 10 inches in Tokyo and the 22lb hammer 115 feet on two occasions. He still

remains active in Highland games, and he was judge at the World Championships at Pleasanton, California, in 2006. He now lives in Southern California with his wife Kelly, who is a successful fitness girl and executive of a world-famous nutrition company. They met at Arnold Schwarzenegger's Classic in Columbus, Ohio, and married soon after. Now they have a bonnie son called Blaze. Francis now judges at World Championships.

Kevin Thom is another who deserves mention, owing to his many successes in some-times difficult circumstances. Hailing from Dumfries, he was a little outside the mainstream of Highland throwers but built a good physique and reputation, winning three British powerlifting championships. Turning his attention to Highland games, this 6 feet 276lb heavy excelled in events such as throwing the 56-lb for height (16 feet 3 inches) and caber tossing. Kevin won the world's caber-tossing championship in 1990. Gradually, he became good at all events, winning the Glenfiddich Trophy amongst others, but his sporting career came to a sudden stop when part of his hand was mangled in an industrial accident. Fortunately, he recovered after missing a couple of seasons, and after that time he was champion at many games on the international circuit. His son is now competing in heavy weights.

There are many other great Scots of recent years who deserve mention: Chris Black, bronze medal in hammer throwing at the Commonwealth Games; Eric Irvine, a great shot putter; and Gordon Forbes and Gordon Martin, superb hammer throwers, are some who come to mind. This is

Highland games heavies: Chris Black, George Patience and Eric Irvine in the Scottish Commonwealth Games uniform.

just a handful of competitors who have given enthusiasts much pleasure in the 1970s and 1980s.

From the mid-1970s, Americans have gradually improved their rankings, and in 1976, 6 feet 5 inches-tall Fred Vaughan of South Carolina threw his bonnet into the international games ring. He had won discus events in the mid-1960s and after graduating in 1968 he won the state discus title and some powerlifting events. Born circa 1944, he read of Highland games in a geographic magazine and after two years' gaining experience in America, he came to Scotland and competed at Lonach Games. Fred made history that day by placing first overall, the first-ever American to win a games championship in Scotland. He went on to become a regular and popular contender in the next decade, competing internationally to World Championship level. Fred was the first American to exceed 80 feet in the 28lb for distance and he did 15.5 feet in the 56lb for height. He founded the North American Scottish Games Association in 1976, an organisation which continues to play an important role in Highland games

Brian Oldfield, born in 1945, created a sensation when, after competing in the Olympic Games shot put in 1972, he turned to professional and competed at numerous games in the USA and Scotland. He was undoubtedly the best stone putter ever seen at Highland games, and at Braemar in 1973 he broke light and heavy stone records, putting the 16lb stone 63 feet 2 inches, a record that still stands unbroken. He also did 40 feet 7 inches with the 28lb Braemar stone, done with a standing putt. At 6 feet 5 inches and around 280lb at his best, he put 70 feet with a glide and his best ever, done with rotation, was 75 feet in 1975. At 6 feet 5 inches and 266lb, he was a very fine figure of a man and full of fun. He introduced the completely new rotation style

Fred Vaughan gives Tom Johnson a lift.

Brian Oldfield, world shot put record breaker.

of throwing that has been copied throughout the world and used by all the best throwers (see Chapter 21).

As far as we know, track-and-field historians have never recorded this important development's link with Highland games. Brian earned a lot of money with the International Track Association before being reinstated as an amateur. As a professional, he put the 16lb shot 73 feet 1 inch

at Meadowbank, Edinburgh, in 1975. Brian's Highland games records include a put with 72 feet 9¾ inches with 17lb at Campbell, California, and 46 feet 5 inches with 25lb at Fergus, Ontario.

Keith Tice of Clovis, California, 6 feet 2½ inches and 265lb, was more like the traditional heavy, travelling to as many games as possible. Born on 22 October 1947, he graduated from Fresno State University and taught history and social studies.

Keith began competing in Highland games in 1969 and won the US title in 1974, then the Canadian Open between 1982 and 1985. In 1981, at the World Championships in Australia, he pushed Bill Anderson all the way, finishing in second place, only one and a half points behind Bill. Amongst his best throws were 57 feet in the 16lb put, and he threw 75 feet with the 28lb for distance. Another fine feat was his 16 feet 6 inches in throwing the 56lb for height.

A very worthy successor to Keith Tice was Jim McGoldrick, a Texan who moved to San Jose, California, and many believe that he has an unequalled record amongst American heavies. At 6 feet 2¼ inches, he was the same height as Tice but while competing in Scotland tipped the scales at a muscular 270lb. Jim was one of America's best amateur discus throwers, winning the national high school championship of 1971 and the national collegiate championship four years later. Not only was he at, or near the top of, the American ranking lists for the discus, his name appeared in the world's top ten. Jim represented his country in Italy, Norway, Sweden, Germany and Russia, with a best throw of 215 feet. Brian Oldfield introduced him to Highland games and in parallel he competed seriously as an amateur during 1978–84 and thereafter as a professional, giving up a banking career to become a full-time heavy. He won the 'Open' at Santa Rosa in 1985, 1986, 1988, 1989, 1990 and 1992.

In Scotland, Jim was known as the 'Californian Cool Cat', but in America his fellow

Keith Tice, America's best in the 1980s, pitched the 16lb sheaf 26 feet 1 inch. His career was ended tragically in a fatal car crash around 1988. He was a much-respected competitor and his contemporaries had 100 kilt belt buckles cast in bronze to commemorate him.

athletes called him 'Chief'. His record of five world championship wins and four-times runner-up has never been beaten. Jim also won six US championships and in four other years he placed second. It was an unequalled record and even after the world title changed hands, the Chief still took top prizes. After many years at the top, the 6 feet 2 inches 265lb athlete was still the greatest caber tosser in the world, although challenged by Robert Troupe. Jim still loves the games scene and always appears at major events. He also finds time to do some coaching and write instructive training articles about Highland games.

In his heyday, he was exceptionally strong, even by weightlifting standards. Jim power cleaned 400lb and bench pressed over 500lb, without the aid of a special shirt and claims a press behind neck of 500lb. He still used 400lb in this lift at over 40 years of age. Many people saw him do such poundages and constantly sang his praises.

For a short while, it looked as though Carl Braun (b. 1967) of Fredericksburg, Virginia, would be the next champion after Jim McGoldrick. Unfortunately, a skiing accident prevented Carl from reaching his full potential. This dashing young man in his mid-20s stood 6 feet 4 inches tall at 264lb and was blessed with an outgoing personality and another distinctive feature – a haircut from hell!

He began competing in heavy events during 1986 and rapidly improved. His hammer throwing was world class and, indeed, he exceeded the record in Scotland, only to be told later that, on re-weighing, the hammer was slightly light.

Carl is a keen all-round sportsman and this was, literally, his downfall. Carl had a bad tumble on the ski slopes and broke a leg. Over-enthusiastic, he began heavy training too soon, his leg had to be reset and he lost the best part of three seasons, during which time new contenders entered the scene. Carl used the 'down-time' productively, setting up a modern gym, and planning to bring the World Championship to Fredericksburg. This ambition was achieved in 1997 when he staged what was, in many ways, the best ever competition for the world title up to that date. His father, who worked in the White House in Washington DC, and his family were an enormous help in organising every aspect of the games.

Carl Braun's prime events were hammer and sheaf pitch, his 30 feet 2 inches with a 20lb sheaf was a world record and he pitched a 16lb sheaf 34 feet 10 inches. Carl threw the 22lb hammer 123 feet and the 16lb hammer 146 feet 3 inches for American records.

Ben Plucknett was another noted American heavy and, like Brian Oldfield, he was a member of the US Olympic team. Ben threw the discus in the 1980 Olympics and a year later did the longest discus throw the world

Chief Jim McGoldrick.

Dave Harrington, Canada.

had ever seen. That year, he set an American record with 237 feet 4 inches and was voted by *Track and Field* magazine as the number-one discus thrower in the world. Indeed, he was ranked in the top 10 for five years, and after an amateur career spanning 21 years, he retired from track and field in 1989 and became prominent in Highland games. At 6 feet 7½ inches in height and weighing 322lb, he was outstanding in throwing the 56lb for height and set many American records between 1991 and 1993. The climax of Ben's wonderful career was in 1993 at Rothiemurchas Games, Aviemore, when Scottish Television filmed him throwing the 56lb 18 feet 3½ inches to create a new world record. He was also excellent in putting, his best being 67 feet 7 inches with a 16lb shot.

In roughly the same era, Canada's most outstanding heavies were Dave Harrington, Dusco (Dan) Markovic, Harvey Barkauskas, Harry MacDonald, George Chiappa and, more recently, Warren Trask, Doug MacDonald, Greg Hadley and Joel Thiesen.

Dave Harrington, 6 feet 2½ inches and 250lb, was Canada's undisputed 'King of the Caber' and from his retreat at Old Chelsea in the Gatineau hills near Ottawa, he ventured forth to compete in as many games as his management consultancy would allow. Dave was born in California around 1946 and was a graduate of Stanford University. His father was a fighter pilot who won the Victoria Cross flying Mosquitoes (Second World War fighter planes) from a base in Britain.

Harrington started competing at Maxville in 1965 and his first full season of heavy events was in 1979. He set his sights on competing internationally and joined the international circuit and the World Series in the early 1980s. Having realised his ambition, he retired in 1985. Dave's best throws included 129 feet 8 inches with the 16lb hammer at Georgetown and 108 feet 11½ inches with 22lb at Vancouver, both in 1982.

The next three successive Canadian Championships went to Dan Markovic, one of the most colourful characters ever to appear at the games. You never knew what to expect from this muscular, deep-chested undercover cop. Born in Tetova, Yugoslavia, in 1956, he threw discus, javelin and shot as an amateur, did a lot of weightlifting, broke records in the Fergus Walk and competed in World's Strongest Man competitions. Ask him about his diet and this joker would tell you that as a very large baby he chewed granite lumps until he could go on to solids, and now his favourites are cow pie and hoot owl juice. 'Big Dan' put the 25lb Fergus stone 47 feet 1 inch in 1986 and his line shooting could beat any fisherman.

The next champion was Harvey Barkauskas, whose family roots were in Lithuania and England. After graduating, he taught physical education and science before becoming keen on lifting weights. Excelling as an all-rounder,

Dan Marcovic, Toronto.

Harvey Barkauskas, of London, Ontario. Born in Wolverhampton, England of Lithuanian extraction. Seven times Canadian champion (1985–1992), losing the title to Harry MacDonald in 1990.

Harry MacDonald. This Big Mac is 6'1" and weighs 325lb.

he competed regularly in open competitions at a high level and now competes in age-group competitions, winning many such 'Masters' Championships.

At the age of 21, Harry MacDonald became the youngest ever Canadian champion, and in his first 10 years as a professional, Harry was the top prize winner at almost 100 games. He won the Canadian Championships five times and he was still competing in a few of his favourite Highland games in 2007. When the Canadian government honoured Highland games with a postage stamp, Harry MacDonald was depicted tossing the caber.

One of his favourite events was throwing the weight for distance and in this he was

Warren Trask of Alma, Ontario. Director, Fergus Games, wearing a maple leaf tartan kilt.

Canadian record holder. He actually broke a *world* record in Australia, where he pulled HMS *Bounty*, a 387-tonne sailing ship, a distance of 25 metres in one minute 36 seconds to exceed the previous record recognised by the *Guinness Book of Records*. Big Mac, as Harry is nicknamed, won a strongman competition in Nova Scotia and was an excellent powerlifter with a squat of 605lb, bench press of 575lb and dead lift of 700lb.

Harry MacDonald threw the 28lb 91 feet 3 inches at Haliburton, the 56lb 43 feet 9 inches, 16lb hammer 133 feet 6 inches and 22lb 108 feet – all in 1996 – and may have done more before retiring. He was a contender in World Highland Games Championships and always gave 100 per cent.

Warren Trask, a 6 feet

4 inches farmer of Alma, near Fergus, excels in throwing the 56lb weight for height (16 feet 1 inch), sheaf pitching (36 feet 6 inches at Maxville) and the Fergus Walk, in which he has broken several world records, his current best being 465 feet with two 200lb. Warren's career has been impaired by the demands of work on his farm and the fact that he has become director of the heavy events at the Fergus Highland Games, one of the world's major gatherings. He competed in the World Masters Championship in 2006, when he led a very fine team of Canadians in Inverness, Scotland.

George Chiappa of Ottawa is 5 feet 10 inches and at his best competed at around 210lb body-weight. His parents came from north-west Italy and he was given a good education at the University of Ottawa. After graduation, he taught physical education and English before becoming a professional athlete and imaginative entrepreneur.

Peter Binks, one of a family of Australian Highland games heavies in the early 1980s.

Historic photo of first World Caber Championships. Eric Hedin (Sweden), Reverend Arnold Pope (USA), Colin Mathieson (Australia).

During his lengthy career, George has competed internationally, including in the world championships in Scotland.

The Southern Hemisphere

There is an excellent Highland games circuit in Australia, producing great champions such as five-times world champion Matt Sandford, the greatest Highland games athlete from 'down under'. Other fine competitors over the years include Aaron Neighbours, Billy and Peter Binks and Joe Quigley.

The first Australian heavy to become famous internationally was Colin Mathieson, who competed at the gatherings in Australia and Scotland for a quarter of a century. He was born in Scotland, and became a sheep farmer, property manager and then a major estate agent in the outback. Colin won the World Caber Champion of 1975 and was British Champion of 1976.

Colin Mathieson, by Doug Fales.

Joe Quigley, pictured on the day he made his debut in international Highland games.

This jovial athlete was first to turn the 19 feet 10 inches, 132lb Sydney Caber – a brute of a stick – and he earned the gratitude of international heavies by promoting several wonderful Highland Games in Australia, in which he still competed with honour even though he was well into his 40s.

Before turning professional, Joe Quigley of Melbourne was a world-class amateur, having been in the Australian Olympic Squad and winning a Commonwealth Games silver medal for hammer throwing. At 6 feet 2 inches and 274lbs, Joe was very good at shot putting, and when he turned to Scottish events he proved to be equally expert in the weight for height. He made an extraordinary debut in international Highland Games when he placed first equal with Jim McGoldrick at the Australian Bicentennial Games.

He made his first appearance in Scotland that season of 1988, and in 1992, as a professional, he won the world championships. In 1993, he took US Open titles and could have won more had he been better at tossing the caber. Quigley was exceptionally strong but just could not perfect his technique and timing in this one event. He had exceptionally muscular legs, which he used to great effect. Joe represented Australia in the World's Strongest Man competition in Hungary in

1988, and he competed in many other countries until a ban interrupted his career. Back in action again after a confusing series of announcements, he was determined to make up for lost time. Unfortunately, he developed some serious back troubles that put an end to his sporting career.

Matt Sandford, Australia.

Matt Sandford, of Hoppers Crossing, Victoria, Australia was born in July 1970. He was 6 feet 3 inches and weighed 250lb (114kg). Five-times world champion, Matt Sandford began training with weights at 12 years of age, and as a youth Matt played football under Australian rules. With the support of his father, he became a successful amateur track-and-field athlete, particularly in shot and discus events. He won state and regional championships in the 10–14 years age group, improving significantly with the hammer as he moved out of this class. He then cut down on shot and discus training in order to specialise in hammer throwing. By training on throws four times a weeks and with two or three weight-training sessions weekly, he won state and national championships for under 18s while still only 15 years of age.

Matt then took a break from hard training and when he resumed competing in 1988 it was as a professional in Highland games. He found the atmosphere quite different from amateur athletics and he enjoyed this much more and trained with renewed vigour.

After gaining experience in the Australian circuit and following coaching from Craig Watson, he travelled to Scotland and immediately made a very good impression during the early 1990s. Although being informed of regular drug testing at Highland games in Scotland, he suffered a big setback with a positive test that entailed an immediate ban. He returned to

Pat Hellior, New Zealand.

THE WORLD HISTORY OF HIGHLAND GAMES

Australia, where he missed the camaraderie of the games and was determined to return in due course and fulfil his ambitions. This he did, and with hard training he won five consecutive world championships between 1999 and 2000, and also the world hammer throwing championship at Aviemore. In addition to titles, Matt broke world records with 16lb and 22lb hammers. During these years, Matt travelled extensively in America and Scotland, competing in numerous world heavy event championships including Finland, Scotland and, of course, New Zealand, taking on all comers. Competing in up to 40 Highland games a year is tough work, and in spite of injuries he won an incredible number of the most important titles.

My lasting memory of Matt is his total focus on the job in hand. He had no time for small talk between throws and was totally calm, even at critical stages. I remember once when he had missed two throws with the 28lb for distance – it was thought that he may take it a bit easier to

Aaron Neighbour.

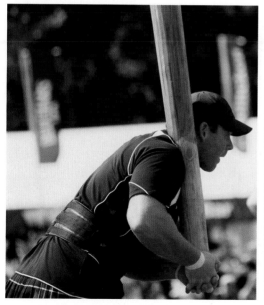

ensure he stayed behind the trig. No way! He made his usual all-out effort, a blur as he spun up to the stop-board and wham! The weight soared into first place and he kept in the throwing area. 'He must have ice in his veins,' commented one of the heavies, shaking his head in disbelief at what he had just seen. That epitomised Matt. He stayed cool and calm and collected the top prizes.

Across the water in Auckland, New Zealand, the current and long-standing champion is 6 feet 1 inch and 242lb Pat Hellior. Before becoming a Highland games heavy, Pat was a prominent track-and-field athlete. He was in the top ten track-and-field lists in all four throwing events and proceeded to break long-standing New Zealand Highland games records. He is also the national record holder in the sheaf pitch. Pat has competed in numerous world heavy event championships including in America, Canada, Finland and, of course, New Zealand, where Highland games took the sports world into the new millennium.

In 2007 and 2008 there has been a greater depth of Highland games talent in America than in any other country in the world, with athletes such as, alphabetically, Harrison Bailey III, Dave Barron, Sean Betz, Larry Brock and Dave Brown – and that's just to the second letter of the alphabet! All these men continually come close to Ryan Vierra, five-times world champion, and sometimes even beat him. In September 2008, America's leading amateur, 23-year-old Eric Frasure of North Carolina, made a sensational debut as a professional, defeating many former champions and record holders.

What follows are some brief biographies of several of the best and most popular athletes on the international Highland games scene at this time.

Bruce Aitken.

*Greg Hadley of Antigonish, Nova Scotia, several times Canadian
Champion and World Championship contender.*

THE WORLD HISTORY OF HIGHLAND GAMES

CHAPTER TWENTY SIX

21st Century Champions – Biographies of the Best

BRUCE AITKEN

Auchenblae, near Stonehaven, Scotland. Born: 11 December 1970. Height: 6 feet 5 inches. Weight: 18 stone 6lb; 258lb; 117.27kg.

In 2005 Bruce won the world championship in New Hampshire and he is the current world record-holder in throwing the hammer, having thrown the 16lb hammer a distance of 156 feet 8½ inches and the 22lb hammer 125 feet 1½ inches. His best with the 16lb stone is 58 feet 4 inches.

He comes from a very successful Highland games family. His father Bob and brother Stephen were both all-round champions who won top honours in heavy and light events. Other male relatives have also been successful. Bruce has won several Scottish Highland games championships and has competed all over the world. He particularly enjoys competing at Fergus Games in Ontario, Canada, while in Scotland his favourite venue is Aboyne.

STEPHEN AITKEN

Stockton-on-Tees, England. Born: 8 August 1966 in Stonehaven. Height: 6 feet 2½ inches. Weight: in his 30s he weighed 18 stone; 252lb; 114.55kg.

Brought up in Scotland, Stephen followed in his father's footsteps. He began competing at Highland games when he was 14 years of age, and when he was 17 he entered the heavy events. He was particularly good at putting the stone and was very fast and athletic. In tossing the caber, he built up good speed and made a sudden stop – solid on his feet and without losing control. In throwing the hammer he used four swings before release and his methods paid off in a long career, in which he won many top awards. Stephen, who was brought up on a farm,

became a cattle auctioneer and still enjoys this occupation.

HARRISON BAILEY III

Easton, near Bethlehem, Pennsylvania, USA. Born: 23 March 1973. Height: 6 feet 3 inches. Weight: 19 stone 9lb; 275lb; 125kg.

Quiet-natured Harrison has been a professional in Highland games for eight years and has been in the world's top six Highland games athletes for the past five years. During a relatively short but very successful amateur career, he set several records in 28lb and 56lb weights for distance and in both hammers. Four of these were world amateur records. Nowadays, his favourite event is throwing the 56lb for height.

This former football player is one of the most dynamic throwers ever, and this is clearly seen in

Stephen Aitken.

Harrison Bailey.

throwing the weights. Although in the past few years he has been breaking records in the professional ranks, he still holds a number of amateur records in throwing the 28lb and 56lb weights for distance. Harrison Bailey III is much sought after by promoters of the world's biggest games, and he has competed with distinction in Highland games from Canada to Brazil and all over the USA and Scotland.

Harrison displays great athleticism and mental concentration in throwing and is popular amongst his fellow competitors and officials. He combines brain and brawn, being very intelligent and articulate, which one would expect as he is principal of an American high school.

JAMIE BARR
Kingskettle, Fife, Scotland. Born: 13 March 1965. Height: 6 feet 2 inches. Weight: 18 stone; 252lb, 4.55kg.

Jamie Barr.

Jamie has participated in a variety of strength events, as did his father, Thomas, before him. Both were power lifters, breaking national records, and Jamie even got a Commonwealth record before turning to strongman events. In this tough sport he became a finalist in the televised *World's Strongest Man*. He has won many of Scotland's strongest man competitions, as late as 2007 when he decided to concentrate more on Highland games.

DAVID BARRON
New York, USA. Born: 23 March 1972 in Denver, Colorado. Height: 6 feet 5 inches. Weight: 19 stone 4lb; 270lb; 123kg.

This dynamic world-class competitor won the world caber tossing championship at Montrose in Scotland. He was runner-up in the World Championship of 2004.

David participated in his first Highland games at 17 years of age and has since represented his country at international games in Iceland, Brazil, Ireland, Canada and throughout Scotland.

He has competed in five world championships and his brother Will is also a top-class heavy. They travel together to participate regularly in circuits across America.

SEAN BETZ
Omaha, Nebraska, USA. Born: 26 June 1976. Height: 6 feet 5 inches. Weight: 20 stone 11lb; 291lb; 132½ kg.

David Barron.

Sean won the World Heavy Events Championships in Bridgeport, West Virginia, in 2008. He is strong in all events and usually places high in each. This sort of all-round ability is essential to win major titles and Sean has previously placed second in American and world championships. He has broken several American records as a professional and has held the amateur world record in the 28lb weight for distance. He was manager of a fitness gym in his hometown but now prefers being a personal trainer as this allows him time to compete in international Highland games.

LARRY BROCK

Charlotte, North Carolina, USA. Born: 13 May 1979 in Fayetteville, North Carolina, USA. Height: 6 feet 3 inches. Weight: 20 stone 5lb; 285lb; 129.55kg.

Larry travels all over America to compete in the most important Highland games. After a great record in track and field athletics, Larry became a teacher, American football player and then a Highland games professional. At the turn of the century, 2007 was his best year to date in winning two American national championships, and also taking third place in the world championships and winning the world stone put championships. 'Big Brock' is a jovial and popular character and during the lunch break at Sacramento Valley Games he was once persuaded to enter the haggis throwing contest. To everyone's surprise he broke the American record with a throw of 136 feet. Most Scottish heavies make their own 'tacky' (the sticky substance which athletes put on their hands to help in gripping the implements) by melting down resin and mixing it with Venice turpentine, but Young Larry is quite a business-man and produces and distributes his own *Magic Tacky*.

Kyrylo Chuprynin.

KYRYLO CHUPRYNIN

Ukraine. Height: 6 feet 5 inches. Weight: 21 stone; 294¾lb; 134kg.

Kyrylo is one of best Highland games competitors regularly appearing on the Scottish circuit and breaking records, including the 56lb weight for height at Braemar. He started competing in 2004 and in 2006 he went to America and competed for the world championships for the first time, placing fourth.

He is one of the many Olympic Games competitors who have competed in Scottish Highland games over the years. He represented his country in the Sydney and Atlanta Olympic Games and, in spite of diversifying to compete in Highland games, he still retains his Ukrainian national discus championship.

Kyrylo is a popular character at the games, with a ready smile and happy disposition, and his English is improving, although sometimes spiced with Scottish slang. He is quite definitely one of the best Highland games athletes in the world.

GREGOR EDMUNDS

Carmunnock, Scotland. Born: 15 April 1977. Height: 6 feet 4 inches. Weight: 22 stone; 308lb; 140kg.

Gregor has had a long and varied career as a strength athlete, winning a junior national Highland games championship, Scottish amateur

Gregor Edmonds.

Alistair Gunn.

athletics Highland games championships, the Scottish Professional Championships and competing in several World Highland Games Championships. This coveted world title eluded him until 2007 when the competition took place on his native heath. Had Gregor Edmunds specialised in Highland games, he could well have had an even more successful career, but for a while he competed in international strongman competitions, living for a year in Finland where he worked closely with Jouka Ahola, a former world's strongest man. Having been runner-up in Britain's strongest man competition, Gregor then reached the finals of television's *World's Strongest Man* competition.

Amongst his many claims to fame, he is one of the comparatively few who have tossed the famous Braemar caber and won the overall competition watched by the Royal Family. Gregor is currently studying for qualifications in sports science.

His best throws at the time of writing are: 16lb putting the stone – 58 feet 6 inches; 28lb weight for distance – 89 feet 3 inches; 16lb hammer – 145 feet; 22lb hammer – 112 feet; 56lb for height – 17 feet; 56lb for distance – 42 feet. The caber is one of his best events.

ALISTAIR GUNN

Halkirk, near John o' Groats, Scotland. Born: 1963. Height: 5 feet 10 inches. Weight: 16 stone 6lb; 236lb; 107.27kg.

Alistair has won many Highland games titles including: World Champion of 1995; World caber titles in 1992 and 1995; three times World Hammer Throwing Champion in 1994, 1995 and 1996; Middle East and Far East Champion; and five-times Scottish Champion. He is probably the best Highland games veteran in the world but prefers to compete in events open to all ages and weights. Pound for pound, he was the best Highland athlete in the world, without any weak event and with extraordinary determination. He is not a big man as far as heavies go, but he had travelled the world toppling most opponents, regardless of their records or size. As a result, he became known as the 'Giant Killer' and he did indeed beat many famous names. He first gained attention when he won the Scottish Junior Championships and turned professional in 1982, later winning five Scottish championships, many international events in various continents and, of course, the world championship.

His best official throws include: 16lb hammer – 150 feet 3 inches (Halkirk, 1996); 22lb hammer – 122 feet ½ inches (Pleasanton, 1996); 16lb stone – 54 feet 7 inches (Luss, 1996); 22lb stone – 47

THE WORLD HISTORY OF HIGHLAND GAMES

feet 11½ inches (Halkirk, 1995); 28lb weight for distance – 87 feet 2 inches (Dunbeath, 1997); and 56lb for height – 15 feet 6 inches (Iceland, 1997).

Like many other Scottish competitors, he has a fine family tree of Highland games competitors. His brother, Murray Gunn, is a high-ranking competitor and their father and grandfather were also games athletes. Even more importantly, one of his ancestors competed in the Olympic Games. Adam Beattie Gunn, born in 1872, won the silver medal in the Olympic decathlon at St Louis in 1904. He was selected to represent Canada, but while competing under the Canadian flag, he was allowed to have his throws marked with the St Andrews Cross.

STEVEN KING

Inveraray, Scotland. Born: 28 January 1960. Height: 6 feet 2 inches. Weight: 258lb, 18 stone 6lbs, 117.27kg.

Born near Oban, at Inveraray, the home of the Dukes of Argyll, this young Scot made his mark when he won the World Hammer Throwing Championship at Fredericksburgh, Virginia, in 1999. It was the first time this championship had been held outside Scotland and it was a very dramatic competition. At the end of it all, he lived up to his nickname, King of the Hammers, and successfully defended the world title he had won at Rothiemurchas in Scotland in the previous year.

Steven King.

Having competed in Highland games for 15 years, his crowning glory was breaking world records, throwing 125 feet 1 inch with 22lb and 153 feet 2 inches with 16lb in 1998. He competed in 47 games that season and broke 32 field records in the process. He also does well in 56lb for height and is a competent caber tosser.

DOUG MACDONALD

Antigonish, Nova Scotia, Canada. Born c.1962. Height: 6 feet 4 inches. Weight: 280lb, 20 stone, 127.27kg.

Being a native of this historic location, Doug grew up being very much aware of Highland games. He tends to shun publicity but being Canadian Champion and with such great talent, he has been in great demand and a big success in games in Scotland, the USA, Ireland and Brazil. In his prime, he was one of the best caber tossers in the world. Douglas has had an interesting life as a physical education teacher and as one of the elite Royal Canadian Mounted Police. He is now a priest. He has been the guiding light in the formation of the Canadian Highland Games Federation.

SCOTT RIDER

London, England. Born 22 September 1977. Height: 6 feet 2 inches. Weight: 18 stone, 252lb, 114.7kg.

Scott was England's best Highland games athlete in 2006–09, and is still improving. He is a

Doug MacDonald.

Scott Rider.

very versatile sportsman who has won national amateur titles and represented his country in several sports. He is one of several Highland games athletes who have competed in the Olympic Games, being in the 2002 Winter Olympic bobsleigh team.

In addition, he also represented England at the 2006 Commonwealth Games in putting the shot and throwing the discus. He reached the final in the shot put and he also won the British indoor championship in this event. This gifted athlete has already won many firsts in Highland events and overall prizes at Scottish games. He competed in the World Championships for the first time in 2007, and did very well. His greatest achievement to date was ending the 2007 season with a win at the famous Braemar Gathering with five personal best throws.

RYAN VIERRA

California. Born 23 August 1968. Height: 6 feet 1 inch. Weight: 300lb; 21 stone 13lb; 136.36kg. Ryan began throwing at high school in Hilmar, California, then at Modesto Junior College, where he was coached by Rob MacKay. Rob had been a Highland games heavy and Coach Mac introduced Ryan to Highland games in 1987, competing as an amateur. He showed promise in 1990 when he tied for first place in the Amateurs Class and realised that promise when he won the following year at the prestigious games of the Caledonian Club of San Francisco in 1990. He turned professional at the end of the 1994 season. In 1996, with perseverance and dedication, he won the world championships in Waipu, New Zealand, and the stone put championship of 1996 at San Jose, California. He continued to win world championships in 1997, 1998, 2005 and 2006, and was placed second in 2007.

His best throws up to 1997 were 59 feet 2 inches with the 18lb stone; 150 feet 7 inches with the 16lb hammer; 119 feet 6½ inches with the 22lb hammer; 45 feet 9 inches in the 56lb for distance; 16 feet in the 56lb for height; and 37 feet in the sheaf toss.

Ryan has competed in major Highland games in countries all over the world, including Scotland, Ireland, Finland, Iceland, Australia, France and New Zealand to name but a few. He has now won the American National Championship 11 times and is still counting. As a result of his worldwide success in Highland games, Ryan Vierra was able to buy a ranch in Stevenson, California, where he could board horses, but it also became a fully equipped centre for training athletes. A special attraction was a well-lit throwing area, ideal for training clinics and one-to-one coaching.

Ryan is 6 feet 1 inch in height and his body weight has gradually increased, reaching 280lb in the 1997 season and up to some ten years later he

Ryan Vierra, America's all-time great.

THE WORLD HISTORY OF HIGHLAND GAMES

weighed approximately 300lb. His status grows with the years. Although by nature he is a quiet man, Ryan Vierra has become a fine ambassador for Highland games and lives up to the public's best expectations of a world champion.

WOUT ZIJLSTRA

Friesland, the Netherlands. Born: 4 August 1964. Height: 6 feet 7 inches. Weight: 21 stone; 294lb; 133.6kg.

Wout is the tallest competitor in world heavy event championships. He started participating in Highland games in 1987 and since then has been competing in these games and strongman competitions all over the world. He has won four Netherlands' Strongest Man titles and in the 1998 World's Strongest Man competition in Morocco he placed third. Wout now competes only in Highland games. For some years the Dutch champion held the world record in throwing the 56lb weight for height with the fabulous mark of 18 feet 8¼ inches.

On a personal level, he has a huge appetite, his favourite meal being meat and potatoes. He loves meat, sometimes eating as much as one kilogram in one sitting. Fortunately, he is a meat inspector, so there is always a good supply to hand.

Thanks to Wout's efforts, there are more than a dozen Highland games held in the Netherlands

Wout Zijlstra of the Netherlands.

each year, and some games have also been held in neighbouring Belgium. A great many Highland games fans have come to Scotland to cheer for Wout in major competitions, sometimes in busloads, and they have marched proudly to the games field behind a pipe band. The Dutch fans are passionate in their support for their champion.

MIKE (ZEE) ZOLKIEWICZ

Springfield, Massachusetts, USA. Height: 6 feet 4 inches. Weight: 19 stone, 9lb; 275lb, 125kg.

Mike takes us to the end of this alphabet of famous games athletes. Like Jim McGoldrick, Kyrylo Chuprinin, Sebastian Wenta and several others, he was a national discus throwing champion before taking up Highland games. In 2003, Mike Zee exceeded the amateur record in throwing the 56lb for height. Unfortunately, he lost it on a technicality. Mike turned professional in 2005 and is building a good reputation in America and Scotland. At Antigonish Nova Scotia in 2009 he created a sensation when he threw the 56lb for height 18 feet 19 inches. Within minutes Wout Zijlstra phoned congratulating him on breaking his record.

Future Stars

Looking to the future, I can foresee progress in all areas. In Europe, Sebastian Wenta, a 6 feet 7 inches athlete, has won 13 national Polish titles in different sports, including shot and discus, and also won the International Strongman Cup. He has already won some major Highland games and is seriously considering concentrating on these events. If he does, we can expect some sensational performances.

In America, 22-year-old Garrit Johnstone, formerly of the University of Tallahassee, won the All-American Championship in shot and discus and has a put of 68 feet to his credit. While studying for a masters degree in politics at Oxford

University in England, Garrit sampled Highland games and liked the experience. He could be the one to beat Brian Oldfield's long-standing stone put record. Tommy de Bruijn, the massive, 6 feet 9½ inches, Belgium champion has become much more active in international events in 2009 but a severe injury hampered him greatly as the season reached its height. Hans Lolkema, Sloten, the Netherlands, was a late starter but has reached top in Holland and Belgium. Placing 2nd in the 2009 European Championships in Bressuire, France, he then participated in the 2009 World Championships and placed sixth.

Bruce Bobb was born in 1977. Proportionately built at 6 feet 6 inches in height, he won many amateur championships in shot and discus but his coaches discouraged him from entering Highland games.

Since 2004, Bruce has been more active and in 2007 he was almost always in the top three in competitions, except for the world championships. Even then, he finished in great style by winning the 56lb weight over bar against the world's best. Craig Sinclair (Drumoak) Sinclair Patience (Tain), and the Perthsire Coulthard brothers are currently the leading young throwers in Scotland.

Bruce Robb, (b.1977), at Oakley, Fife, represented Scotland in amateur events as Scotland's shot-putting and discus champion.

THE WORLD HISTORY OF HIGHLAND GAMES

Highland Games Heavy Events Championships

In 1973, Lord Aberdeen presided over the founding event of the World Highland Games Heavy Events Championships and afterwards the title was officially registered on 25 May 1973.

Considerable support was also given by Sir Billy Sneddon, Australia's Speaker in Parliament, and the Premier of Queensland hosted the World Championships in Melbourne when the historic decision was made to form an international body to represent traditional athletes. Thereafter, the championships have been organised annually and without interruption, with 2009 being the 30th year.

Great athletes from home and abroad have competed in the world championships. Many Olympic Games competitors and Commonwealth medallists and champions from nearly every continent have entered the lists, including giant Okonkwo, an African Olympian; Olympic veteran Petur Gudmundsson of Iceland; Jouko Ahola of Finland; England's Geoff Capes; and Ukraine's double-Olympian Kyrylo Chuprynin. Others of exceptional standard include Bill Anderson MBE and Jim McGoldrick of the USA, national and international and five-times world champion. Matt Sandford of Australia is another five-times world champion and, most recently, Ryan Vierra has joined the elite band with five world titles. Nobody has yet exceeded this feat.

National and international organisations have recognised and supported these events and civic heads and dignitaries of the highest calibre, including foreign ministers and ambassadors, have attended these world championships. The international Highland Games Federation's other associated games have also been attended by royalty.

The World Highland Games Heavy Events Championships has a pedigree second to none.

The World Heavy Event Championships

Dates, winners and venues

1980	Los Angeles, California	Grant Anderson, Scotland
1981	Melbourne, Australia	Bill Anderson, Scotland
1982	Prestonpans, Scotland	Grant Anderson, Scotland
1983	Lagos, Nigeria	Geoff Capes, England
1984	Carmunnock, Scotland	Geoff Capes, England

1985	Carmunnock, Scotland	2000	Waipu, New Zealand
	Geoff Capes, England		Matt Sandford, Australia
1986	Carmunnock, Scotland	2001	Pleasanton, California
	Geoff Capes, England		Matt Sandford, Australia
1987	Clarkston, Scotland	2002	Pleasanton, California
	Geoff Capes, England		Matt Sandford, Australia
1988	Aviemore, Scotland	2003	Antigonish, Nova Scotia
	Jim McGoldrick, USA		Matt Sandford, Australia
1989	Aviemore, Scotland	2004	New Hampshire, USA
	Jim McGoldrick, USA		Bruce Aitken, Scotland
1990	Glasgow*, Scotland	2005	Fergus, Canada
	Jim McGoldrick, USA		Ryan Vierra, USA
1991	Callander, Scotland	2006	Pleasanton, California
	Jim McGoldrick, USA		Ryan Vierra, USA
1992	Callander, Scotland	2007	Inverness, Scotland
	Joe Quigley, Australia		Gregor Edmunds, Scotland
1993	Callander, Scotland	2008	West Virginia, USA
	Jim McGoldrick, USA		Sean Betz, USA
1994	Callander, Scotland	2009	Edinburgh, Scotland
	George Patience, Scotland		Aaron Neighbour, Australia
1995	Kilmarnock, Scotland	2010	Victoria, British Columbia
	Alistair Gunn, Scotland		Larry Brock, USA
1996	Waipu, New Zealand	2011	New Hampshire, USA
	Ryan Vierra, USA		Dan McKim, USA
1997	Fredericksburg, Virginia		
	Ryan Vierra, USA		
1998	Oulo, Finland		
	Ryan Vierra, USA		
1999	Pleasanton, California		
	Matt Sandford, Australia		

The Caledonian Club of San Francisco has indicated that it will bid for the hosting of future World Championships events. Over 50,000 spectators have attended these games on the occasions when this club has hosted the World Championships.

THE WORLD HISTORY OF HIGHLAND GAMES

CHAPTER TWENTY EIGHT

The Games' Golden Girls

Female competitors in the traditional events are a fairly recent innovation and, initially, were a subject of much debate. Traditionalists in Scotland still do not include such events in their programmes. It is quite unusual throughout Europe, but we do sometimes see women competing in games such as those at Callander, Killin, Aviemore and Glenarm, and in Germany and the Netherlands.

In the USA, such women's events are now quite common. Charles Black was one of the first men to encourage such female competitions and many will remember that Shannon Hartnett started her career as a (145lb) 'heavy' throwing with the men at Santa Rosa in California, where she lived at that time.

When the ladies were given a competition of their own, there was some negative feedback as there were a number of complaints on both sides. Some women thought they had been stuck in a corner of the field, not realising that there were restrictions of space for safety reasons. They found the implements too heavy and the hammers too long. They said they had not been given the same publicity and attention as the men, who in turn called them 'attention seekers' and 'picnic athletes', insinuating that the women did not train as hard and regularly as the men.

The incredible Shannon Hartnett with the Caledonian Club of San Francisco's trophy.

Shannon Hartnett
www.shannonhartnett.com

Multi World Champion
in Scottish Games

Bodybuilding

USA Olympic Bodsled

World's Strongest Woman
competitor

The greatest contribution in getting real recognition for women in Highland games came from the aforementioned Shannon Hartnett, who became a truly superb all-round athlete. This athletically built, sun-tanned Californian girl was totally dedicated to sport and fitness, training as hard as many men would. Her polished technique in the throws contrasted with the feeble and clumsy efforts of some others, making these women realise that if they wanted to be respected they would have to train hard. She also broke ranks with the women who mostly did not want their weight, age, marital status and employment mentioned in publications or commentaries. Shannon set standards, and a new breed of real athletes emerged. From these small beginnings, women's events are now popular all over the USA and Canada.

Shannon was practically unbeaten in Highland games championships, setting and breaking every known record. She had her own all-women *Body Central* commercial gym, which was officially voted the best gym in Sonoma County. The gym sponsored Shannon's own sports teams and was an excellent part of the local community. In 2002, she signed for a professional women's football team but she still had time to study and become a qualified marine biologist who went on to study dolphin life in the Caribbean.

Shannon trained long and hard to become part of a team to make a well-planned and valiant attempt to reach the summit of Mount Everest. It was a perilous assault and as the team neared its goal it encountered severe storms and even a fatality. The team never quite made it and frost-bitten and bitterly disappointed they gave up; nevertheless, it was a great achievement. Shannon Hartnett had proved her worth, from the depths of the sunny Caribbean to the freezing heights of Mount Everest, but still there was more to come. She excelled in the *Glamazons* television programme made at Universal Studios, Florida. She placed third and had she not had a disastrous first event, may have won. Shannon competed in the first World's Strongest Woman competition and again placed very well.

Although best known for her prowess in Highland games, one of Shannon's greatest achievements was winning a place in America's Olympic bobsleigh team at the 2002 Winter Olympics.

There were tears in many eyes when Shannon retired from Highland games in 2006. But times and attitudes towards women competitors had changed forever.

One day in 1994, a package dropped through my letterbox. In this mail there was a letter and magazine with a cover-photo of a beautiful all-American girl, proudly illustrating an article entitled 'Salute to Women in Sport'. Little did I know the future effect of this article. The girl was the letter writer and she wanted to compete in Highland games, not as a Highland dancer or piper, but in the heavy events! Donald Dinnie would not only have turned in his grave; he would have been spinning!

To support her request, the young woman, Cindy Morrison (b. 1959), enclosed her list of performances at Florida Highland

Cindy Morrison of Florida, USA.

THE WORLD HISTORY OF HIGHLAND GAMES

Games, her powerlifting results and a picture of her squatting. It was a beauty. I called it 'the Screaming Skull', for here she was sweating, howling and 'busting a gut' – the very attributes displayed by Highland games champions. I decided to give her a chance.

Newspapers were full of Cindy's photos, accompanied by front-page headlines. Radio and television clamoured for interviews. Having taken a law degree, it was evident that Cindy was no 'dumb blonde'. Although she had no previous media training, her responses were instinctive and her co-operation at photo shoots was very productive. Even when she flatly turned down any provocative posing, she declined with good humour that avoided confrontation.

Cindy was the first woman to lift one of the McGlashen Stones at Callander, and she did it with a smile.

She had a strange notion of travel to Highland games. When I told her that my organisation would provide transport, she imagined herself riding on a hay cart with her legs dangling over the edge, travelling through mountains and glens to the tunes of the bagpipes!

At the games, the crowds loved her and vocal locals gave their full support. One particular man at Garnock Games had been too long in the beer tent and every time Cindy appeared he shouted some off-colour remarks when her kilt flared out as she spun to throw the weight. It was amusing at first but became wearisome and in exasperation she exclaimed to the judge, 'That's what happens when cousins marry'.

In the lounge at the American Old-time Strongmen's Banquet in New York, Cindy asked strongman Derek Rogers about tearing telephone directories. Derek found a thick New York directory and, to cut a long story short, after a little coaching, Cindy tore it in half.

Having achieved her ambitions at Highland games, she was honoured in her hometown and received a message of congratulations and a personally signed photo from Hillary Clinton.

Cindy, who has some German and Cherokee blood in her veins, moved on from Highland games and has added to her amazing background in old classic cars, jousting, escapology, crocodile wrestling in Florida's Everglades, fire-eating and walking on glass.

Looking serious as she goes into battle, Cindy explains 'This is jousting not jesting'.

Canada's current champion is the French-Canadian Josee Morneau of Winnipeg. Josee has won several world championships in arm wrestling and, like the two women mentioned above, has often competed at Highland games in Scotland. She comes from a rural background and she built up her strength from an early age with strenuous farm work normally reserved for men. The ability to turn her hand to all kinds of difficult tasks earned her a place in the *World's Strongest Woman* television programme and, of course, she had already laid the foundations for the physical versatility required to be a champion in Highland sports.

Josee Morneau of Canada.

Josee loves the international lifestyle that takes her all over Canada and the USA then over to Scotland, Ireland and other parts of the world. Josee Morneau is always immaculate, even after a long, hard journey, and while on tours she has early breakfasts and is fully made-up, bright-eyed and ready to go.

Summer Pierson of Phoenix, Arizona, is one of the USA's top discus throwers and a member of America's World Cup team. As I write, she is America's, and probably the world's, best woman 'heavy'. Looking every inch a champion, Summer is a popular competitor wherever she goes and, like the others featured here, she is a great ambassador

Julie Dunkley of the UK and Summer Pierson of the USA.

representing her country. If she continues to improve at the present rate, she will undoubtedly be a great champion in years to come.

In 2008, Mindy Pockoski has topped American ranking lists. Trained by her husband, Mike, a well-known professional athlete, they recently moved from North Carolina to Las Vegas.

Britain is fortunate to have the charming Julie Dunkley of London as Britain's top-ranking woman in Highland games. She has been the UK's best shot putter and, having represented Britain in many international events and Commonwealth Games, she is recognised as one of the country's best amateur athletes. Julie is also one of the world's strongest women, having placed fourth in such a television competition.

Very professional on the competition field, Julie is always friendly and outgoing. Her rapid improvement in Highland games mirrors the progress of Scott Rider, who she married. They make a great couple.

These lovely, talented ladies have definitely earned their place in the history of Highland games.

CHAPTER TWENTY NINE

Wider Horizons

Over the past half century, I have devoted a great deal of time, money and energy to promoting Highland games on an international basis. Initially, I enlisted the aid of Scottish champions such as Jay Scott and Bill Anderson, then over the years others helped, including Colin Matheson in Australia, Dave Harrington and Dan Markovic in Canada, and Wout Zijlstra and Manfred Muelenhaus in Europe. In the USA, a vital role was played by the Caledonian Club of San Francisco and its champions, from Keith Tice and Jim McGoldrick right through to Ryan Vierra. In Canada, Fergus Games led the way, with Warren Trask and Lynn Boland-Richardson making a massive contribution, the latter with her excellent photographs and prolific writings. With such allies, a transformation has taken place and now the world champions, banded together in the International Highland Games Federation, are steadily progressing, raising standards and increasing international participation. This rather personalised section records the efforts of these people over the years.

In the immediate post-Second World War era, international Highland games were at a low ebb. In Scotland there was a struggle to get back to normal. An entertainments tax had been introduced and Highland games suffered badly. The tax was resented but worse still, unpaid organisers of local Highland games were, understandably, unwilling to become involved in such tax matters. However, in the following period of relative stability there was greater affluence, and improved and cheaper air travel made international athletics much more attainable for those engaged in Scottish sports. The late 1950s and early 1960s were particularly exciting times as many moved from being active competitors in strength sports and concentrated more on the promotion and development of Highland games.

Nor was the Scottish scene neglected. Indeed, one of the most ambitious Highland games projects was presented in 1962 at the Kelvin Hall in Glasgow. Largely sponsored and publicised by a daily newspaper, for three weeks the arena was packed every night to watch splendidly produced indoor Highland games presented by Archie McCulloch, a very experienced commentator. In total, some 54,000 people watched a star-studded cast including champion dancers such as Betty Turkington, Marjory Rowan, Billy Forsyth and Sandy McNidder. There were pipe bands marching through the 'castle' gates with another band on the ramparts, while on one side of the arena the moon appeared to shimmer on a loch. Heavies included Jay Scott, Bill Anderson, Jock McColl and Charlie Allan, while world-famous wrestlers such as Ian Campbell, Clayton Thomson, Justice Ross and Andy Robin created mayhem on the mat. Another major effort was an immense International Boys' Brigade Highland Games in 1963, with hundreds of boys from all over the world competing in the traditional events. This took place at Glenalmond, a famous Scottish school.

The international circuit was the start of a new lifestyle for many involved in Highland games, typified when, after doing a very successful show in Shrewsbury, the athletes were driven at speed through the night to get on a plane to the Bahamas for a Highland games. In those days, such jet-setting was rather special. The heavies were a versatile lot. After the heavy events, Jay Scott danced with two bonny Scots lassies – the trio were trained by a professional teacher, Valda, wife of Jimmy McCue, weightlifting champion of Scotland. Also representing Scotland was a young boxer who was to become prominent in Highland games. His name was Douglas Edmunds.

In 1964, Bill Anderson, Jay Scott, Sandy Sutherland, Louis McInnes, Jock McColl and Andy Robin participated in a six-week American and Canadian tour, presenting Highland games as part of a spectacular 'Wonderful World of Sport'. It was a tremendous experience, full of excitement and unrehearsed fun. The stories could fill a book. The itinerary included places such as New York State, Baltimore, Washington DC, Rochester, Montreal and Toronto. There were many important visitors, one of whom was Frank Tunney, the big-time wrestling promoter, and after watching a bout which we had specially arranged for his visit, he gave Andy Robin the chance of a lifetime. Andy got a contract with a tilt at the Commonwealth professional title, which Andy won. Then he took an opportunity to wrestle a bear! Long after, when Andy returned to Scotland, he bought and wrestled Hercules, the huge bear, which became world famous when it escaped and went missing, evading capture until giving up in its own time.

The International Sports Exhibition at Crystal Palace in 1965 gave another opportunity to innovate, with the first floodlit Highland gathering. On this occasion, and at many other international games, Arthur Rowe, the Olympic shot putter from Yorkshire, joined the team. While in the south, the opportunity was taken to present another Highland games, this time at Wimbledon to mark the centenary of the London Scottish Golf Club.

The Highlanders were becoming more interested in major international events. There was a big drive for trade exports in the late 1960s and the group was already well established internationally by 1969 when, in conjunction with the British Embassy in Sweden, it promoted a series of five Highland games in and around Stockholm. Princess Alexandra was guest of honour.

A significant point in the dateline was a response to an article in a newspaper asking for suggestions on the promotion of Britain and British goods in overseas countries. Conscious of the possibilities of commercial sponsorship, a letter was written on behalf of the Highlanders, pointing out the appeal of Highland games as a family event, with cultural and sporting items suitable for men and women, young and old. It also indicated how some of the games activities

The McVities Team in Stockholm in 1968.

THE WORLD HISTORY OF HIGHLAND GAMES

could be adapted to limited space and to huge stadiums. The idea appealed to McVitie's, the well-known biscuit firm with Scottish roots, and, to cut a long story short, a Highland games team was put together as part of British Week in various countries. One of these took place in Tokyo.

The Kilt and Kimonos

The McVitie's Games in Japan during 1969 were nothing short of sensational. The spectacle was featured frequently on television and royalty of two nations attended. It led to numerous bookings on the other side of the world and was a major factor in the growing globalisation of Highland games.

The sponsors were delighted with the results, for in just two days in the Japanese capital they sold £4,000 of biscuits in two stores alone. The demand became so great they had to fly in extra supplies from their depots in Australia – all this as the result of the publicity given to the Scottish team.

The export drive was opened by Her Royal Highness Princess Margaret, who was accompanied by Lord Snowdon, and on the very night of our team's arrival we were invited to 'go to the pictures' with the Royal couple and were later invited to a reception with these popular personages. The games took place at Toshimaen, a complex in Tokyo with numerous halls, tracks, swimming pools, ice-skating rinks, a trampoline centre and, of course, the huge athletic stadium where we were almost overwhelmed by a crowd of 20,000 on the first day and 22,000 on the following day. On the opening day,

Tokyo bound. This was also the first day of computerised checking in at Heathrow Airport.

His Royal Highness Prince William of Gloucester made a spectacular entry when he arrived by helicopter and alighted suitably kilted, in keeping with the grand occasion. He was introduced to the key members of the team, many of who are still widely remembered. On the second day there were no less than five members of the Imperial Japanese Royal Family, including Princess Chichibu of Emperor Hirohito's family.

Prince William presented trophies to the team, which included the massive Dave Prowse, who afterwards appeared in many films; Bill Anderson was later awarded the MBE for his contribution to British sport. Charlie Allan, a professor at Strathclyde University and publisher of Scottish books was there; Billy Forsyth, who became Chairman of the Official Board of Highland Dancing; dancers Doug Duncan, Arleen Stuart and Margaret Murphy; television strongman Graham Brown; Charlie Simpson; professional wrestlers Ian Campbell and Clayton Thomson – a closely knit group.

This group not only competed at Highland games but also performed in stores and on rooftop gardens of skyscrapers. An extended session in television studios resulted in seven programmes on Fuji Television. Another highlight was a visit to a dojo, where Grand Champion Wakanohana, holder of the Emperor's Cup, conducted a sumo school. After watching the huge wrestlers training, the largest of them challenged the Scottish heavies to meet him in

A media event in Tokyo.

combat. To the amazement of all, Charlie Simpson accepted with alacrity but was thrown almost as fast. Bill Anderson reluctantly agreed to wrestle and won in back-hold style.

This greatly embarrassed the Japanese and was a severe loss of face for the loser. In a bid to help the Japanese save face, Bill agreed to try sumo style. The two faced up to each other and on the signal the sumo star shot forward like a bullet and Bill braced himself for the impact. He hardly budged as the huge Japanese wrestler crashed into him and the Scot retaliated, trying to heave the big man off the floor. The sumo wrestler stood as firm as Bill had a second earlier and, struggle as he might, the Aberdonian just could not get his opponent off the ground. The latter was pulling at

Bill at the dojo.

Bill's kilt, and as it started to give way, Wakanohana stepped in to terminate the bout. It may have been an unsatisfactory ending but it glossed over the earlier embarrassment.

Bill spoke of his difficulty in lifting the huge man: 'I was not lacking in strength,' he explained. 'I lifted the outside but the mannie on the inside kept his feet on the ground!' Masses of flesh had been raised, but to no avail.

The Highlanders were treated like stars in the hotel and asked to join in a Japanese wedding party. Once again, the group showed their versatility, on this occasion by providing music and dance. The Japanese were so impressed that they miraculously produced beautifully wrapped presents for the Scots, which turned out to be lovely kimonos.

Stories from such a trip could fill a book but there is one that simply must be shared.

At one stage of the proceedings, having looked at the timetable, the Japanese timekeeper ordered the band of the Royal Highland Fusiliers on to the field. They were concentrating on their entry and at the same time Charlie Allan was in the act of running with a 25-foot long, skinny caber, concentrating solely on turning this unusual 'stick'. He never saw the band even as he made his effort. Fortunately, the observant Drum Major saw

Bill Anderson tries sumo wrestling in Tokyo.

THE WORLD HISTORY OF HIGHLAND GAMES

Charlie and reacted instantly. 'Drum corp – *mark time*,' he roared above the sound of the pipes and drums. The well-trained soldiers obeyed and the caber landed between the drummers and the pipers. 'For-*ward*,' the Drum Major ordered, and they did to the sound of tumultuous applause.

The bandsmen did not agree with the heavies that this should be made a permanent part of the presentation.

There was a sequel later in the Meadowbank stadium in Edinburgh when the Royal Highland Fusiliers band had been booked for another Highland games. As they lined up for the opening parade, we called to the Drum Major asking if he remembered us. He looked perplexed for a moment then it dawned. 'Hi men,' he addressed the band. 'Do you remember the b******s that nearly had us clobbered wi' a caber in Tokyo?' They did, and responded with a derisory drum salute, a few good-natured cat calls and some unearthly screeches and screams from the bagpipes.

Ask a silly question and you will get a silly answer.

May the Force Be with You

Few people know that Darth Vader, the villain of *Star Wars* films, was a Highland games athlete competing in many events at home and abroad. Dave Prowse, former British weightlifting champion, said that he got the part because of his controlled, purposeful walk, which he copied from his initial approach to tossing the caber! Dave had a good career in film and television, appearing in horror movies, comedy thrillers, *Casino Royale* with David Niven, *A Clockwork Orange* and other cult films.

Away from film studios, at 6 feet 7 inches in height and 18 stone in weight, he looked very well in kilt and, like most strong men, he was excellent at throwing the 56lb for height and tossing the caber – and he was no slouch in wrestling. He received his first coaching from Jay Scott and Jock McColl; later Charlie Allan gave him some assistance. Of all the strong men alive today, Dave was the earliest to lift both Dinnie Stones

ABERDEEN HIGHLAND GAMES 6p
Hazlehead Park   Saturday, 9th June, 1973

Dave Prowse.

together, which he did in front of television cameras. His first appearance in the heavy events was at Leeds Highland Games, along with Arthur Rowe. On this occasion, he won the 56lb weight for height with 15 feet, which was excellent at that time, and took third places in 22lb stone and caber. It was a fine start to a career in Highland games.

From 1976 to 1989, Dave was a household name as the Green Cross Code Man, in a major road safety campaign. Dave represented Britain in world weightlifting championships, took part in the World Caber-tossing Championships

Dave (Darth Vader) Prowse was a champion weightlifter and international Highland heavy.

in Aberdeen and became a regular member of the famous Highland games team that went to Sweden, California, Tokyo and elsewhere. Major hip surgery, with some complications, has slowed him down, but he is still active and keeps in touch with former sporting colleagues.

Developments in Scotland

Back to Scotland, and in Aberdeen, Highland games had been defunct for more than half a century and needed a star attraction to make them unique amongst the many games in the North East, still the stronghold of such gatherings. Always trying to maintain balance with progress and development at home as well as abroad, in 1970, after discussions with Arrol Winning, noted local authority parks director, we proposed a World Caber-tossing Championships. Sponsorship was crucial and we obtained much appreciated assistance from John Burns, later to become well known in Highland games. John was a power in the whisky industry and he was responsible for introducing sponsorship from Grants Ltd to the world championships. Through our internatonal connections, we were able to attract important overseas entries such as Eric Hedin, the Scandinavian Champion, the Reverend Arnold Pope of the United States, Dave Prowse and Colin Mathieson of Australia, the first from overseas to win the title. We retained official links with Aberdeen Games for many years.

In 1970 a small but important international mini-Highland Games was organised in association with the Commonwealth Games at Meadowbank, Edinburgh. This took place immediately before the paraplegic events and several Commonwealth competitors took part in the traditional competitions, as they have done over the years. Some of these amateurs, such as Chris Black, George Patience and Eric Irvine, have gone on to become amongst the best professional athletes of national and international circuits.

Heavies have long enjoyed overseas trips, which extend the season and give them opportunities to travel and even earn a pound or two, so it was with great pleasure that many of the group got together in 1971 for another McVitie's Games, this time at the famous Golden Gate Park in San Francisco, with Princess Alexandra and the Right Honourable Angus Ogilvie as guests of honour. Included in this event were stars such as Bill Anderson, Ian Campbell, Clayton Thomson, Billy Forsyth, Doug Duncan, Graham Brown and Dave Prowse.

This was an extremely significant occasion, although the importance of the contacts was not recognised at that time. The Californian intermediary was Malcolm Ramsay, then Chief of the Caledonian Club, a most helpful and friendly man, and after the games he acquired some of the equipment and considerably extended the club's hitherto somewhat limited programme of heavy events. As a direct result, their Californian Games at Santa Rosa and then Pleasanton now have what is believed to be the most comprehensive line-up of heavies competitions in the world today. There are classes for novices, advanced amateurs, world-ranking professionals, masters and women. It is well organised and superbly presented, currently attracting the best athletes and huge crowds of spectators every year.

In 1972, the International Highlanders asked Lord Aberdeen, Chieftain of Aberdeen Games, and his wife, Lady Aberdeen, to travel to Australia for an additional, one-off, world championship in caber tossing with the current champion defending his title, and with the event returning to Aberdeen as usual without further interruption. Lord and Lady Aberdeen accepted the invitation and accompanied the team to Australia in March

1973, when the championships took place at Geelong. The tour also included Highland games which Colin Mathieson had specially arranged in Melbourne, Sydney and Canberra. While in Australia, discussions took place with organisers and officials and, as a result, the World Highland Games Heavy Events Championships was legally registered on 25 May 1973.

Australia

In Victorian times, Dinnie, Fleming, Cameron and Johnstone were amongst the heavies who attended annual games at towns such as Geelong, Sydney, Ringwood and Canberra. Since then, Australia has produced many world champions, including, for example, Flora Stuart Grubb in Highland dancing in 1960, Lynn Dickson in 1970 and Scottish-born Colin Mathieson, a property manager in Mudgee, New South Wales, who won the World Caber-tossing Championship in 1975. Bill Docherty, doyen of pipe bands in Victoria, annually arranged dozens of events that delighted expatriate Scots and native Australians. There has also long been a thriving running circuit in Australia, attracting the best professional runners from Scotland.

Heavy events were boosted in 1981 when heavies from various parts of the globe gathered for the World Heavy Events Championships. Since then, Joe Quigley became World Heavy Events Champion in 1992 and Matt Sandford of Melbourne won *five* world heavy event championships and Aaron Neighbours won the world title at the great Homecoming Gathering, Edinburgh 2009.

When the 1980 World Championships took place near Los Angeles in the USA, accompanying Colin Matheson was Sir Billy Sneddon, who made a successful bid to host the World Championships in 1981. Sir Billy was the Speaker in Australia's Parliament and he opened many doors for the Scots when they went 'down under'. Dick Hamer,

the Premier of Victoria, hosted the World Championships in the Junction Oval, Melbourne, and after Canberra Highland Games, Sir Billy took the Scots to a reception held for them at the house of Australia's Prime Minister, Malcolm Fraser. When his butler opened the premier's door, there was a big surprise. The man, who came originally from Thurso in Scotland, immediately recognised the Scottish heavy Charlie Simpson who, when not competing, was a policeman in Thurso.

That evening during deliberations, it was proposed that there should be formed an official, athlete-orientated organisation to progress matters for the benefit of top-level traditional athletes. The idea was unanimously approved and I agreed to administer this if others co-operated. While the event sponsors were keen and gave every encouragement, none of the heavies were able to accept responsibility for the various chores that were necessary to achieve success. They were right in declining; they were focused world-class athletes and such responsibilities would have interfered with their training. This would be an international federation functioning to promote cognate strength sports and Highland games. It would not be an organisation for games committees, as the Scottish Games Association already looked after this. The main emphasis of the new body would be to foster the traditional and cognate sports internationally, and giving opportunities for the athletes would be a prime concern. Sir Billy agreed to lead the International Highland Games in the southern hemisphere, and his impact was substantial.

There, in Australia, Bill Anderson crowned his illustrious career by winning the world championships that was recognised by the heads of state, the Honourable Brian Dixon, Minister of Sport, civic dignitaries and the media.

George Shepherd, former editor for the

famous annual *Braemar Book*, asked Betty Gillin, popular Scottish television personality, to write a review of the fast development of international heavy events and to highlight the Australian tour.

In her comprehensive report on worldwide games, she wrote:

> The ubiquitous Doug Edmunds, a popular heavy athlete, accepted a promoted post in Nigeria and promptly began promoting Scottish activities. He gathered a hard-working committee and secured the cooperation of the Minister of Sport. Thus assisted he produced for three years [1980–1982] well-organised Highland games with high calibre international entries with varied backgrounds, creeds and colours.

Writing of the Australian tour, she commented:

> Such prestigious events don't just happen by themselves and the catalyst in this and many other overseas events is David Webster, a former strength athlete and Olympic and Commonwealth Games official. He has been organising major Highland games since 1961 and has taken teams on extensive tours.

Betty Gillin's conclusion was:

> The fact that Highland games have spread all around the world, providing sport, music and colourful family entertainment is something that should give us all great pride. It is doubtful if any other ethnic festival could rival such a record.

Part of the group went back to Sweden several times to strengthen the links first forged in 1968. This continued until the early 1990s, with many exchanges of international competitors. On the little island of Gotland, the Scots competed in the Femkampf's five events, and strength tests; the Swedes returned the compliment by competing at Highland games in Scotland. At this time, Douglas Edmunds was at college and still had his eye on amateur records but we kept in touch and this was but the first step in a long and successful sporting and business partnership that put strength athletics on a major worldwide footing.

The original plan was to extend the season, with some early and some off-season games. These were truly international events, and with the influx of top-line foreign stars from power-lifting and weightlifting, several strength events, especially with strong men in mind, were included so they could still have a guaranteed income even though they were taking on the Scots in traditional events.

With a little standardisation of equipment and regular competition, the main men became very good and the popularity of the open-strength competitions led to their inclusion in the international circuit of Highland games. The best Scottish strongmen and some foreign guests were invited to compete in a battery of five strength tests, separate from, but between and alongside, the throwers who maintained their traditional competitions with cabers and hammers.

The New Millennium

There have been several ambitious World Series events over the years but the millennium year was targeted as being very special. It lived up to all expectations. That special year started with the Hogmanay extravaganza at Waipu, described earlier, and the summer season opened at Fredericksburg, Virginia, where Carl Braun, formerly the United States' best hammer thrower, was supremo of their excellent games and very popular with international heavy athletes. This was one of several televised Highland games that featured in a series of programmes on American and Canadian television for consecutive years. Made by Marsh View Productions in Connecticut, they were called *Ultimate Heavy Athletics*. On more than one occasion, Ken Soudans' Highland games programmes were the highest rated shows of the day on America's ESPN2 airing. Ken stated: 'In only ten airings on ESPN2 we have been seen by more than 6.5 million viewers.' It was superb advertising for Scotland and its Highland games.

Such television coverage puts our media companies to shame. It appears that the only way to get good coverage in Scotland is to include some fanciful trappings in place of authentic and colourful traditions and concepts that have already stood the test of time.

Next on the Millennium international circuit was an outstanding new games at Lord Antrim and Viscount Dunluce's lovely Glenarm Castle in County Antrim, Northern Ireland, with large and welcoming crowds on both days. Northern Ireland has several annual events, the main one being at Glenarm. This event continually attracts crowds of around 30,000, often followed by one or two full feature-length television programmes after the games.

Lynn Boland Richardson's Hall of Fame is a great feature at Fergus for real enthusiasts. It contains hundreds of photographs of Highland games.

As in other years, there were international Highland games, a few days apart at Callander and Killin. At the former, non-profit-making organisations frequently raise £12,000 to £15,000 for local charities. Killin Games, taking place in beautiful Breadalbane, is singled out here for special mention. These well-organised midweek games are always very enjoyable. The natural arena has a background of mountains and forest and good hosts make everybody feel welcome. It is amazing that this very small town can attract a midweek attendance of some 5,000 people year after year. It is a real blessing for the rural community.

Since the start of the new millennium, immediately after Killin Games, some of the leading heavies flew to Canada. By 2007, this Canadian segment had developed into a trilogy of Highland games. With little sleep after a transatlantic flight, our groups met up with their

Canadian colleagues to attend and compete at Maxville, Glengarry and then Montreal, before heading to Fergus, Ontario, where some 44,000 people gathered for the annual celebrations. Athletes must have strength and endurance to compete six days out of ten and squeeze in a transatlantic flight.

Fergus Highland Games, started in 1945, is the brainchild of Alex Robertson. Fergus is a special place. All year round, huge permanent signboards at main road entrances to this little town proudly proclaim *Fergus, Home of the Highland Games*.

On the days leading up to the games the main street is bedecked with tartan and shop windows have appropriate displays. On games days there are thousands of participants and numerous pipe bands, and nearly 1,000 dancers fill the custom-made arenas with sound and colour. Top international Highland games competitors appear in the various activities and there is a plethora of high-standard Scottish entertainers. The organisers are well supported by competitors as organisation is good and hospitality is of a high order; Warren Trask, the athletic director, and committee official Lynn Boland Richardson see to that.

Sticking with millennium travels, as they are fairly typical of the era, German events were next on the itinerary as the season wore on. These are more modest in scale, two or three being part of other British projects, mainly with trade and cultural emphasis. Nevertheless, they are enjoyable and give a variety of heavies an opportunity to travel and to gain foreign competition experience.

The international circuit continued with what many believe is the world's biggest annual Highland games, staged in northern California by the Caledonian Club of San Francisco. Celebrations begin with band concerts and other events on Friday evenings before Labor Day each year and continue through the weekend.

Over the years, crowds have grown considerably, and average at around 50,000. While some organisers tend to inflate their reports of attendances, it is believed that the figures quoted here are genuine. The committee for these Caledonian Games regularly 'import' dancing judges, personalities, great international athletes and officials. There were over 60 heavy event competitors at Pleasanton in 2000. For many years the games were held at Santa Rosa, north of San Francisco, but they are now held in the wine country at Pleasanton. Each discipline has its own space and there is a special display area in front of a massive covered grandstand, which shields spectators from the unrelenting sun. It is an eye opener for those attending for the first time.

A fairly typical large group of heavy event competitors and officials at the Caledonian Club's games at Pleasanton.

THE WORLD HISTORY OF HIGHLAND GAMES

Those in the international group were just getting over jet lag when it was time for the final Millennium event of the World Series. This time, the exotic destination was Rio de Janeiro, Brazil. There, the St Andrews Society President, Jimmy Frew, had been working hard at promoting its first Highland games. They had an excellent pipe band and some very fine Highland dancers, all resplendent in the best traditions of Highland dress and all Brazilians.

Spectators sat on a terraced and banked setting that overlooked a field with four lines of coconut palms, and the throwing events took place in the centre with two rows of palms down each side. Ian McPhail and his lively Scottish country dance band have long been popular in Brazil and were there again to help create a great Scottish atmosphere. The heavies were extremely popular and a month later they had an invitation to return. They accepted and they enjoyed themselves even more.

One never knows quite what might happen at overseas locations when it is their first attempt at Highland games. In Brazil, when the events were over and it was time for the prize-giving, the crowd swarmed into the arena and crowded round the stars, shaking their hands, slapping their backs and asking for autographs. Then when Lord MacDonald, Lord of the Isles, had graciously distributed the prizes, Ian McPhail and his excellent band struck up 'Auld Lang Syne'. St Andrews Society members quickly formed a circle round the field and sang in the traditional manner. The heavies joined in and then the Brazilians too. It really was a very touching experience. When Brazil's first games and the millennium season was all over, emotions were released and as Charlie Allan, former champion heavy, declared, 'If there was a dry eye in the place it wasnae Davie Webster's'.

Later, relaxing at the famous Cococabana Beach, athletes reflected on the changes from the time emigrants spent months on crowded boats from Scotland to the Americas and from Nova Scotia to the Antipodes. We compared this with the ease that, in every month from September 1999 until October 2000, the athletes went overseas and enjoyed Highland games and competitions in the furthest corners of the world.

Globalisation

Many aspects of people's lives are changing rapidly. Technological advances are being made at a bewildering pace. It is clear to all just how much has changed in one lifetime. Many children are now becoming 'couch potatoes', more interested in computer games than physical activity. This, and labour-saving devices at home and at work, has resulted in obesity taking the place of athleticism – as a nation we are fat rather than fit.

It is perhaps time to pause and briefly reflect on how changes are affecting Highland games. The greatest change, of course, is globalisation. The ancient informal rural activities of the Highlands are now a worldwide phenomenon, attracting audiences of hundreds of thousands

Competitors from different nations at Glenarm Castle, Northern Ireland.

and exceeding most high-profile British sports. Nowadays, Scottish competitors and officials in all Highland games disciplines are regularly invited overseas to participate, and overseas competitors will arrive in and depart from Scotland throughout the summer. There are many frequent flyers in the games fraternity.

Over the past 50 years, great efforts have been made to actively encourage Highland games at home and abroad. These efforts have met with some success thanks to the co-operation of some very fine organising committees and to some very enthusiastic Scottish 'exiles'.

A quick review of the current situation reveals Highland games in many remote, exotic places in every continent. There are well over 30 days of games scheduled on the west coast of America, good circuits in the east and a scattering through-out the whole country. In one newspaper count in Canada a few years back, there were over 120 games. Europe has developed astonishingly. Iceland led the way with a very extensive circuit, with games nearly every summer weekend. Sweinung Tansted has regular events in Norway and Wout Zjilstra, who has an army of fans who often follow him to Scotland, has built up a very fine circuit of 12 to 15 games in the Netherlands. This includes games at Lisse, Apeldorm, Swifterbank, Dordrecht, Hank and Beckum. The Stegeman family of Hengelo also have some good games, so it is a very healthy picture. France is coming into the picture with several Celtic/Breton games attended by Wullie Baxter and his athletes. Bressuire is the main centre, with the picturesque chateau being a wonderful setting for splendid Highland gather-ings. Jean Louis Coppet, acting for Ajef, their national governing body, has done a terrific job in securing some world-class athletes who attract very large crowds. His European Championships have been very successful.

With assistance from Wout Zjilstra of the Netherlands, Belgium is now on a firm footing with Tommy de Bruyne and his wife, who is a very able organiser. They have been promoting excellent Highland games since 2005 and have splendid support from the community and also the local authorities. Now they are organising official Belgian championships for men and women. Tommy, massive at 6 feet 9½ inches, now competes internationally.

Ukraine is unique, with fine annual television coverage of Highland games. It is believed that Ukraine's television features Scotland's heavies *more* than both main Scottish television channels combined. Again, it is a woman who plays an important role. Not only does Olena Obeka, formerly an international high jumper, organise

Crowds in Bressuire, France.

THE WORLD HISTORY OF HIGHLAND GAMES

the events and direct the television programmes, she is also the manager of leading competitors.

The newest kids on the block are from Germany and below is a more in-depth report to show how much Highland games have developed here in a comparatively short time.

The German Dimension

In the Middle Ages, *baum werfen*, a sport similar to tossing the caber, was practised in Germany. Instead of a long log, the Germans used a squared, untapered length of wood. It was recorded that the mighty Dirk Dammers was their greatest champion of putting the stone and their version of the caber. This sporting hero died in Buesen in 1533. Carl Diem, a German sports historian, wrote of such very early Highland games as practised by Scots.

In the early 1950s, there were a number of Highland games in Germany, mostly with Scottish regimental connections. These gatherings seemed

Wilhelmshaven, Germany: Anderson and Weir support Aitken, Freebairn and Webster.

to be either one-off events, or would take place for a few years and then cease.

My personal experience of Highland games in Germany began in 1989 when a group of Scottish athletes travelled to Wilhelmshaven in north-west Germany. The athletes – Stephen Aitken, John Freebairn, Walter Weir, Alan Anderson and their leader – were faced with several problems, all of which were overcome, thanks to the athletes' versatility and good humour.

The local organisers had little knowledge of Highland games and had arranged that daily events would take place in a large car park. They were not worried about broken hammer shafts and cabers but hastily changed the venue when public safety issues were explained. Next, they publicised that the games would be demonstrated in Circus Lauenburger, a fine family circus being staged before large audiences in a big top; this did indeed take place, but with a very limited programme of games events.

Throwing the weight for height was the favourite item, along with some impromptu strongman stunts. The final Highland games were done in the proper surroundings, and included army pipe bands, Highland dancers and the heavies. It was a resounding success, with happy-go-lucky Stephen Aitken being a very popular winner.

From time to time the Scottish Tourist Board included some minor demonstrations of events

Manfred der Highlander von Neiderrhein.

such as caber tossing and ceilidh dances in their German promotions, and while these were rather low-key events, they did help to publicise the concept of Highland games as incentives and corporate activities for commercial companies.

In spite of the passing of time since those great British Weeks in Japan, America and Canada, the export councils and Chambers of Commerce had not forgotten the Highland games, and towards the end of the millennium Germany came into the picture.

Omar Orloff was the star of the Berlin games.

In 1998, the British Chamber of Commerce introduced Highland games as part of the annual British Day celebrations they were organising in Hamburg, which gave heavy events considerable exposure and, importantly, some continuity of publicity. The inclusion of the heavy brigade's Highland games in this new era of British Day was the brainchild of Sue Austin on the staff of the British Chamber of Commerce, and these events proved to be a catalyst for further development. The knock-on effect of the venture was immediate. Before the end of the first event at Hamburg, two agents anxious to arrange a whisky-sponsored Highland games in Berlin approached the International Highland Games Federation administrator, who arranged for Jamie Barr, a second-generation Highland games athlete, to be brought in on an organisational basis. The results were very gratifying. There were large crowds and great sport in the German capital.

Graham's chest was so big he could set a saucer and a cup of tea on it and not spill a drop. Here he settles for a soft drink.

Many of Europe's best throwers competed and a new star, Omar Orloff, came to light. Although residing in Germany at that time, Omar came from Poland and later returned to his homeland. Fortunately, he competed in Scotland, so enthusiasts could see for themselves that his fine reputation was not in any way exaggerated.

The Berlin Games lasted for several years until there was a change of venue and the sponsor moved on to a different project.

After the success in Hamburg, the heavies and their sports were included at British Days in Krefeld and later Konigstein. The venue for Hamburg is at the elite polo club in Flotbek. In Krefeld, the beautiful castle precincts of Burg Linn are used and at Konigstein another castle, the Burgruine, was a fitting background.

Big in size but small in number, the 'heavies' fill a significant part of the arena programmes, appearing some five times each day. Their demonstrations of all the heavy events are done as friendly competitions and the sportsmanship displayed appeals to the audiences. The personalities of the athletes are important from an audience viewpoint, and in Germany at the beginning of the new millennium Graham Mullins, Forbes Cowan and Jamie Barr were amongst the most popular. These strongmen greatly enjoyed their sport and their enthusiasm was infectious. They were great ambassadors for Britain, who gave 100 per cent

THE WORLD HISTORY OF HIGHLAND GAMES

effort. Rivalry was keen within the arena, but away from the field of dreams they all had amusing nicknames, which changed from time to time depending on current activities and comments. The easiest nickname to understand was that of amateur thrower Walter (Wattie) Weir. Graham Mullins of England represented the Auld Enemy and had more than his share of leg pulling, but he gave as much as he got. Scandinavian heavies, led by Jouko Ahola, the then World's Strongest Man, observed that Graham's huge torso, topped by a 64-inch chest, made his limbs look small and said his proportions were like a spider – so they called him 'Spiderman'.

In a jape during a Canadian visit, Graham was one of the trio of titans who, when invited to a function that emphasised 'dress informal', bought some outsize women's dresses, applied elaborate lipstick and, without shaving, attended the function, to the amusement of all. Mullins was the funniest of these Clanvestites and his friends dubbed him 'Tranny'. However, after his spectacular film appearances in Ridley Scott's epic, kids everywhere knew him as 'the Gladiator' – but that was before the film *Shrek* came along. Graham's spitting image of the character was immediately obvious – only a mother could tell them apart. Naturally, he became 'Shrek' to all and sundry!

Sue Austin, the British Chamber of Commerce coordinator, said more than once that our dour, intimidating Fifer was such a nice boy. To his teammates he became Jamie (Nice Boy) Barr. Surely Sue must be the only person who described him thus with sincerity, but actually, *she was dead right*. The most articulate athlete was Colin B(r)ayne, but what would you call Forbes Cowan, the toughest of the tough, 6 feet 4 inches of might and muscle? Only 'Sir' or 'Mr Cowan, sir'! Forbes is now a very busy motorcyclist, racing on an international circuit.

The popularity of these men received a great boost when seven Highland games heavies were auditioned and selected for parts in the Stephen Spielberg blockbuster *Gladiator*, directed by Ridley Scott. Amongst other athletes, Graham Mullins, Forbes Cowan, Gordon Smith and Sebastian Abbatiello performed with distinction, each playing at least two different roles in this thrilling film.

There is no doubt that the British Days have been successful and such success can be measured in various ways. For example, the events at Hamburg and Krefeld usually attract between 19,000 and 20,000 spectators and in addition to the promotion

A trio of Titans. Graham Mullins, Oliver Reed, Forbes Cowan.

Gladiators Gordon Smith and international athlete Pauline Richards.

of trade and commerce, charities benefit significantly, receiving donations of nearly 40,000 euros.

Since the early German British Days, there have been a number of guest athletes from Germany and other parts of mainland Europe. This initiative started with the usual invitations to the biggest and strongest men in the audience to come on the field and try their strength and testify that the weights were genuine. One of these was Manfred Muehlenhaus, a husky ice hockey player and coach from Kempen. He came out of the crowd at Krefeld and later became a key figure in the development of Highland games in Germany. It was immediately clear to the Scottish athletes that this was a man of high potential as an athlete but what was not immediately apparent was his resolution and tenacity. These qualities resulted in him recruiting training partners, forming a Kempen Highland games club, organising local games and then inviting overseas guests. One of his athletic colleagues was the son of a farmer who allowed them to train in one of his fields. They have built a hut in which they can store equipment, use as a changing or meeting room, with a table and seats so they can chat and have a drink after training. Around this table, the strength athletes planned to expand their activities and the first Kempen Highland Games took place in 2003. Before this, the only other German-

Leading throwers and officials at prize giving in Kempen.

organised Highland games in Germany was at Maachen, originating in 2001.

The growth of Highland games in Germany in the new millennium has been quite remarkable. On the first day of the second Kempen Highland Games, 64 young male athletes paraded, led by a pipe band, to the town square for the Burgomaster's (mayor) official opening of the games.

It was like our old-fashioned March of the Clansmen. They came from the east to the west of Germany, the Netherlands and Belgium; all but a few wore kilts. After the opening ceremony, the German 'Highlanders' returned to what we would call the village green for a celebration of traditional Scottish activities. This was Kempen's first two-day games, with groups and novice competitions on the first day and championships on the second. On the second day, 20 good athletes from Germany, Holland, Scotland and New Zealand were divided by ability into two groups and competed in the traditional Scottish events.

The German emphasis is on participation; spectators are not charged but, if interested, they are encouraged to take part in future competitions, providing they will wear kilts in order to maintain tradition. 'Only kilties can play' is the rule of the day. It is very gratifying for the Scots to see such development and dedication, with a true feeling and respect for our ancient traditions.

At the games in Kempen, the Clan der Ebronen were impressive, well organised and professional. They were uniformly dressed with good kilts and black T-shirts bearing an attractive insignia. After the second meeting at Kempen,

Mustering for the March of the German 'clansmen' in Kempen.

THE WORLD HISTORY OF HIGHLAND GAMES

we were invited to officiate at the first International Highland Games, held in 2005 at the big racecourse in Halle, in the eastern part of Germany.

Peter Stegeman putting the stone in Germany. Inset: Gerd Stegeman.

The smallest of three large posters.

Led by their clan chief, Sven Ebert, the clan's marketing was incredible. A beautifully designed poster was prominently exhibited around the town and there, displayed on the end of high-rise flats, were the biggest-ever Highland games posters. The largest started just above a row of shops and then covered the next six storeys! It was the biggest image of a caber tosser ever seen. Their efforts certainly proved effective; the official estimate was that around 28,000 people attended this first Halle International Highland Games.

On the first full day of these games, 13 'clans', each with approximately ten representatives, accompanied by two pipe bands and officials, marched around the town square, a busy market place, then onwards through the town to the racecourse. It was a long march but spirits were high and there were no complaints. In one part of the arena there was a superb medieval village with a smithy, other working craftsmen and the Clan Ebronen chief's tent.

Advertising Halle's Highland Games.

The blacksmith seemed to be linked with a massive machine, a ballista that would have been used for catapulting big stones or fireballs at ancient fortresses. At night, festivities went on after the games and this machine hurtled a fireball a distance of about 70 metres to set fire to a huge wicker man, the resulting bonfire lighting the following proceedings. Under the stars, pipe bands played and torches held aloft by some muscular, kilted German athletes illuminated the areas unlit by the bonfire's flames. The highlight of the night was an incredible fireworks display, choreographed with the pipes and drums as the bands played 'Highland Cathedral'.

Pyrotechnic experts produced a shower of brilliantly coloured sparks and flames that formed what looked like the inside of a dome in a church or cathedral. There were Scottish-based fun competitions for the clans, a very large and well-supported amateur heavy event competition using 16lb stone, 16lb hammer, 28lb weight for distance,

The Shah of Persia at Glenmuick Games.

42lb weight for height and a medium-sized caber. However, the professionals from various European countries used all the standard weights and had an impressive long, thick, caber. The caber had been well dried and the Dutch Stegeman brothers, Peter and Gerd, both got 12 o'clock throws.

The host clan was represented by a huge, 130kg athlete known as Mozart, which he said was his real name. In spite of very vocal local support for Mozart, Manfred Muehlenhaus beat him and took second place. The overall winner of the first Halle International was the experienced 32-year-old Dutchman, Ivo Degeling, who had already participated in over 200 games, many of these in Scotland.

From small beginnings, a fine German circuit has emerged, with Highland games in Kempen-Neiderrhein, Hamm, Westfalen, Halle, Saale, Ossweil, Machern, Duisburg, Büsen, Angelbachtal, Obermain Stetten, Pfaffenhofen/Buxheim-Bavaria and Rüsselheim. British Days at Hamburg and Krefeld still include Highland games heavy events on an annual basis. Although centred on heavy events, many of the games include pipe bands and other attractions. In 2009 it was estimated that there were over 30 Highland games in Germany.

Another Level of International Games

There has long been a practice of entertaining visitors to Scotland by presenting demonstrations of Highland dancing, piping and heavy events. Royal visitors from home and abroad have commented favourably on this, Queen Victoria being especially enthusiastic.

With the growth of international travel, it is not surprising that in the late 1970s the Scottish Tourist Board organised a major project to attract Americans to Scotland – for while British tourism was doing very well, the British Tourist Board policies ensured that London was the gateway to the whole of Britain. *This policy failed to maximise Scottish potential.* During the American promotions, Hamish Cathie of Travel Scotland discussed with the director of leisure, recreation and tourism of Cunninghame District Council, a strategy to present not only demonstrations of Highland games but also active participation in the activities by the visitors, with scaled-down equipment. The plan was to cater for commercial firms interested in staff incentive schemes. There would be flexibility to cater for large or small groups competing with each other on a team or individual basis, or with a purely recreational approach. The first main venue for the experiment was Glamis Castle, where the Queen Mother was brought up. In addition to the games, a tour of this fascinating building and fine Scottish catering added to the concept.

This plan for incentive corporate tourism was a success and soon other venues were booked for similar games at other locations. Our favourites venues included Dalmahoy, Blair Castle (ancient seat of the Dukes and Earls of Atholl), the Indoor Riding School and Wheel Garden at Gleneagles Hotel, Hopetoun House (the fine Scottish stately home overlooking the Firth of Forth), Lennoxlove, Oxenfoord Castle, Rothiemurchus Highland Estate, Thirlestane Castle, Formakin, Traquair (dating back to the 12th century), Scone Palace (the crowning place of Scottish kings), Huntly Castle, Drum Castle, Dalmeny and Mavis Hall Park (at the time of writing, the most successful so far). These are just a few of the places where private Highland games have been a big success.

CHAPTER THIRTY

Conclusion

Progress of Highland games can be measured in a number of ways: improved records, geographic spread, number of participants, number of games, size of crowds, quality of organisation, and so on. I am happy to say that a review of these is encouraging.

One factor that is given scant attention in Scotland is the varying classes or categories of competition. In other countries, and particularly in the USA and Canada, the importance of these has long been recognised. There are very often amateur, professional, women and masters' divisions and invitation championships. In Scotland, the classes are generally local and open only.

There is no doubt in my mind that the introduction of different categories is important from many points of view and should therefore be encouraged. When I attended the second World

A group at the World Masters Championships in Inverness in 2006. Bill Anderson MBE, centre front. Immediately behind him is Warren Trask of Canada. On either side of Warren is M. Muehlenhaus of Germany and Anthony Lordi of Switzerland. Also pictured are David Webster, Steve Clark, Gord Walsh, Jamie Barr, Kevin Fast and Dirk Bishop.

Masters Championships in Sacramento, California, the late Bill Butler told me that there were around 120 heavy event competitors in total, including all the usual classes.

The Masters competition in Scotland in 2006 attracted over 100 entries. Credit must be given to people such as Bill Scruggs of America and Gerry Reynolds, the on-the-spot man at Inverness. One of the beauties of the Masters category is that we see many old favourites extending their careers, which gives new fans the opportunity of seeing great names from the not-so-distant past.

We must not be too complacent. There are still, and always will be, many problems.

It is costly to present first-class Highland games, and it is voluntary committees that do almost all of the work. Almost all the games are well organised at a local level, but there is a limit of what can be expected from people giving many hours of their time at no cost to those who benefit most from their services. I strongly believe that there are roles and responsibilities for national and local government.

I accept that there is never enough money to go round for all the important services that are required, but I am extremely surprised at the distribution of money in terms of benefit to the community. Comparisons are usually invidious in such matters and it may appear that I am disparaging some activities. That is not the case. I am simply saying that Scotland as a country benefits more from Highland games than most other sporting and cultural activities. Decide for yourselves: apart from the likes of football and perhaps a few other sports, which sports attract more than our traditional ones?

The crowds at nearly every Highland games in Scotland outnumber even the biggest athletic meetings. In cultural terms, vast amounts are spent on dance, yet there are many more Highland dancers, audiences for Highland dancing and tourists coming to Scotland to support these dancers. Where is the justice in this? In music it is the same story. For a large number of Scots, there is nothing in orchestras to compare with massed pipe bands.

Financial grants of many millions have been given to such activities in Scotland. From a tourist's point of view, there is no contest – the number of public appearances, from Edinburgh Tattoos, Cowal and Braemar down to the small games so important to rural communities, traditional activities win hands down. When politicians travel abroad, they enjoy the support of pipe bands and pipers, rather than government-financed professional orchestras. It is not a situation of 'one or the other'; all I am looking for is a fair division of existing, available resources, *after proper research*.

The emphasis is important. There will not be the best use made of limited finance if there are ill-informed decision makers. Amongst the few grants previously given to Highland games have been those for events introducing inappropriate 'spin' and with less genuine Highland games content.

Tourism and Highland games are closely linked. Every time Scottish tourism suffers from some disaster, be it a terrorist attack somewhere in the world or foot and mouth disease, Highland games also suffer. Indeed, some games have had to be cancelled because of such events. The games are also very weather dependent, so heavy rain and flooding can be disastrous. Mostly, we have no control over such matters, but sometimes this is not the case.

Constantly increasing legislation and very demanding statutory regulations are decided disincentives to voluntary organisers and local committees. Of course, there should be precautions in public events, but looking honestly and fairly at Highland games, it appears that – generally speaking – the old Scottish declaration that 'they are looking for snow and there is none falling' seems quite appropriate. A realistic appraisal and a common sense approach would make life easier for hard-working, unpaid organisers.

Sadly, at the time of writing, there is little government support of any kind for Highland gatherings and games. National sports councils change their priorities and aims with the passing of time. There is little wrong with this, *providing they include traditional Scottish activities as part of the equation*. For example, it is understood that winning medals internationally is a stated objective of **sport**scotland (the national agency for sport in Scotland) at this time but while others receive grants for training and overseas competitions, our international Highland games athletes never receive such government support. *Without this, the gap between Scots and the rest of the world will widen and Scotland's wonderful heavies may be in danger of becoming an extinct species.*

There is a very good case for support.

Apart from providing competitive sport at all levels, there are very high participation numbers in Highland games. There has often been 800 participants in various activities at a single Highland games. There can be as many as 900 dancers at Highland games in Scotland and the same in North America. There are usually well over 1,000 pipers at Cowal Games in Dunoon. *Participant figures are far ahead of the vast majority of grant-receiving bodies.*

The quasi-government bodies of today could help maintain and perpetuate these age-old activities in line with their aims, whether it be to win international medals, encourage active physical recreation, fight childhood obesity, provide community services or attract tourists and service those who visit our shores. Our Scottish traditional activities are very versatile: they add to the quality of life in a very healthy and fulfilling way.

It is sad to see that the Scottish and British governments give less to Scottish Highland games than state and local governments give in Canada and the USA.

This matter needs proper attention. The scale of deterioration (in some respects) over the years is incredible. In past times, competitors had the choice of a dozen Highland games in Scotland at peak weekends in the season. Crowds of up to 70,000 attended. There has been a reduction of 12 games in Scotland in two years. This is only one of the warning signs. Gerry Reynolds, a most enthusiastic organiser, says, 'The games are like the Titanic heading for an iceberg, and nobody is listening.'

Like our country, the games have had a chequered history. Over the years, commercial interests have motivated changes, and recently in Scotland there has been talk of what was termed 'sexing up' and introducing fanciful concepts. This seems ridiculous since overseas traditional Highland games are flourishing more than ever in their long history. The games are all about tradition and this will be our lifeline. We have deep roots. Highland games will survive.

However, Highland games deserve much more government help than they are being given. This is not about party politics; it is about gaining rightful tangible recognition for this part of our rich heritage. Thankfully, there are already a few glimmers of hope from a more nationalistic government.

Throughout the history of our games, family tradition is very noticeable. The many generations of MacCrimmon pipers are a classic example; the McHardys, the earliest heavies; the many Nicolsons from Tighnabruaich; the Gunns, then the Andersons – Ed, Jim, Bill, Craig and Steve. In dancing, World Champion Wilma Tolmie married pipe major George Michelson, then their offsprings – Ailsa, Deryck, Gareth, his wife Donna – and then their families are all involved. The same applies to other teachers such as Myra Miller-Richardson, her daughter Jane and her granddaughter, Kira. Organisers, too – I could go on and on. It is a family affair, probably in our genes from clans of the past, which were such an important part of our proud nation.

Highland games with hammers and cabers, dancing, Strathspeys and reels, bagpipes and tartans are all internationally recognised as symbolic of Scotland and our pride of race and place. Few countries have such potent images – a living reality, not an ancient memory. Out, we say, with the inverted snobbery of those snide critics who fear association with all things Scottish! Highland games and their traditions are jewels in our crown. We must perpetuate them for posterity.

Biggest and Best

In July 2009 in Holyrood's Royal Park, Edinburgh, there took place the largest clan gathering since 1822, when King George IV visited Scotland. The Gathering was the main event of Homecoming Year and the centrepiece, licensed by the International Highland Games Federation, was the 30th World Highland Games Championships.

A respected national daily newspaper reported that a crowd of more than 60,000 flocked to the capital and that of those 47,000 of the 'Sporran legion', attended the Games. It was said that as a conservative estimate the event generated over £8,000,000 into the Scottish economy. With 124 different clans and societies, massed pipe bands, four hundred Highland dancers, and the heavies (enlarged throughout on a huge 'jumbotron' screen), this historic event was regarded as 'the biggest and best' by public and participants alike.

Lord Jamie Sempill with World Championship athletes and international officials.

Roll of Honour

Many of the world's greatest strength athletes have competed in international circuit Highland games. There have been Olympic finalists, world record holders, Commonwealth Games medal winners, Guinness Book of Records entrants, physique champions, continental and national title holders, World's Strongest Men and international legends in various sports. These are detailed below, but the list is not exhaustive.

Argentina
Christian Gonzalo Martinez

Australia
Colin Mathieson, Peter and Billy Binks, Joe Quigley, Joy Dobson, Bill Lyndon, Nathan Jones, Matt Sandford, Aaron Neighbour

Austria
Manfred Hoeberl, Franz Beerbaum

Belgium
Filip Scherlippens, Tommy De Bruyn

Brazil
Jaier da Silva Gomez

Bulgaria
Evgeny Popov, Elle Petkova

Canada
Dave Harrington, Dan Markovic, Harry MacDonald, Warren Trask, George Chiappa, Tom Magee, Greg Ernst, Chuck Haase, Hugo Girard, Doug MacDonald, Josee Morneau, Glen Dewtie, Greg Hadley, Jamie Peppard, Joel Thiesen, Steve Clark, Pastor Kevin Fast, Christoph and Marcus Wand, Lyle Barrow, Matt Doherty, Matt Richardson, Dirk Bishop

Czech Republic
Jaromir Nemec, Jiri Zalondek

Denmark
Henning Thorsen

England
Geoff Capes, Mark Higgins, Mark Procter, Graham Mullins, Jamie Reeves, Adrian Smith, Paul Lupton, Russ Bradley, Bill Pittuck, Carl Sullivan, Andy Bolton, Lee Bowers, Dave Miles, Rob Dixon, Steve Brooks, Fraser Tranter, Laine Snook, Beth Talbot, David Dowson, Scott Rider, Julie Dunkley, Gemma Taylor

Estonia
Karl Loobas, Valdec Susi, Jaan Kirsipuv, Paul Lepik

Faro Islands
Regin Vagadal

Fiji Islands
Derek Boyer

Finland
Ilkka Nummisto, Markku Sounenvirta, Ilkka Kinnunen, Heini Koivenemi

France
Alain Prebert, Eric Allagill, Marc Messeant, Phillipe Cassader

Germany
Rudy Kuster, Heinz Ollesch, Manfred Muhlenhaus, Jorgen Sticklebrug

Iceland
Petur Gudmundsson, Jon Pall Sigmarsson, Magnus Ver Magnusson, Hjalti Arnason, Andreas Gudmundsson, Torvi Olafsson, Audunn Jonsson, Solvi Fannar, Saemunder Samundersson, Omar Sigurdson, Kejarten Gudbjartsson, Bjorgen Palifson, Gudbrander

Ireland
Glenn Ross, Emma James, Francis Kirkby, Ray O'Dwyer

Italy
Sebastian Abbatiello

Japan
Michael Abdullah

Latvia
Raimonds Bergmanis

Lithuania
Arvydas Svegsda, A. Pintinas

Namibia
Anton Boucher

Netherlands
Tjalling Van Den Bosch, Ab Wolders, Ted Van Der Parre, Huub Van Eck, Mark Daalmann, Siem Wulfse, T. Tuunter, Berend Veneberg, Wout Zilstra, Jarno Hamms, Gorrid Vissor, Hank Stepanov, Peter Baltus, Geritt and Peter Stegeman. Ivo Deneling, Ralph Koniger, Hans Lolkema

New Zealand
Colin Cox, Pat Hellier, Matt Rossiter, Scott Green, Steve Barry, P. Hart, M. Cotrell

Nigeria
Chris Okonkwo, Iron Bar Bassie

Norway
Sweinung Tangsted, Od Heugan, Svend Karlsen

Poland
Omar Orloff, Jaroslav Dymak, Mariusz Pudzianowski, Sebastian Venta, Anneta Florcyk,

Russia
Mikhail Koklyaev

Samoa
Joe Onosai

Scotland
Bill Anderson MBE, Grant Anderson, Jay Scott, Gordon Forbes, Charlie Allan, George Patience, Francis Brebner, Chris Black, Gordon Martin, Alistair and Murray Gunn, Kevin Thom, Eric Irvine, Forbes Cowan, Jamie Barr, Kenny Simmonds, Stephen King, Douglas and Gregor Edmunds, Iain Murray, Brian Bell, Davie Sharp, Lee Maxwell, Rab McNamara, Rab Clark, Stuart Murray, Pauline Richards, Gordon Campbell Smith, Lawrie and Colin Bryce, Stephen and Bruce Aitken, Walter Weir, Susan Bisland, Steve Anderson, Jackie Young, Malcolm Nimmo, Bruce Robb, Craig Smith, Fraser Ewing, Malcolm Cleghorn, Mhairi Porterfield, Bernadette McKinley, Alison Rodger, Craig Sinclair, Kyle Randall

South Africa
Gerrit Badenhorst, Wayne Price

Spain
Julio Jiminez

Sweden
Torbjorn and Magnus Samuelsson, Eric Hedin, Gosta Jacobson, Kim Wahlstrom, Anna Rosen

Switzerland
Anthony Lordi

Ukraine
Vasil Virastuk, Kyrylo Chuprinin

USA
Fred Vaughan, Keith Tice, John Sells, Tom Carmichael, Tom Johnstone, Jim McGoldrick, Bill Dunn, Bill Kazmaier, Paul Ferency, Ben Plucknett, Phil Martin, Carl Braun, Ryan Vierra, Robert Troupe, Cindy Morrison, Shannon Hartnett, Karl Dodge, Grizzly Brown, Iron Bear Collins, O.D. Wilson, Terry Brennan, Rich Costello, Gary Mitchell, Mark Phillipi, Karl Dodge Kurt Pauli, Rev. Chris Rusher, Steve Pulcinella, Art McDermott, Jeff Bain, David Brown, Jim Parman, Harrison Bailey III, Dave Barron, Steve Conway, Mark Robinson, Ken Lowther Mike Smith, Jill Mill, Gene Flynn, Mark Herisay, Ron McKie, Danie McKim, Gene Flynn, Adriane Blewitt, Jeremiah Strand, Aaron Thurman, Andrew Hobson, Larry Brock, Sean Betz, Mike Zolkiewicz, Bill Crawford, Matt Vincent, Rusty Price, Summer Pierson, Eric Frasure, Mike and Mindy Pockoski

West Indies
Basil Francis

Wales

Gary Taylor, Mark Webster, Christian Clay

VIPs and guests of honour at our events

Charles and Camilla, Prince of Wales and Duchess of Cornwall, at the World Championship 2009.

Prince Edward at our Commonwealth Highland Games

Princess Alexandra and Right Hon. Angus Ogilvie at Golden Gate Park, San Francisco

Prince William of Gloucester and Princess Chi Chibu, sister of Emperor Hirohito in Tokyo

10th and 11th Dukes of Atholl (Patrons) Lord and Lady Aberdeen in Australia

Sir Billy Sneddon, Australia's Speaker in Parliament in Australia

Hon. Dick Hamer, Premier, Victoria

Prime Minister of Australia, Minister of Sport, Nigeria. Foreign Minister of Iceland

Alex Salmond, Scotland's First Minister

Alexander, Earl of Antrim

Randal McDonnell, Viscount Dunluce

Lord Jamie Semple

Ray and Cinda D'Amante, New Hampshire

Stage, television and sporting personalities include Mark McManus (*Taggart*), Diana Rigg (*The Avengers*), Hazel Irvine, Julie Graham, Johnny Beattie, Andy Cameron, Bill McCue (opera singer), Sir Jimmy Saville, Arnold Schwarzenegger, Betty Gillin, Tom and Jack Alexander, Ken Buchanan (boxing champion), Terry Butcher (international footballer), John Beattie (rugby internationalist and commentator) and Cobra, Rocket (Pauline Richards), Wolf, Barbarian and Hawk from television's *Gladiators* programme.

Honoured athletic directors, judges and officials

Australia
Bill Lyndon, Colin Mathieson

Belgium
Sabien Desmet De Bruyn

Brazil
James Frew

Canada
Lynn Boland Richardson, George Chiappa, Rod Hadley, Leo MacDonald, Don McEachran, Roddy McLeod, Warren Trask

France
Monsieur Jean Louis Coppet

Germany
Manfred Muehlenhaus

Hungary
Adam Darazs

New Zealand
Don Ewen

Norway
Trond & Hanne Nilsen

Scotland
Wullie Baxter, David Birkmeyer, Francis Brebner, Dr D. Edmunds, Chas Grant, Ian McPherson, Walter Weir

Ukraine
Olena Obeka

USA
Steve Conway, Peter Hoyt, Jim Jardine, John Johnstone, Jim Pauli, Malcolm Ramsay, Mark Robinson, Randall J. Strossen, PhD

International drug testing
Dr W. Crawford and Christoph Wand

Dated Developments of Scottish Gatherings and Games

Where there is no country listed in an entry, the event will have been in Scotland. Although this is by far the most extensive review of its kind, it is not complete and research is ongoing. It is hoped that those with additions or corrections will assist by providing authenticate information. The dates given are the earliest dates I have found for those specific gatherings. I would also point out that there is some confusion in the methods of indicating the 'age' of the games. Some committees quote the anniversaries, others quote the number held (e.g. if a games began in 1998, then 2008 would be the 11th games, but the 10th anniversary).

1829 BC	Tailtin Games in Ireland at Telltown, County Meath. Dates before 700 BC have also been quoted
6th century AD	Scots from Ireland settled in Scotland before the demise of the Tailtin games
1040	Tradition asserts that a dance over crossed swords was performed after the battle of Dunsinane
Circa 1058	King Malcolm Canmore's gathering, Creag Choinoch, Braes o' Mar. Winning hill racers named
1314	Ceres Games at the Bow Butts after Bannockburn
1513–42	King James V is said to have attended Highland games including putting the stone, caber tossing, wrestling and archery at the Royal Castle Park, Stirling
1554	Inveraray Castle Games. Mary, Queen of Scots present. It has been claimed that for many centuries annual Highland games have taken place at the Duke of Argyll's Inveraray Castle. This has been backed by evidence of such activities related to other noble Scottish families
1500s	Clan Fraser Games at Beauly
1500s	Games to honour Lord William Harwood, King Henry III's envoy
1525	Mentions of Highland reels in published reports
1605	Strathmiglo Games, Fife
1618	John Taylor, the Water Poet, visiting Braemar wrote 'The high-land games and minds, are high and great.'
1618	King's Book of Sports. Issued by King James I/VI
Circa 1650	Lairds of Glenlyon's (mother's) funeral games at Chesthill. Internment delayed one day because of competitions
1652	Burntisland Highland games, it is claimed, originated from St Peter's Market on that date
1652	Inverkeithing Games linked with foot races at Lames Fair, Fife, Scotland
1770s	Creek Indians taught Highland Games by Scottish soldiers in American Wars of Independence
1729	St Andrew's societies formed in Charleston, USA. Later formed in Philadelphia in 1747 and New York in 1756. They influenced future development in the USA. See also 1971
1745	Jacobite Rebellion leading to Act of Proscription in 1747, banning Scottish traditions. Highland Clearances and widespread emigration
1747	Aberdeen Town Council appoint Francis Peacock as official dancing master
Pre 1775	Georgia, USA. Scottish soldiers and

	Creek Indians competed in Highland and running events
1775–83	American Wars of Independence
1778	Highland Society formed in London. Bagpipe competitions, etc.
Circa 1780	Scottish Society formed in Alexandria, Virginia
1781	First Highland Society Gathering at Falkirk Tryst (held in conjunction with cattle sales)
1781	There were important piping competitions at the above tryst
1784	Loch Lomond Bagpipe Competition. Ref. Faujais St Fond (1741–1819)
1788	Northern Meeting, Inverness, instituted. At first there were Highland Balls, etc. In 1816 there were athletic events and in 1822 games were held on the level stretch under the Hill of Birds, Glengarry. Full scale Highland games from 1840
1800	Formation of the Braemar Wrights Walk. Marches and associated activities in the district
1804	Strathglass Highland Games. Heavy events winner was William Fraser, a priest who became first Bishop of Antigonish in 1827
1816	Braemar. Wright Friendly Society constituted 18 January. Braemar Castle still occupied by Redcoats
1817	Wrights Walk re-designated as Braemar Highland Society.

There is clear evidence of separate piping, dancing and heavy event competitions in the early years of the 19th century, and there are also some examples before this era. The Napoleonic Wars, Britain's colonial conquests and the Anglo–US war, when the British burned the White House, restricted overseas development of Highland games at that time.

1819	St Fillan's Games by Lochearn, Scotland
1819	Highland Society formed in Glengarry, Canada, forerunner of the current games at Maxville
1822	Formation of Lonach Highland and Friendly Society
1822	King George IV's visit to Scotland, involving Sir Walter Scott, sparked a cultural revival. Strathfillan Games representatives attended events
1822	McDonnell of Glengarry's Highland Games
1823	Annual games near Peebles, mentioned in Lockhart's life of Sir Walter Scott
1823	Institution of Lonach Highland and Friendly Society
1824	Athole Society and Gathering instituted for local inhabitants. Professionals excluded. Blair Atholl[1]
1827	St Ronan's Games, Innerleithen, formalised. Source: old letter heading in Bryce Scott's collection. Not 1835 as claimed elsewhere
1830s	Highland Games in Lancaster and other Canadian towns
1832	The games portion of Braemar Gatherings formalised its traditional sporting events
1836	First full-scale Lonach Games
1836	First sportive meeting of Highland Society of New York, Elysian Fields, Hoboken. USA
1838	Prince Edward Island Games – similar history to Atholl Gathering in Scotland
1838	Caledonian Society of Halifax, Nova Scotia, formed
1839	First Caledonian Society in Australia. Founded in Sydney
1939	Toronto Highland Games, Canada
1840	First full-scale Highland games at Northern Meeting, Inverness, Scotland
1841	Galashiels Games
1841	Leith Gymnastic Games (traditional events) by Edinburgh, Scotland
1842	Tomintoul Highland Games, Banffshire, Scotland
1842	Taymouth Gathering for Queen Victoria and Prince Albert. Scotland
1842	Dunkeld Games. Queen and Consort attend
1843	Aberfeldy Highland Games, Scotland
1844	Inveraray Highland Games, Argyllshire

1844 Caledonian Games at Guilbault's Gardens, Montreal

1847 Laggan Highland Games, Inverness-shire. Queen Victoria and Prince Albert attended

1847 St Andrew's Society of Ottawa formed. See 1877

Highland games in their modern form existed and were well documented during the reigns of George III, George IV and William IV. Queen Victoria became very interested in the games during the 1840s and maintained her interest over the years.

1848 Queen Victoria and family's first visit to Braemar Gathering and Games. Held at Invercauld

1848 Cape Breton Games, Nova Scotia

1848 Highland Games, Otago, New Zealand

1849 First annual Perth Highland Society Games, South Inch, Perth, Scotland. Two days.

1849 Detroit St Andrew's Society Games, Michigan, USA

1849 Alva Highland Games, Clackmannanshire, Scotland

1850 Dunbeath Highland Games, Caithness, Scotland. Annually after 1852

1850 Edinburgh Highland Games

1850 Highland Games, Lord Holland's Park, London. Queen Victoria attends

Early 1850s
Informal Games in Boston, USA (Caledonian balls began in 1847)

1850 Strathallan, Scotland

Circa 1851
Kilbirnie Highland Games, Ayrshire. See also 1982

1852 First Annual Highland Games, Lord Holland's Park, Kensington, London. Queen Victoria attends

1852 Thornton Highland Games, Scotland. Also stated as 1864

1852 Pitlochry Highland Games

1852 Glenisla Highland Gathering, Scotland (annually)

1853 Jedburgh Border Games, Scotland

1853 Formalised Boston Caledonian Club Highland Games

1853 Auld Yule Highland Games, Fourdon, Aberdeenshire, Scotland

1854 Banchory Highland Games, Scotland

1854 Thornton Highland Games, Fife, Scotland

1854 Waipu, New Zealand. Landing of the Nova Scotian Scots Informal Highland Games (formalised in 1871)

1855 Jedforest Games, Lothmay Park, Scottish Border Games

1855 Montreal Caledonian Games, Quebec, Canada

1856 Perth Highland Society Annual Games, Scotland

1856 Dunbeath Highland Games (one source quoted 1853)

1856 Glenisla Highland Games

1856 Sydney Highland Games, Australia

1857 First Forfar Games, Soctland. Some say earlier but *Scotsman* newspaper of 1860 shows otherwise

1857 New York City's Caledonian Society's first proper annual Highland Games

1857 Lumphanan Highland Games

1857 First Geelong Highland Games, Australia

1858 Alva Highland Games. 1862 is also claimed as a being the first

1858 Cruden Highland Games, Scotland

1858 Philadelphia Society Caledonian Games

1859 Queensburgh, Canada

1859 Dundee Highland Games

1860 Angus and Mearns Games, Montrose, Scotland

1860 Halifax, Nova Scotia

1860 Bendigo Highland Games, Australia

1861 First Earlston Games, Easter Green, Earlston, Scotland

1861 Newark Highland Games, USA

1861 Highland Society formed in Antigonish, Nova Scotia, Canada

1861 Maryborough Highland Gathering, Australia

1862 Caledonian Society formed in Otago, New Zealand

1862 Edinburgh Society Highland Games, Woodburn Park, Morningside, Scotland

1862 Camphill Athletic Games. Champion was Donald Dinnie

1862	Clova Gathering
1862	Chatham Highland Games, Canada
1862	Club of True Highlanders Highland Games at Beaufort House, London. Dinnie competed
1862	Kincardine O'Neil Highland Games, Scotland
1862	First Drumblair Highland Games, Forgue, near Huntly, Scotland. Became very important games
1863	Antigonish Highland Games, Nova Scotia, and until present (World Heavy Events Championship celebrated the 140th anniversary of these games in 2003)
1863	Dublin Highland Games.
1863	First St Andrew's Society of Ottawa Games
1863	Ballater Highland Games
1863	Johnstone Annual Tournament of Athletic Sports (traditional – caber, hammer, etc.)
1864	Birnam Highland Games, Birnam House Park, Scotland
1865	Turakina Highland Games, New Zealand
1865	First Denny Scottish Games, East Borland, Denny, Scotland
1865	First Alva Games, Scotland. 1849 and 1858 have also been quoted
1865	Royal Patent Gymnastic Highland Games, Edinburgh
1865	*End of American Civil War*
1866	Brooklyn Caledonian Club formed in New York, USA
1866	First Caledonian Club of San Francisco Highland Games
1866	Taymouth Gathering and Games for Queen Victoria, and annually for several years afterwards
1866	First Tillicoultry Gymnastic Games (these gymnastic games were essentially Scottish Games)
1867	Nairn Athletic Games, Scotland
1867	Aboyne Highland Games
1867	First Annual Tournament of National Games, Academy Park, Greenock, Scotland
1867	First Brooklyn Highland Games
1867	International Gathering and Games in New York. Canada vs. America
1867	First St Andrew's Highland Gathering, Detroit

1867	Milwaukee Highland Games and Scottish Festival, Wisconsin, USA
1867	Maryhill Highland Games, Glasgow
1867	First Strathmore Central Athletic Meeting, Couper Angus, Scotland
1868	Couper Angus Highland Games, Scotland
1868	Turriff Highland Game, Scotland
1868	First Sydney Highland Gathering and Games, New South Wales, Australia
1869	First Airth Games, Scotland
1869	Caldercruix Gymnastic Games, Scotland
1869	Carnwath Games and Races
1869	National Sports and Highland Games, Kelvinside, Glasgow
1869	Huntly Games, Scotland
1869	Crofthead Gymnastic Games, Old Mansion House, Crofthead, Scotland
1869	Royal Patent Games, Edinburgh
1869	Victoria Games, British Columbia
1869	Culter Games, near Aberdeen, Scotland
1869	Perth Highland Society Games
1870s	(and almost certainly earlier) Highland Games in Aberdeen
1870	Johnstone Highland Games, Renfrewshire
1870s to 1880s	
	Games at Brussels, Dundas, Ingersoll, London, Lucknow, St Catherine's, Stratford, Woodstock in Ontario and Fredericton in New Brunswick. In Australia: South Pacific Highland Games in Geelong., City of Newton Highland Games, Ringwood Highland Games Jubilee Park, Melbourne, Australia
1870	Comrie Games, Strathearn, Scotland
1870	First Crieff Games. 4,000 spectators in spite of bad weather
1870	Bucherybush by Portlethan, north-east Scotland
1871	Argyllshire Highland Gathering
1871	Dunoon Highland Games, Scotland (not Cowal – see 1894)
1871	Falkirk Highland Games, Scotland
1871	First Annual Highland Games at Crystal Palace, London, England
1871	First Annual New Haven Games, USA
1871	First Hudson County Highland Games, USA

1871 Waipu Highland Games, North Island, New Zealand, formalised after informal games since 1854

1872 First Airth Highland Gathering

1872 Buffalo Caledonian Society Highland Games., USA

1872 Syracuse Caledonian Club first Highland Games, New York, USA

1872 First Argyllshire Gathering

1873 Argyllshire Gathering and Games

1873 Warwick Highland Games, Australia

1873 Braes of Gight, Scotland

1873 First Warwich Highland Games, Australia

1873–4 Donald Dinnie won medals at Aberdeen Games, Scotland

1873 First Alexandra Athletic Club Games, Cumbernauld Road, Glasgow, Scotland. Dinnie, Fleming, etc.

1873 Richmond Caledonian Club Highland Games, Virginia, USA

1873 Highland Games inaugurated at Princeton University, USA, in honour of George Goldie

1874 Ardross Castle Games, Scotland

1874 First Garmand Highland Games

1874 Scranton Highland Games, USA

1874 Providence Caledonian Games, Rhode Island

1875 First Luss Highland Gathering

1875 Birnam Highland Games, Perthshire. Also stated as 1870

1875 South Canterbury Caledonian Games, South Island, New Zealand

1875 Waimate Caledonian Games, South Island, New Zealand

1876 Kinross Highland Gathering

1876 First Norwich Caledonian Club Annual Games, Connecticut, USA

1876 Stirling Highland Games, Toronto

1877 Linlithgow Gymnastic Games, Academy Park, Scotland

1877 Society of Ottawa Grand Scottish Gathering. Earlier games claimed.

1877 Golspie Highland Games, Inverness-shire, Scotland

1877 Caledonian Society of Mainland, British Columbia. First games at Langley

1877 Skye Highland Games, Portree, Scotland

1877 Lorn Ossianic Games, Scotland

1878 Schenectady and Troy Highland Games, New York

1878 Fochabers Highland Games, Scotland

1878 Oban Highland Gathering, Argyllshire, Scotland

1878–9 Blackford Highland Games, Scotland

1879 Strathallan Highland Games, Bridge of Allan, Scotland

1879 Upper Strathearn Highland Games, Laggan Park, East end of Comrie

1879 Forth Sports (Highland Games) Scotland

1880 First Bute Highland Games, Rothesay, Scotland

1880 Vale of Leven Annual Games, Scotland

1880 Saline Highland Games, Scotland

1880 Ratcliffe Caledonian Games

1880s Balquidder, Lochearnhead and Strathyre Highland Games, Lochearnhead, Scotland

1880 Abernethy Highland Games, Loch Lomond

1880 Winnipeg's first annual Games

1880 Stockton Highland Games

1881 Strathpeffer Highland Games, Scotland

1881 Cleveland Highland Games, Ohio

1881 Caledonian Club of Holyoke Highland Games, Massachusetts

1881 Lake Linden Caledonian Club Games, Michigan

1881 Fall River Highland Games, Massachusetts

1881 Paterson Games, New Jersey, USA

1882 Black Isle Highland Games, Scotland

1882 Greenock Games, Scotland

1882 Strathardle Highland Gathering, Perthshire, Scotland

1882 Minneapolis Highland Games, Minnesota

1882 Kingussie Games, Inverness-shire

1882 Burns Club Annual Games, Burns Club, Fishkill, New York

1882 Saughton Highland Games, Scotland

1883 Haddo House Highland Games, Aberdeenshire, Scotland

1883 Portland, Oregon, USA

1883 Sacramento Caledonian Games, California, USA (Later Sacramento Valley Scottish Games)

1883   St Louis Caledonian Games, USA

1883   Ashburton Caledonian Society Games, New Zealand

1884   Dunedin Caledonian Club Games, New Zealand

1884   Queensland Caledonia Society, Brisbane, Australia

1884   First Dunecht Highland Games, Scotland

1884   Brisbane, Australia. Dinnie exhibited

1884   Hamilton Highland Games, South Island, New Zealand

1884   Riverton Caledonian Games, New Zealand

1884   Wyndham Caledonian Society Games, New Zealand

1884   Palmerston Caledonian Sports, New Zealand

1884   Riverside Caledonian Games, New Zealand

1884   Oamara Caledonian Sports, Otago, New Zealand

1884   Timaru Caledoninan Games, New Zealand

1884   Christchurch Caledonian Society Games, New Zealand

1884   Melbourne Highland Games, cricket ground, Australia

1884   Ballarat Highland Games, Australia

1884   Goulburn Highland Games, Australia

1884   Inverell Highland Games, Australia

1884   Maryborough Highland Games, Australia

1884   Gympie Highland Athletic Games, Australia

1884   Bundaberg Athletic Games, Australia

1885   Edinburgh Highland Society Games, Powderhall

1885   Caledonian Games, Washington DC

1885   Hartford Highland Games, Connecticut

1885   Rochester Caledonian Club Games, New York

1885   Caledonian Club of Yonkers Highland Games, New York

1885   Coutermanora, Athletic Games, News South Wales, Australia

1886   First Halkirk Highland Games, Caithness, Scotland. The 100th Games were held in 2003

1886   Brodick Highland Games, Arran, Scotland

1886   Edinburgh Exhibition Highland Games

1887   First Highland Society of Edinburgh Highland Games

1887   First Annual Spring Games, Highland Athletic Association, Manayunk, Philadelphia

1887   Blackburn Athletic Sports, Scotland

1887   Arbroath Highland Games

1887   Dunecht Highland Games, Aberdeenshire, Scotland

1887   First Dornach Highland Gathering

1887   Gartmore Highland Games, Scotland

1887   Temuka Caledonian Highland Games, South Island, New Zealand

1887   Newcastle Exhibition Highland Games

1888   Glasgow Exhibition Highland Gathering

1889   Athletic Sports if 4th Battallion Argyll and Sutherland Highlanders

1889   A Monster Highland Gathering, within The Tour De Nestle, Paris, 17 and 18 October 1889 Over £700 will be given as prize money (details taken from leaflet courtesy W. Baxter)

1890   First Dutton Highland Games, Ontario, Canada

1891   Johannesburg Highland Games, South Africa

1891   Beuly Highland Games, Scotland

1893   Inverness Highland Games, Scotland

1894   First Cowal Gathering, Dunoon, Scotland

1894   Wangerie Highland Games, North Island, New Zealand

1895   First Annual Gathering, Central Park, Aberdeen. See also 1897

All these formalised and structured Highland games were held before the first modern Olympic Games in 1896

1896   Bowmore Highland Games, Islay, Scotland

1897   Airdrie Highland Games, Scotland

1897   Auchterarder Highland Games, Scotland

1897   Armadale Highland Games, Scotland

1897   Avoch, Black Isle Highland Games

1897   Birnam Highland Games, Perthshire. Also stated as 1870

1897   Balfron Highland Games, Scotland

1897   Bon Accord Highland Gathering, Kittybrewster, Aberdeen

1897   Burghhead Highland Games, Morayshire, Scotland

1897   Clydebank Highland Games, Scotland

1897   Cramond Bridge Highland Games, Scotland

1897   Dornoch Highland Games, Scotland

1897	Drymen Highland Games, Scotland
1897	Falkirk Highland Games, Scotland
1897	Invercarron Highland Games
1897	Inverkeithing Highland Games, Scotland
1897	Kilmarnock Highland Games
1897	Kirkintilloch Highland Games, Scotland
1897	Leslie Highland Games, Fife, Scotland
1897	Natal Caledonian Society Programme of Sports, Lord's Grounds, Durban, South Africa
1897	Methil Highland Games, Fife, Scotland
1897	West Calder Highland Games, Scotland
1897–8	Donald Dinnie in South Africa. Caledonian Games at Bloemfontein, Cape Town, Dundee, Durban, Johannesburg, Kimberley, Krugersdorp, Ladysmith, Natal, Newcastle, Pietermaritzburg, Port Elizabeth, Pretoria
1898	Aberdeen Autumn Games, Scotland
1898	Drumblair Championship Games, Scotland. Belt, trophies, good prizes.
1898	Galston Highland Games, Ayrshire, Scotland
1898	Govan Police Games, Glasgow, Scotland
1898	Lanarkshire Police Sports, Motherwell, Scotland Dundee Highland Games
1898	Glasgow Highland Games, Scotland
1898	Motherwell Highland Games, Scotland
1898	Ross Highland Games, Hamilton, Scotland
1899	Auchterarder Highland Games, Scotland
1899	Athena Caledonian, Games, Oregon, USA. Revived 1976
1899	Dalbeattie Highland Games, Scotland
1899	Oamaur Caledonian Society Games, New Zealand
1899	Airdrie Police Games, Scotland
1899	Partick Police Gathering. Glasgow, Scotland
1899	Aberdeen Police Games, Scotland
1899	Leeds Highland Games, England
1899	Oamaru Caledonian Society Games, New Zealand

In the late 19th century, Wick, Thurso and every Caithness village or district held Highland Games. Caithness, Dunbeath, Halkirk and Mey still survive.

There were annual Highland Games at College Green, off High Street, Glasgow, and a large annual Gathering at Maryhill, Glasgow, but they came to an end before 1900. There were

other games held at Banchory, Birnam, Blairgowrie, Dundee, Dunoon, Edzell, Forfar, Fort William, Helensburgh, Inverness, Johnstone in Renfrewshire, Tranent, Lairg, Inverness-shire, Lanark, Nethybridge, Oban, Pitlochry, Plains, Tain, Tillietudlum and over the border in Leeds and Liverpool.

For 20 to 30 years after the American Civil War there were as many as 125 Highland games in America. There were over a hundred Highland games in Canada before the end of the 19th century.

During the Victorian era there were Highland games in all the major Scottish towns and also in a great many villages. In the Buchan area, in the north-east of Scotland, there were games at Auchnagatt, Bonnykelly, Culter, Crichie, Cruden, Crudie, Delgaty, Ellon, Fraserburgh, Fyvie, Gamrie, Garmont, Hatton, Helensburgh, Landside, Maud, Mintlaw, Muchalls, New Aberdour, New Blyth, New Deer, New Pitsligo, Peterhead, Plaidy, Rosehearty, Ratham, Slains and Turriff. This is quite incredible to those who know that area. Many places mentioned were little more than hamlets but people would travel far in simple conveyances of the day, and there were sometimes crowds of around 7,000.

John Watt, a popular competitor, thought nothing of cycling 90 miles from Stirling to win some light events, then cycling home that evening.

1901	First Corncockle and Lochmaber Highland Games
1901	Alexandria Highland Games, by Loch Lomond, Scotland
1901	Galston Games, Ayrshire, Scotland. One of the first games of the season
1901	Lochaber Highand Gathering, Scotland
1901	Aberfeldy Highland Games, Perthshire, Scotland
1901	Drumblair Highland Games, Scotland
1902	Newcastle Highland Games, England. See also 1969

1903–22   See also list of 43 games at which Bryce and Knox competed in this period

1904   Assynt Highland Games

1905   Kirkconnel Games (51st games in 1955)

1905   First Rothienorman Highland Games

1908   Scottish National Exhibition Highland Games, Saughton, Edinburgh

1908   Dunfermline Highland Games

1908   First Annual Gatheiring of London Highland Association, Stamford Bridge, UK

1911–12   Alex Munro competed in North American Highland Games

1913   Glengarnock Highland Games, Garnock Valley, Ayrshire

Immediately prior to the First World War there were hundreds of Highland games in Scotland.

1920s   Markinch Highland Games, Fife

1921   Invergordon Highland Games

Circa 1922
        Gordon Castle Games rescusitated. Once one of the leading games in north-east Scotland

1922–3   Scotland – In addition to the larger and best known gatherings there were also games at Aberdeen, Aboyne, Airth, Alloa, Almond Valley, Alva, Birnam, Bathgate, Bannockburn, Blackridge, Biggar, Callander, Carronsmore, Ceres, Comrie, Clyde, Crieff, Dennyloanhead, Douglas, Edinburgh Police, Garthaven, Gartmore and Aberfoyle, Comrie, Glasgow Eastern, Glenluce, Dundee FC Games, Haddo House in Aberdeenshire, Inverkeithing, Inverness, Kincardine, Kirkcaldy, Kirkconnel, Kippen, Lochaber, Lochmaben, Lockerbie, Lonach, Longcroft and District, Luss, Millport, Nairn, Newburgh- Foreran House, New Pitsligo, Oban, Sanquhar, Skye, St Ronans, Saughton, Solway, Stirling, Stornoway, Stranraer, Strathallan, West Calder and Winchburgh

1923   Round Hill Highland Games, Connecticut, USA

1924   Gilmorton Games, Recreation Park, Gilmerton, Edinburgh, Scotland

1926   Strathendrick Highland Games, Scotland

1927   Hatton of Cruden Annual Games, Scotland

1927   United Scottish Society Gathering and Games, Orange County, California, USA

1930   In Buchan the following small towns and villages still hosted traditional Highland Games: Banff, Bogmuchals, Boyndie, Ellon, Gammond, Gordon Castle, New Byth, New Pitsligo, Turriff Rothienorman and the Buchan Gathering

1930   Southern California Highland Gathering and Games

1930   First Old Meldrum Highland Games

1930   First United Societies of Southern California Highland Gathering and Games

1930   First Kilmallie Highand Games, Annat Park, Loch Eil

1930   Games introduced to Braw Lads Gathering, Galashiels, Scotland

1933   Brandon Highland Games, Canada

1934   Central New York Scottish Games, Lake Onondaga, USA

1935   First Aberlour Highland Games

1939   Last Inverurie Highland Games until revived in 2003

War years

1940s   Aberlour and Strathspey Highland Games, Scotland

1940s   Killin and District Highland Games, possibly earlier. Revived 1994

1942   Modesto Highland Games and Gathering, California, USA

1945   51st Highland Division Highland Games, Verden, Germany

1945   Glenfinnan Highland Games, Scotland

1945   Pacific North-West Highland Games, Enumclaw, Washington, USA

1946   Fergus Highland Games and Scottish Festival, Ontario, Canada

1946   First Dingwall Highland Gathering. Abeyance 1962–78

1947   New Hampshire Gathering of the Scottish Clans

1947   Highland Brigade Highland Games, Edinburgh, Scotland

1948	Glengarry Highland Games, Maxville, Ontario

1948 Glengarry Highland Games, Maxville, Ontario

1950 Hastings Highland Games, North Island, New Zealand

1850 First Shotts Highland Games

1952 Daylesford Highland Gathering, Victoria, Australia

1952 Portland Highland Games, Oregon, USA

1954 Blackford Highand Games

1954 Alloa Highland Games

1954 Cupar Highland Games

1954 Alyth Highland Games

1954 Crook of Devon Highland Games

1954 Oxton Highland Games

1954 Leslie Highland Games

1954 Couper Angus Highland Games

1956 First Grandfather Mountain Highland Games and Gathering, Linnville, North Carolina, USA

1957 Fresno Highland Games, California, USA

1957 City of Newtown Highland Gathering, Geelong, Victoria, Australia

1958 Spokane Scottish Festival and Tattoo, Washington, USA

1958 Ross Highland Games, Tasmania, Australia

1959 Ligonier Highland Games, Pittsburg, Pennsylvania, USA

1959 First Festival of Scotland Highland Games, Clapham Common, London, UK

1960 First Scottish Heavy Field Events Championships, Scottish Amateur Athletic Association

1960 First Adelaide Highland Games, South Australia

1960 First Lesmahagow Annual Highland Games

1960 Bellingham Highland Games, Washington, USA

1960 Colonial Highland Gathering, Fairhill Maryland, USA

1961 Long Island Scottish Games, Old Westbury, New York, USA

1961 Salado Highland Highland Games, Texas, USA

1961 Aberdeen Highland Games revived

1962 Peterhead Highland Games, Aberdeenshire, Scotland

1962 Indoor Highland Games (1 week), Kelvin Hall, Glasgow

1963 Rocky Mountain Highland Games, Denver, USA

1963 Boys' Brigade World Highland Games, Glen Almond, Scotland

1964 First Shrewsbury Highland Games, England

1964 Nassua Highland Games, Bahamas

1964 Cobourg Highland Games, Donegan Park, Ontario, Canada

1965 Leeds Highland Games (revival) Yorkshire, England

1965 International Highland Games, Crystal Palace, London, England

1965 London/Scottish Centenary Highland Games, Wimbledon, England

1965 Scotland – Jedburgh, Inveraray, Tobermory, St Ronans, Armstaig, Dornach, Strathallan, Newtonmore, Fort William, Creiff, Glanfinnan, Cowal, Strathardle, Aberdeen, Aboyne, Braemar, Argyllshire (Oban), etc.

1965 DELCO Scottish Games, Devon, Pennsylvania, USA

1966 Phoenix Highland Games, Arizona

1966 Dunedin Highland Games and Festival, Florida, USA

1966 Manitoba Highland Gathering, Western Canada

1966 Loch Lomond Highland Games, Balloch

1967 Delco Scottish Games, Devon, Pennsylvania, USA

1967 Houston Highland Games, Texas, USA

1967 Monterey Highland Games, California, USA

1968 Kansas City Highland Games, Missouri, USA

1968 Thousand Islands Highland Games, Brockville, Ontario (previously in New York State)

1968 Tacoma Highland Games, Washington, USA

1968 Alma Highland Festival and Games, Michigan, USA

1968ca. Durness Highland Games, Sutherland, Scotland

1968 Swedish Highland Games. Five locations

1968 Corby Highland Games, Northhamptonshire, England

1969 Tokyo Highland Games, Tosheamean Park, Japan

1969 Cutty Sark Highland Games, Newcastle, England

1969 Cutty Sark Centenary Highland Games, Greenwich. Including international caber contest

1970	Dundee Highland Games, Scotland
1970	Commonwealth Highland Games, Pre. Para. Games, Edinburgh, Scotland
1970	Monterey Highland Games, California, USA
1970	Bath and West Highland Games, Shepton Mallet, England
1970	Sacramento Highland Games, California, USA
1970	Auckland Highland Games, New Zealand
1970	First Virginia Scottish Games, Alexandria, Virginia, USA
1971	First Annual Charleston, Scottish Games and Highland Gathering, South Carolina, USA
1971	Highland Games, Golden Gate Park, San Francisco, USA
1971	First Annual Scottish Games and Gathering, South Carolina, USA
1972	Queechee Scottish Festival, Vermont, USA
1972	Ozark Highland Games, Arkansas, USA
1972	Dallas Scottish Highland Games, Texas, USA
1972	St Paul Scottish Country Fair, Minnesota, USA
1972	First City of Ottawa Highland Games, Canada. See also 1847
1972	World Heavy Events Championships. Registered
1972	East Coast Highland Games, Australia
1973	Tam o' Shanter Scottish Games and Festival, USA
1973	Dalesford Highland Gathering, Victoria, Australia
1973	First Maxville Highland Games, Ontario, Canada
1973	Stone Mountain Scottish Festival and Highland Games, Georgia, USA
1973	Canberra Highland Games, Australia
1973	Sydney Highland Games
1973	South Pacific Highland Games, Australia. Previously Geelong H.G. see 1884
1973	City of Newtown Highland Games
1973	Ringwood Highland Games, Jubilee Park, Ringwood, Melbourne
1973	McLean Highland Games, Australia
1973	Europa Cup (Athletics) Highland Games, Edinburgh, Scotland
1974	First Irvine Annual Highland Games, Kilwinning, Ayrshire
1974	First Virginia Highland Games, Alexandria, USA
1974	Utah Scottish Festival and Highland Games, Salt Lake City, Utah, USA
1974	San Diego Scottish Games, California, USA
1974	Virginia Scottish Games, Alexandria, Virginia, USA
1974	Marin County Highland Gathering, California, USA
1974	Waco Highland Games, Waco, Texas, USA
1974	Coburg Highland Games, Ontario, Canada
1975	First US Invitational Championships, Santa Rosa, California, USA
1975	Georgetown Highland Games, Ontario, Canada
1975	Jakarta Highland Gathering, Indonesia
1975	Irvine New Town Highland Games, Irvine (until 1995)
1975	First Dundonald Highland Games, Ayrshire, Scotland
1975	First Annual Cambridge Highland Games, Cambridge, Canada
1976	First Annual Orilliia, Scottish Festival, Ontario, Canada
1976	Highland and Island (Gotland) Games, The Foreshore, Largs
1977	Calgary Highland Games, Alberta, Canada
1976	First Oklahoma Scottish Games and Gathering, USA
1976	First Gateway Highland Games, St Louis, Missouri
1976	Loon Mountain Highland Games, New Hampshire. Gathering of the Clans, USA
1977	Glens Falls Gaelic Festival, New York, USA
1977	Queen's Silver Jubilee Games, Blair House, Dalry, Scotland
1977	Isle of Mull Children's Highland Games. Ran for around 12 years
1977	First Jacksonville Highland Games, Florida, USA
1977	Scottish Highland Games, Holland
1977	Adirondack Scottish Games, Glen Falls, New York, USA
1977	Flora Macdonald Highland Games, Red Springs, North Carolina, USA
1978	Capital District Highland Games, Altamont, New York, USA
1978	Williamsburg Scottish Festival, Virginia, USA

1978	Long's Peak Scottish Highland Festival, Lake Estes, Colorado, USA
1978	Savannah Scottish Highland Games, Georgia, USA
1978	First Orlando Scottish Highland Games
1978	Ohio Scottish Games, Ohio, USA
1978	Nazeing Highland Games, England
1978	Metro Highland Games, Bradford, England
1978	Wageningen Highland Games, Holland
1978	Fort Ticonderoga Memorial Scottish Gathering, New York, USA
1978	Orrilla Scottish Festival, Ontario, Canada
1979	Celtic Festival of Southern Mainland, Huntington, USA
1978	Ardrossan Games, Scotland
1979	Savannah Scottish Games, Georgia, USA
1979	Mallaig and Morar Highland Games
1979	Tidewater Scottish Festival and Clan Gathering, Norfolk, Virginia, USA
1979	Waterville Highland Games and Gathering, Maine, USA
1979	Jacksonville, Scottish Highland Games and Gathering, Florida, USA
1979	Pacific Highland Clan Gathering and Games, Chine, USA
1979	Campbell Highland Games, California, USA
1979	Maine Highland Games, Brunswick, USA
1979	South Maryland Festival and Gathering, St Leonard, USA
1979	Pomona Highland Games, Southern California, USA
1979	Putney Highland Games
1979	Tomintoul and Strathhavon Highland Games (see also 1842)
1980	Oklahoma Scottish Highland Games and Gathering, Tulsa, USA
1980	New Brunswick Highland Games, Oromocto, Canada
1980	Trenton Acadian Scottish Festival, Maine, USA
1980	Waxhaw Scottish Games, North Carolina, USA
1980	Highland/Viking Games, Lord Glasgow's Kelburn Castle, Largs, Scotland
1981	International Clan Gathering Games, Edinburgh, Scotland

1981	Cawdor Castle Highland Games. There were many games here over the years
1980	Scottish Highland Games, Vlissingen, Netherlands
1980	Acadian Scottish Festival, Trenton, Maine, USA
1981	San Fernando Scottish Heritage Highland Games, Los Angeles, California, USA
1982	Collins Scottish Gathering, Colorado, USA
1982	Great Smokey Mountains Highland Games, Gatlinburg, Tennessee, USA
1982	Honolulu Highland Games, Hawaii, USA
1982	Council of Europe, Scottish Highland Games, Lamego, Portugal
1982	West Texas Highland Games, Lubbock, Texas, USA
1982	First World Series Highland Games: Atholl Gathering, Blair Castle, etc. Kilbirnie Highland Games (finals at Carmunnock Highland Games)
1982 until 1997	Revival of annual Highland games in Kilbirnie, Ayrshire. Previously held during the 1850s
1982	Revival of Annual Atholl Games and Gathering
1982	Alaska Scottish Games, USA
1983	Scottish Heritage Gathering, Longwood Gardens, Pennsylvania, USA
1983	Lagos Highland Games, Nigeria
1983	Kentucky Scottish Weekend, Carrolton, USA
1983	Pike's Peak, Highland Games and Celtic Festival, Monument, Colorado, USA
1983	Aurora Scottish Games, Colorado, USA
1983	Selma Scottish Festival, Alabama, USA
1983	First Sarnia Supreme Highland Games
1984	Vermont International Highland Games, Essex Junction, USA
1984	Capital Region Highland Games, Mooneys Bay, Ottawa, Canada
1984	First Annual Scottish Festival and Games, Key Biscayne, Florida
1984	Payson Scottish Festival, Utah, USA
1984	Berkshire Indoor Highland Games, Pittsfield, Massachusetts, USA
1884	Plana Highland Games, Texas, USA
1984	Litchfield Scottish Festival, St Andrew's Society of Connecticut, USA

1984	St Andrew's Society of Connecticut Scottish Festival, Goshen, USA	1987	Clarkston International Highland Games, Glasgow
1984	Vashon Island Highland Games, Washington, USA	1987	First Viking and Highland Games, Kelburn Castle, Largs
1984	World Series of Highland Games promoted in Scotland. Four venues scheduled	1987	Hong Kong St Andrew's Society Highland Games, Hong Kong
1984	North Lanark Highland Games, Ontario, Canada	1987	Glasgow Highland Games, Kentucky, USA
1984	First Scottish Junior and Novice Championships, Beith, Scotland	1987	Annapolis Valley Highland Games, Canada
		1987	Payson Scottish Festival, Utah, USA
1984	Hamilton Highland Games, South Island, New Zealand	1987	Batesville Highland Games, Arkansas
		1987	First Indiana Highland Games, Fort Wayne, Indiana, USA
1984	Brockton Highland Games, Massachusetts, USA	1988	In a review for *Scotland's Runner* magazine, Highland games organisers estimated that there were around 130 games in Britain. All but a few of the games were in Scotland
1984	Kingsville and Gosfield Highland Games, Ontario, Canada		
1985	Brenton-Parker Scottish Festival and Games, Mount Vernon, Georgia, USA		
1985	Bundanoon Highland Games, Australia		Bicentennial Highland Games, Sydney, Australia
Circa 1985			
	Nuremberg Highland Games, Germany	1988–9	Wilhelmshaven Highland Games, Germany
1985	Great Smokey Mountains Gatlinburg Highland Games, Tennessee, USA	1988	Beloxi Highland Games, Mississippi
		1988	First Highland Games, Fort Wayne, Indiana, USA
1985	Molson Highland Games, Barrie, Ontario		
1985	Fort Worth Highland Games, Texas, USA	1988	South Texas Gathering and Games, McAllen, Texas, USA
1985	Paso Robles Highland Games, California, USA		
1985	Amherst Highland Games, New York, USA	1989	First in new series Chatham Highland Games, Ontario. There were earlier games; this starts 14 consecutive games up to, and beyond, 2003
1985	Biloxi Highland Games, Mississippi, USA		
1985	Dumfries and Galloway Highland Gathering		
Mid 1980s	Scottish Tourist Board estimated gross number of spectators at Scottish Highland games around half a million	1989	First British Days in Hamburg, Germany
		1989	First Sons of Scotland (Dist. 16) Highland Games, Delta, British Columbia, Canada
1986	First Galloway Games, Stranraer, Scotland. For approximately 10 years		Formakin Highland Games, Bishopton
			During 1990 the following Highland games were announced in North America: Claremore, Oklahoma; Barrie Highland Games, Ontario; Northern Alabama Scottish Festival, Huntsville, Alabama, USA
1986	Carmunnock Highland Games, by Glasgow, Scotland		
1986	Commonwealth Highland Games, Edinburgh, Scotland		
1986	Highland Games, Leuven University, Belgium	1990	McHenry Highland Festival, Garrett County, Maryland, USA
1986	Scottish Festival and Highland Games, Arlington, Texas		
		1990	Garden Festival Highland Games, Gateshead, England
1987	Earlshall International Highland Games, Fife		
1997	Trossachs International Highland Games, Kinlochard	1990	Edinburgh Highland Games, Scotland. Approximately 12 in four years
1997	First new series of Callander Highland Games	1991	Renfrew District International Highland Games, Scotland
1987	Blantyre Highland Games		

1991	First Canmore Highland Games, Rocky Mountains, Alberta, Canada
1991	First Banff Highland Games, Centennial Par,. Banff, Canada
1991	First Fredericksburgh Highland Games, Virginia, USA
1991	Glendevon International Highland Games
1992	First annual Columbus Scottish Festival, City Park, Indiana, USA
1992	An American list of Highland Games scheduled for this year includes games in: Orlando, Arizona, South East Florida, Pozo, Dunedin, Hawaii, Sacromento Valley, Ozark, Southern Maryland, San Louis Obispo, Kentucky, McAlester H.G.. St Paul MN, Corte Madera CA, Albuquerque, Savannah GA, Fairhill MD, Alma MI, Gatlinburg TN, Houston TX, Marysville CA, Auroora CO, Ferndale WA, Glen Falls NY, Arlington TX, Millington N.J, Kansas City MO, Salt Lake City, Utah, Havre de Grace, MO, Downers Grove IL, New Market, AL, Devon PA, San Marcos CA, Big Bear Lake CA, Obertin, OH, Enumclaw WA, Eagle River Alaska, Detroit, Monterey CA, Spokane WA, Easton MA, Nashville TN, Denver CO, Liverpool NY, Columbus IN, Brunswick ME, Westbury NY, Altamont NY, Santa Rosa CA, Salodo TX, Treasure Island H.G, FL, Pensacola FL.
1993	Scottish Highland Games of Mississippi, Jackson, USA
1993	Tucson Celtic Festival, Arizona, USA
1993	Loch Prado Games, Chino, California, USA
1993	Anne Arundel Scottish Highland Games, Annapolis, Maryland, USA
1993	Princess Anne Scottish-Irish Festival, Maryland, USA
1993	Scotland Highland Festival, Scotland, Connecticut, USA
1993	Highlands and Islands Scottish Games and Festival, Biloxi, Mississippi, USA
1993	St Andrew's Scottish Scottish Festival, Goshen, Connecticut, USA
1993	Yuba-Sutter Highland Games and Festival, Yuba City, California, USA
1993	Celtic Day in the Park, Staatsberg, New York, USA
1993	Redlands Scottish Festival, California, USA
1993	Alabama Highland Games, Montgomery, Alabama, USA
1993	Scot's Settlement Festival, Highlandtown, Ohio, USA
1993	New York Scottish Games and Celtic Festival, Liverpool, New York, USA
1993	Celtic Highland Games and Clan Gathering, Myrtle Creek, Oregon, USA
1993	Quechee Scottish Festival, VT, USA
1993	Ashbourne Highland Games, Derbyshire, England
1993	Parklands International Highland Games, Giffnock, Renfrewshire
1993	Thistle in the Park Scottish Festival, Kalamazoo, Michigan, USA
1993	High Desert Celtic Festival, Redmond, Oregon, USA
1993	Days of the Scots, Hunt, Texas, USA
1993	Chevrolet Celtic Classic Highland Games, Bethlehem, Pennsylvania, USA
1993	Estes Park Highland Games, Long's Peak Scottish Highland Festival
1993	First Annual Celtic Highland Games, Millside Park, Myrtle, Creek, Oregon, USA
1994	Revival of Killin Highland Games
1994	Highland Games, Magnum Beach Park, Irvine
1994	First Disabled Highland Games, Kilwinning, Ayrshire
1995	First North Berwick Highland Games
1995	Kilmarnock Highland Games
1995	First Annual Eastern Sierra Celtic Festival and Highland Games, Mammoth Mountain, California, USA
1995	Haliburton Highland Games, Head Lake Park, Ontario, Canada
1995	Ayr International Highland Games
1995	Tartan Sertoma Chatham-Kent, Tecumseh Park, Ontario, Canada
1995	Scottish Highland Games of Mississippi, USA
1995	First Fredericksburgh Highland Games, Virginia, USA
1995	First Omaha Scottish Festival, Nebraska, USA

1995	Ferndale Highland Games, California, USA
1995	Alaskan Scottish Highland Games, Anchorage, Alabama, USA
1995	Chicago Highland Games, Illinois, USA
1996	Richmond Highland Games and Celtic Festival, USA
1996	East Renfrewshire Highland Festival, Crookfur Park, Scotland
1998	International Highland Games, Oulo, Finland
1998	First of series of Highland Games in Germany. Now annually in Berlin, Hamburg, Krefeld, Kempen, Halle, etc.
1998	Current Australian events include Berwick Highland Gathering, Nunawading Highland Gathering, Scots School Bathurst Highland Games NSW, Geelong Highland Games, Ringwood Highland Games, Bundanoon Highland Games, Maclean Highland Gathering, NSW, Maclean Highland Gathering, Sydney Highland Games
1998	First Annual Ulster-Scots Highland Games Newton Stewart, Northern Ireland
1998	First Swifterbank Lowland Scottish Games. There are now some 15 annual games in the Netherlands
1999	World Hammer Throwing Championships in Fredericksburg, Virginia, USA
1999	Ronneburg Castle, Frankfurt, Germany. Scottish Convention Bureaun Games
2000	Highland Games, Rio de Janeiro, Brazil (revival, Highland games there in Victorian times)
2000	First Annual Highland Games, Glenarm Castle, County Antrim, Ireland
2000	First Annual Dixon Scottish Games and Gathering, California, USA
2000	Millennium Youth Highland Games, Stirlingshire, Scotland
2000	Sixth and last in series of Fredericksburg Highland Games and Irish Festival, Maury Stadium
2000	Fort Erie Celtic Festival, Ontario
2001	First World Masters Championships, Fort Smith, Arizona, USA
2001	Mintlaw Highland Games

2001	Renfrewshire Highand Games, Paisley, Scotland
2001	First annual Maachen Highland Games, Germany
2001	Museum of Country Life Highland Games, East Kilbride, Scotland
2002	First Scottish Festival and Celtic Gathering, Bridgeport, West Virginia, USA
2002	European Heavy Events Championships, Netherlands
2002	First Brazil Highland Games in this century.
2002	Second World Masters Championships, Sacramento, USA
2003	First Energy Highland Games, Macae, Brazil
2003	Highland Games, Sneek, The Netherlands
2003	European Heavy Event Championships, Den Halder, The Netherlands
2003	First annual Highland Games at Kempen, Germany
2003	Aberdeen Highland Games, New South Wales, Australia
2003	Third World Masters Championships, Springfield, Illinois, USA
2003	Revival of Inverurie Highland Games, first since 1939
2003	European Highland Games Championships, Bressuire, France
2003	First annual Beckum Highland Games, Ne Hengelo, Netherlands,
2003	At least eight games in Netherlands, six in Germany, four in Ireland, six in Iceland. In Scotland, amongst others: Aberdeen, Aboyne, Airth, Alva, Balloch (Loch Lomond) Balmoral, Ballater, Balquider, Blair Atholl, Blairgowrie, Braemar, Burntisland, Callander, Cowal (Dunoon), Gourock, Crieff, Forres, Glengarry, Inveraray, Inverurie, Kenmore, Killin, Lonach, Luss, Loch Lomond, Milngavie, Morvern, Pitlochrie, Roseneath and Clynder, Stirling, Strathardle, Taynuilt, Tomintoul, Trossachs
2004	International Highland Games Federation accepted for membership by the Federation of Indigenous Scottish Sports and Games
2004	La Force Ecossaise, St Hernin, France
2004	Belgisch Highland Games, Reinaert Park, Destelbergen, Belgium
2004	Spokane Highland Games, Washington, USA
2004	Formation of the Canadian Highland Games Athletes

2005	First official Internationale Highland Games, Halle, Germany
2005	British Columbia, Canada. Highland Games at Victoria, Komtex Valley, Coquitlam and Perticton, which has a perpetual trophy going back to the 1970s
2005	Alberta has around eight Highland Games
2006	Pozo Whisky Highland Games, USA
2006	First Bad Lausick Highland Games, near Leipzig, Germany. It has been said that there have been around six or seven Highland Games in New Zealand in the recent past. Waipu, Turukind, Invercargill, and Paerdoa being mentioned specifically. Dunedin Games have ceased
2009	The Homecoming year, where a series of events took place to attract those of Scottish ancestry to visit the country. The main event was the clan gathering which took place in Holyrood park

[1] Athole and Atholl are two of several spellings for the district and the small town at various times.

Numerous events have commenced in North America and Canada during the last five years and these are currently being surveyed. It is hoped to update this original study in due course.

Some indicative attendances at Highland games

These are largely based on press reports but successful efforts were made to check some of the figures, particularly the exceptional ones for Thornton.

Boston

| 1870–80s | 20,000. In Victorian times, often around 15,000 |
| 1905–22 | 10,000–20,000 |

New York

1886	15,000
1893	10,000
1923 onwards	Solely track and field, no Scottish events. Numbers diminished and last games in 1923, approximately 1,000 attended; yet 3,000 attended the Scottish Ball that same evening

Grandfather Mountain

| 1956 | 7,000 |

Caledonian Club of San Francisco, Santa Rosa

| 1986 onwards | 30,000, rising at Pleasanton in the 21st century to generally around 35,000–40,000 |
| 2002–2005 | Record upwards of 50,000 |

Spokane, USA

| 2004 | 1,000 |

Scotland

Haddo House Highland Games

| 1907 | 5,000 attended. These games are still popular 50 years later |

Aboyne

1922	15,000
1923	16,000
1924	15,000
1925	12,000
1927	11,000
1930	20,000
1957	10,000

Argyllshire

| 1931 | 7,000 |

Auchterarder

| 1904 | Over 3,000 |

Ballater

| 1925 | 7,000 |

Blairgowrie

| 1930 | 5,000 |

Braemar

1919	12,000–15,000
1922	10,000
1925	Record crowd
1927 and 1928	20,000. First post-war games record. Was said to be 30,000 but one report said 42,000 in 1952.
1962	20,000–25,000

Burntisland

| Often 10,000 |

Ceres

1923	15,000

Clyde FC

1923	10,000

Cowal

1908	7,000
1909	20,000
1912	Friday: 5,000, total 20,000
1925	Day 2: 15,000
1926	20,000

Crieff

1926	10,000
1930	8,000

Venue for the Scottish Heavy Events Championships. Attendances for 20 years, 1960–1980. The committee is to be congratulated on the precise nature of the figures

1960	7,718
1961	8,071
1962	8,335
1963	8,916
1964	3,578
1965	8,190
1966	7,485
1967	7,643
1968	8,838
1969	9,307
1970	9,355
1971	9,166
1972	10,621
1973	9,698
1974	8,575
1975	9,300
1976	9,621
1977	8,254
1979	7,742
1980	7,188

Murrayfield, Edinburgh

Amateur Highland games with many Empire Games stars

1958	35,000

Edinburgh Police Highland Games

1923	5,000

Forfar

1860	5,500
1922	15,000
1930	10,000

Greenock Annual National Games

1879	10,000

Leith

1866	14,500
1868	over 15,000

Linlithgow Gymnastic Games

1877	1,000

London Highland Association Gathering and Games, Stamford Bridge

1906	10,000

Montrose

1922	7,000
1925	6,000

Newmacher

1913	2,000
1923	2,000

Patent Games, Edinburgh

1869	9,000

Pitlochry

1925	5,000
1933	8,000

Rothiemurchas, Aviemore

1980s and early 1990s International Highland Games attendances: 4,000 to 7,000

Shrewsbury

1964	30,000

Stirling

1923	3,000

Thornton

1904	20,000
1905	nearly 60,000
1906	over 40,000
1908	65,000
1909	50,000
1912	40,000

1913	50,000
1919	70,000
1922	20,000
1930	10,000

Meikleour

| 1930s | 4,000 |

Redhall, Fordoun

| 1850 | 650 |

Rothienorman

| 1922 | 6,500 |

Saughton

| 1919 | close on 20,000 |

Strathallan

1913	a record attendance, but no figures quoted
1919	8,000
1922	16,000
1926	16,000
1930	10,000

Stirling

| 1923 | 3,000 |

St Ronan's

| 1831 | 4,000 |

Vale of Leven Annual Games

| 1880 | 4,000 |

Douglas, Isle of Man

| 1930 | 30,000 |

Fergus, Ontario

Record attendance approx. 50,000

Bundanoon Highland Games

These games claim Australia's highest attendances with around 25,000 spectators

Glenarm Castle Highland Games, Northern Ireland

Approximately 30,000 spectators each year, with a large television audience in Ireland. Cancelled in 2007 due to bad weather. There are now a number of much smaller Highland Games in Ireland.

German Highland Games in British Days, Hamburg and Krefeld

19,000–20,000

After Hamburg in 2002, 37,000 euros donated to charity.

On the first day of the second Kempen Highland Games in Germany, 64 young male athletes paraded with a pipe band to the town square for the official opening of the games. They came from the east to the west of Germany, the Netherlands and Belgium; all but a few wore kilts. The following day, 20 good athletes from Germany, Holland, Scotland and New Zealand were divided by ability into two groups and competed with merit in traditional Scottish events. Several of the best German athletes now compete at Highland Games in Scotland.

Strange but True

The *highest* Highland games in the world are the Eastern Sierra Games at Mammoth Mountain, Mammoth Lakes, California, USA. At 9,000 feet above sea level, they are truly high land games. The *lowest* games are the annual games at Swifterband, the Netherlands, which are seven metres below sea level.

The *smallest* Highland games, advertised as such and open to the public, were at the Drovers' Inn, Loch Lomond. Owing to the restricted size of the site, wrestling was the main event.

The *largest* attendance recorded in Scotland is 70,000 people at Thornton Games in 1919. The largest games in America are thought to be at Bethlehem, Pennsylvania. There are no admission charges and the attendances are said to exceed 100,000.

The first Highland games of the new millennium was at Waipu, New Zealand, on 1 January 2000.

The first throws of the millennium were caber tosses by Francis Brebner (Scotland) and Doug MacDonald (Canada) at one second past midnight at Waipu on 1 January 2000.

The last throw of the old millennium was by Russ Murphy (USA) in Hawaii, a fraction before midnight on 31 December 1999, *after* the throws in Waipu in 2000.

The first annual Highland games in Australia is held in Sydney, on 1 January each year.

Since 1 January 1992, a New Year heavy events competition has been held at Alma, Ontario, often in deep snow.

The *largest* heavy is probably Billy Morse of Antigonish, Nova Scotia. The *tallest* athlete who competed at Highland games in Scotland was Ted van der Parre of the Netherlands, who is over seven foot tall.

In 1898, there were over 500 bicycles at Dunecht Highland Games in Aberdeenshire. This was a smaller than average Highland games, and it was said that at the larger games there were thousands of bicycles. Special buses were also run from Aberdeen to the games, a distance of around 14 miles.

The Scottish Heavy Events Championships

Lachlan Macpherson (b. 1811 at Laggan) appears to be the earliest claimant to the Scottish Heavy Events Championship but it has been impossible to confirm. The McHardys on the Braes of Mar and the Lonach hills were widely recognised as the best heavies in Scotland during the 1800s. Alistair McHardys became the first generally accepted Scottish champion, sharing honours with Tom Menzies. Over the years, championships have been held at various games and sometimes the most successful thrower over the whole season was proclaimed champion. The following information is based on extensive research of records kept by games committees and also on newspaper reports up until 1955 and onwards, when the winner at Crieff Highland Games became the official SGA Scottish Champion.

1840s	Thomas Menzies was a top prize winner, along with Alistair McHardy (1825–87)
1844–50	Alistair McHardy
1850–4	John Tait (1829–96)
1854–5	William Tait (1836–1899)
1856–69	Donald Dinnie (1837–1916)
1870	James Fleming (1840–87)
1871–6	Donald Dinnie
1877	George Davidson (b. 1853)
1887	Kenneth McRae (b. 1850)
1890–1900	George Hardy Johnstone (b. 1864)
1901	James Morrison (1874-1945)
1902	George Hardy Johnstone
1903–14	Alexander Anthony Cameron (1877–1951)
1914–19	No championships because of the First World War
1920s	James (Jim) Maitland and Sergeant Major Robert (Bob) Starkey
1927	Robert Starkey (1890–1956)
1929	Edward Anderson (1903–1966)
Mid-1930s	George Clark (1908–1987)

1937	Robert Shaw (1908–1975)
1938 and until after the Second World War (1939–45)	
	George Clark and Bob Shaw shared honours
1950–2	Jack Hunter
1953	Ewen Cameron (1927–95)
1954	Henry A. (Sandy) Gray (b. 1929)
1955	John L. McLellan (b. 1914)
1956–7	Alexander (Sandy) Sutherland (b. 1930)
1958	Jay Scott (1930–97)
1959–1962	William (Bill) Anderson (b.1937)
1963	Arthur Rowe (b. 1935)
1964	Bill Anderson/Arthur Rowe
1965–6	Arthur Rowe
1967–8	Bill Anderson
1969	Bill Anderson/Arthur Rowe
1970	Bill Anderson
1971	Arthur Rowe
1972–8	Bill Anderson MBE
1979	Hamish Davidson (b. 1952)
1980	Bill Anderson MBE
1981	Geoff Capes (b. 1949)
1982	Geoff Capes/Grant Anderson (b. 1945)
1983–5	Grant Anderson
1986	Grant Anderson/Geoff Capes
1987	Bill Anderson MBE
1988	Geoff Capes
1989	Eric Irvine (b.1961)
1990	Francis Brebner (b. 1965)
1991–3	Alistair Gunn (b. 1963)
1994	George Patience (b. 1959)
1995–6	Alistair Gunn
1997	Bruce Aitken (b. 1970)
1998	Stephen Aitken (b. 1967)
1999	Alistair Gunn
2000	Matt Sandford (b. 1970)
2001	Alistair Gunn
2002–3	Bruce Aitken
2004	Ryan Vierra (b: 1968)
2005–10	Gregor Edmunds (b. 1977)
2011	Scott Rider

Bibliography

Books focusing on heavy events

The Games: A Guide to Scotland's Highland Games by Charlie Allan; Famedram Publishers Ltd.; Dunbartonshire; 1974.
Charlie, twice World Caber Tossing Champion, writes with enthusiasm and personal experience of the different games, events and the personalities. A calendar of Scotland's games in 1974 is matched with a map showing their locations and a short entry about each gathering.

Sporting Scotland: Scotland's past in action by John Burnett; National Museum of Scotland; Edinburgh; 1995.
John Burnett, of the NMS, is well known for his keen interest in past and present sporting matters. Highland games are but a relatively small part of this very interesting pocket size publication, but the overall coverage gives readers a very good knowledge of sport in the everyday life of past generations of Scots since the middle ages.

Highland Gatherings by Sir Iain Colquhoun, Bart. DSO and Hugh Machell; Heath Cranton Ltd.; London; 1927.
This coverage of important gatherings like Braemar, the Northern Meeting at Inverness and the Luss gathering are essential reading for those seriously studying Highland games.

Men of Muscle by Charles Donaldson; originally published in the Glasgow *Evening Times*; Glasgow
Fine biographies of heavy event athletes from the 1850s–1901.

The Scottish Highland Games in America by Emily Ann Donaldson; Pelican Publishing Co. Inc.; Louisiana; 1986.
This 253 page hardback covers the usual Highland games attractions but goes further and includes Scottish fiddling, other components of the games, a pronunciation guide and a 14 page section on 'The Games in Scotland' by David Webster.

Highland Games Sketchbook by Douglas A. Fales; Borealis Press; Ontario; 1982.
An unequalled collection of Highland games sketches by this professional Canadian artist of folk subjects. His art work captures leading heavies such as Canadian and American champions like Harrington, Vaughan, Short and McComas. British stars are also featured. There are excellent portrayals of dancers, pipers and officials. The lists of Highland Games in North America and Scotland will be of interest to sports historians.

'e Games: A History of the Halkirk Highland Games by James B. Gunn Jnr; Halkirk Highland Games Association; 2003.
Halkirk is a village in Caithness near John O' Groats. Highland games have been held there since 1886 and although its population is only 1,500, many thousands are attracted to their annual games. Few villages in the world can boast of economically important attractions like 'e Games and this well illustrated publication will be a revelation to those who have not been involved in such a project. The author is one of the Gunns' o' Gerston who have been active in organising and competing

since the 1920s. The term ''e Games' is north east Doric for 'the Games'. 'e is pronounced like 'the' but without the 'th'.

History of Cowal Highland Gathering by W.L. Inglis; Dunoon; *c.*1959.
Contains detailed descriptions of this gathering from its earliest days. Piping is particularly well documented with lists of pipers and pipe band competition winners.

Highland Games: The Making of the Myth by Grant Jarvie; Edinburgh Education & Society; Edinburgh; 1991.
The author is a highly respected Professor of Sports Studies at the University of Stirling and this publication gives an academic perspective of Highland games. Potential readers should not be put off by inclusion of 'Myth' in the title; it is **not** a debunking of Scottish traditional sports.

The Athletic Sports of Scotland by W. McCombie Smith; A. Gardner; Paisley; 1891.
The author, a school teacher, was Donald Dinnie's son-in-law and Dinnie's greatest critic. Apart from this, it is an excellent, and the earliest, worthwhile Highland games reference book.

The Highlanders of Scotland by Kenneth Macleay FSA; John Mitchell; London; 1872
A series of exceptional Highlanders were painted by Macleay and the subjects included several famous Scottish athletes. The biographical notes on these men, written in 1868, and their Highland dress are very enlightening.

*Scottish Sports and how to exel** in them by John James Miller; John Lang & Co.; Dundee; 1908 (*spelling as in the title).
Mainly describes heavy events and participants but also descriptions of light events.

Caledonian Games in Nineteenth-Century America by Gerald Redmond; Fairleigh Dickinson University Press; New Jersey; 1971.
This is a major contribution to Highland games literature, as it evaluates the early impact of Caledonian games in introducing and developing American track and field athletics. Giving detailed references and evidence Prof. Redmond shows how the Scots introduced events like throwing the hammer, putting the shot, triple jump and pole-vaulting to colleges, universities and the general public.

The Sporting Scots in 18th Century Canada by Gerald Redmond; Associated Universities Presses Inc.; Washington DC; 1982.
In 347 pages Redmond clearly shows how Scottish immigrants made their traditional sports into important Canadian festivities now considered indigenous to their environment.

Scottish Athletes and Athletics by Bryce W. Scott and A.W. Campbell. Serialised by the *Aberdeen Weekly Journal*; Aberdeen; 1928.
Written by two well-known athletes, the first section is by Scott, a champion 'leaper' and vaulter, while Campbell was a heavy and dealt with the throwing event in the second section. Their enthusiasm for sport and respect for their rivals are clearly seen in the text.

Sports and Pastimes in Scotland by Robert Scott Fittis; Alexander Gardner; Wakefield; 1891. Republished by EP Publishing Ltd; 1975.
It deals with 'the habits manners and customs of bygone generations of Scotsmen of all ranks and classes.'

Athletics and Football by Montague Shearman; Longmans, Green and Co.; London; 1888.
This volume in the 'Badminton Library of Sports and Pastimes' series of books gives an overview of amateur athletic events at that time and is helpful in comparing the wider development of these activities.

Scottish Highland Games by David Webster, illustrated by John Gardner; Collins; Glasgow and London; 1958.
There were two different soft bindings one in tartan and the other with mock leather. Although the heavies are most strongly featured, Highland dancing and piping are also covered.

Scottish Highland Games by David Webster; Reprographia; Edinburgh; 1973.
Quite different from the previous publication, this larger format hardback was lavishly illustrated with old and modern photographs in all disciplines. In addition to biographical and anecdotal material it also listed champions in the various categories and has been widely used as a reference book.

Donald Dinnie, The First Sporting Superstar by David Webster and Gordon Dinnie; Ardo Publishing; Aberdeen; 1999.
Researched at great length by the authors, the true story of Donald Dinnie and his travels round the world, challenging all comers, is stranger than fiction. This well-produced hardback has a wealth of rare photographs and little-known facts. Of particular interest are the fascinating accounts by Donald Dinnie, not by a reporter or ghost writer, but in his own words. He competed in an incredible range of events at the highest standards, amassing more than 11,000 prizes in his very lengthy career.

The Games by Skye Highland Games Committee; West Highland Publishing Company; Portree; 1998.
Celebrating the 121st year of these games. Contains a wealth of interesting information in its 116 pages.

Books focusing on traditional Scottish dancing, pipers and piping

The MacCrimmon Pipers of Skye: A Tradition Under Siege by Robert Bruce Campbell; Highland Media Group; Wirral; 2000.
On the spot research and up to date information technology has helped Bruce Campbell to collect more information than had previously been widely available.

The Traditional and National Music of Scotland by Francis Collinson; R.K.P. Publishing; London; 1966.
This substantial publication describes Gaelic labour songs, mourning music, the Coronach, lowland vocal music, bagpipes, fiddle, and harp. There is also a good index.

Traditional Gaelic Bagpiping 1745–1945 by John Gibson; McGill-Queen's University Press; Montreal; 2002.
Very well researched 406 pages with comprehensive bibliography and index.

Manual of Scottish Country Dances by Alasdair MacFadyen & working party; MacFadyen, Mackenzie and Macpherson; 2009
These well-known members of the Royal Scottish Country Dance Society reproduced *Frederick Hill's Book of Quadrilles and Country Dancing*, a long-lost and historically important manuscript originally written in 1841, but not published until 168 years later. The Royal Scottish Country Dancing Society have also produced numerous publication describing the great variety of traditional country dances.

The MacCrimmons of Skye by Fred T. MacLeod; Henderson & Hamilton, Edinburgh; 1933.
The MacCrimmons of Skye have been described as a cornerstone of piping history and this book contains a wealth of information and interesting legends.

A History of the Clan Mac Crimmon by G.C.B. Poulter; The Clan Mac Crimmon Society; Camberley; 1938.
These oft quoted booklets lists the famous hereditary pipers of the MacLeods of Dunvegan, along with informative notes and anecdotes.

Highland Dancing: The Official Textbook of the Scottish Official Board of Highland Dancing; Thomson and Sons Ltd.; Edinburgh; 1955.
The basic steps, movements and positions comprise most of the text but the rudiments of music, dress for Highland dancers and competition rules are also covered. A noteworthy selection of photographs show the great J.L. McKenzie illustrating the positions.

Scotland's Dance by H.A. Thurston; G. Bell and Sons; London; 1954.
Includes historical information and descriptions of Highland dances and Scottish country dances, bibliography, numerous appendices and a comprehensive index.

Background information

History of Highland Dress by John T. Dunbar; Oliver and Boyd; Edinburgh; 1962.
Detailed description, beautifully illustrated, including full page colour reproductions of classic images. Has an appendix, bibliography and index.

The Scottish Gael by James Logan; Smith, Elder and G. Cornhill; London; 1831.
A historical and descriptive account of the inhabitants, antiquities and natural peculiarities of Scotland.

Sport En Etniciteit by Christiaan Olyslager; University of Leuven; Belgium; 1989.
Unpublished thesis on shinty and Highland Games in Scotland.

Sketches of the Highlander by Gen. David Stewart of Garth; A. & W. Mackenzie; Inverness; 1822.
Word sketches of the character, manners of Highlanders and the state of the Highlands and Highland Regiments. A very useful and is a recognised classic on these topics.

Other good sources of information

Milo magazine and the associated website, www.ironmind.com, give more regular news of major heavy events than any other periodical.

For many decades *The Braemar Gathering Annual* has been a continuous source of information about games in general and, naturally, their own gathering in particular. This fine annual is now produced by Craig Nisbet, Dee Publishing, St Andrews.

Some other books published by **LUATH** PRESS

Wherever the Saltire Flies

Kenny MacAskill and Henry McLeish
ISBN 978-1905222-68-1 PBK £8.99

 For Scots living in Scotland today, the idea of a society of exiled and ancestral Scots in another country conjures up varying images of nostalgia and sentimentality for their homeland.

For emigrant and ancestral Scots around the world, Scottish societies offer a chance for like-minded, passionate people to join together in celebrating past and contemporary Scotland.

Based on a series of lively interviews with members of Scottish societies, *Wherever the Saltire Flies* charts a memorable journey in the ever-evolving concept of Scottish identity. Providing genuine support and inspiration, these societies play a huge part in the preservation of Scottish culture and the worldwide promotion of Scotland, and the people involved are as much a part of a Scottish history as those of Scotland.

Wherever the Saltire Flies *gives a health check on Scottish societies around the world, and it appears they're flourishing.*
THE SCOTS MAGAZINE

Warriors and Wordsmiths: The Birth and Growth of Democracy

Linda MacDonald-Lewis
ISBN 978-1906307-27-1 PBK £6.99

 What did William Wallace and George Washington have in common?
How did we earn the right to choose our own leaders?
Which two documents brought us from medieval days of feudalism to present day democracy?

The origins of democracy, often claimed for the Ancient Greeks or the Magna Carta, are still a severely contested terrain. Linda MacDonald-Lewis steps onto this battlefield to contend that democracy really began in Scotland. She identifies the Declaration of Arbroath of 1320 as the landmark document that laid the foundation for the American Declaration of Independence of 1776.

From the Scottish Wars of Independence, political and religious feuds and upheavals, we reach the shores of America. This epic voyage reveals surprising and fascinating insights into how the destinies of such far flung people and places were all tied together in a relentless fight for freedom.

On the Trail of Scotland's History

David R Ross
ISBN 978-1905222-85-8 PBK £7.99

Popular historian David R Ross tracks Scotland through the ages, detailing incidents, places and people that are key to Scotland's history. Leading his readers to ancient monuments and the stories surrounding them, Ross guides us on a quest to discover the essentials of Scottish history – and to find things we never knew existed.

From William Wallace's possible steps, the legend of King Arthur and the reign of Robert the Bruce, to rugged battlegrounds, moors and mountains, to Scottish film locations, Ross's journey around Scotland links the past to the present, bringing us face-to-face with the elements that have created the Scotland of today.

An essential read for those who are passionate about Scotland and its mysterious and beautiful tapestry of history and landscape.

... an entertainingly outspoken companion for any inquisitive traveller round this nation.
THE HERALD

On the Trail of Scotland's Myths and Legends

Stuart McHardy
ISBN 978-1842820-49-0 PBK £7.99

A journey into Scotland's past through the awe-inspiring stories that were at the heart our ancestors' traditions and beliefs.

As *On the Trail of Scotland's Myths and Legends* unfolds, mythical animals, supernatural beings, heroes, giants and goddesses come alive and walk Scotland's rich landscape as they did in the time of the Scots, Gaelic and Norse speakers of the past.

Visiting over 170 sites across Scotland, Stuart McHardy traces the lore of our ancestors, connecting ancient beliefs with traditions still alive today. Presenting a new picture of who the Scots are and where they have come from, this book provides an insight into a unique tradition of myth, legend and folklore that has marked the language and landscape of Scotland.

This remains an entertaining record of the extent to which history is memorialised in the landscape.
THE SCOTSMAN

Scottish Roots: Step-by-step guide for ancestor hunters

Alwyn James
ISBN 978-1842820-90-2 PBK £6.99

Scottish Roots provides an excellent, comprehensible step-by-step guide to tracing your Scottish ancestry. Using the example of two Scots trying to discover their roots, Alwyn James illustrates how easy it is to commence the research process and gradually compile a worthwhile family tree. Few countries can compare with Scottish record keeping in the past 250 years and the author explains how to go about searching for family records He navigates the reader through the first steps of sourcing family details, making contact with distant relatives and preparing to collate any new information.

Now in its 20th year of publication, this new and updated edition of the guide includes information on how to access family data utilising electronic resources and the internet – a must if conducting research from an overseas base. An indispensable companion for anyone delving into their Scottish family history.

Rooted in Scotland

Cameron Taylor
ISBN 978-1905222-89-6 PBK £7.99

The idea of home can be associated with the notion of an ancestral homeland, a place where something greater than any one individual began. It is difficult to overestimate just how powerful an experience visiting an ancestral homeland can be.

CAMERON TAYLOR

There are several good guides to tracing your Scottish ancestry and many serious historical studies of emigration. *Rooted in Scotland* takes a different perspective. Its starting point is that your sense of connection with Scotland has meaning and legitimacy, and that the journey of discovery that is ancestral research helps you understand who you really are.

Whether you live in the US, Canada, New Zealand or Australia, your Scottish ancestry is worth exploring and celebrating. This book will help you do both.

Scots in Canada

Jenni Calder

ISBN 978-1842820-38-4 PBK £7.99

The story of the Scots who went to Canada, from the 17th century onwards.

In Canada there are nearly as many descendants of Scots as there are people living in Scotland: almost five million Canadians ticked the 'Scottish origin' box in the most recent Canadian Census. Many Scottish families have friends or relatives in Canada.

Thousands of Scots were forced from their homeland, while others chose to leave, seeking a better life. As individuals, families and communities, they braved the wild Atlantic Ocean, many crossing in cramped under-rationed ships, unprepared for the fierce Canadian winter. And yet Scots went on to lay railroads, found banks and exploit the fur trade, and helped form the political infrastructure of modern day Canada.

… meticulously researched and fluently written… it neatly charts the rise of a country without succumbing to sentimental myths.
SCOTLAND ON SUNDAY

Scots in the USA

Jenni Calder

ISBN 978-1905222-06-3 PBK £8.99

The map of the United States is peppered with Scottish place-names and America's telephone directories are filled with surnames illustrating Scottish ancestry. Increasingly, Americans of Scottish extraction are visiting Scotland in search of their family history. All over Scotland and the United States there are clues to the Scottish-American relationship, the legacy of centuries of trade and communication as well as that of departure and heritage.

Scots in the USA discusses why they left Scotland, where they went once they reached the United States, and what they did when they got there.

A reminder of the days when Scots were inventors, entrepreneurs and pioneers, by the time you turn the last page, if you're not Scottish you'll want to be.
THE DAILY RECORD

Details of these and other books published by Luath Press can be found at:
www.luath.co.uk

Luath Press Limited
committed to publishing well written books worth reading

LUATH PRESS takes its name from Robert Burns, whose little collie Luath (*Gael.*, swift or nimble) tripped up Jean Armour at a wedding and gave him the chance to speak to the woman who was to be his wife and the abiding love of his life. Burns called one of 'The Twa Dogs' Luath after Cuchullin's hunting dog in Ossian's *Fingal*. Luath Press was established in 1981 in the heart of Burns country, and now resides a few steps up the road from Burns' first lodgings on Edinburgh's Royal Mile.
Luath offers you distinctive writing with a hint of unexpected pleasures.

Most bookshops in the UK, the US, Canada, Australia, New Zealand and parts of Europe either carry our books in stock or can order them for you. To order direct from us, please send a £sterling cheque, postal order, international money order or your credit card details (number, address of cardholder and expiry date) to us at the address below. Please add post and packing as follows: UK – £1.00 per delivery address; overseas surface mail – £2.50 per delivery address; overseas airmail – £3.50 for the first book to each delivery address, plus £1.00 for each additional book by airmail to the same address. If your order is a gift, we will happily enclose your card or message at no extra charge.

Luath Press Limited
543/2 Castlehill
The Royal Mile
Edinburgh EH1 2ND
Scotland

Telephone: 0131 225 4326 (24 hours)
Fax: 0131 225 4324
email: sales@luath.co.uk
Website: www.luath.co.uk

ILLUSTRATION: IAN KELLAS